A GUIDE TO THE
GHOST TOWNS AND MINING CAMPS
OF NYE COUNTY, NEVADA

A GUIDE TO THE
GHOST TOWNS AND MINING CAMPS
OF NYE COUNTY, NEVADA

SHAWN HALL

DODD, MEAD & COMPANY / New York

Copyright © 1981 by Shawn Hall
All rights reserved
No part of this book may be reproduced in any form
without permission in writing from the publisher
Printed in the United States of America

1 2 3 4 5 6 7 8 9 10

Library of Congress Cataloging in Publication Data

Hall, Shawn, 1960-
   A guide to the ghost towns and mining camps of Nye
County, Nevada.

   1. Cities and towns, Ruined, extinct, etc.—Nevada—
Nye County—Guide-books.   2. Nye County (Nev.)—History,
Local.   3. Nye County (Nev.)—Description and travel—
Guide-books.   4. Mines and mining—Nevada—Nye County—
History.   I. Title.
F847.N9H34   917.93′34   81-1570
ISBN 0-396-07955-5 (pbk.)   AACR2

*To the memory of
John Wayne,
who made the West
so appealing to me through
his many films.*

Acknowledgments

Many people have been instrumental in the preparation of this book. They all deserve recognition. Foremost would have to be my mother, who helped keep my spirits up when things seemed hopeless. Her constant support was very influential in the completion of this guide.

Extensive historical and photographic help came from William Metscher, president of the Central Nevada Historical Society. He provided continuous support and was an invaluable source for obscure points of interest on many of the sites. For the last three years, Bill and I have been in constant touch. I will be forever in his debt for his generosity.

For photographic assistance, I would like to thank Mrs. Eslie E. Cann and Judith M. Rippetoe of the Nevada Historical Society, Heidi LaPoint of the Western History Research Center at the University of Wyoming, and Mati A. Stephens of the MacKay School of Mines at the University of Nevada at Reno.

I would also like to thank a number of other people who helped me with information: Mrs. LaRue Carter (White River Valley), Mr. and Mrs. Austin Wardle (Tonopah), Mr. and Mrs. Butch Fuson (Tonopah area), Mr. and Mrs. Nick Bradshaw (Tonopah area), Bob Work (Reveille), Leland Hendrix (Railroad Valley), A. D. Hopkins, Jr. (Pahrump Valley), Jim Marsh (Las Vegas), Charles Palmquist (Ione), Sharon Pauley (Manhattan), Bill Phillips (Ione), Helen Uhalde (Adaven), Brooke Whiting (University of California at Los Angeles), Dorothy Wilson (Gabbs area) and Julie Zimmerman (Wilson's).

Special thanks to Wayne and Jean Hage and all of the hands of the Pine Creek Ranch who made my stay in Nye County the best experience of my life. Working on a ranch gave me more of an idea of what the Old West was really like than any ghost town could.

I want to thank all of the above people—and anyone else I might have missed. I look forward to seeing everyone once again when I travel in Nevada during the coming years.

Contents

Preface — xi
A Short History of Nye County — xiii
Nye County's Ghost Towns and Mining Camps — 1
Map — 2–3
Glossary of Mining Terms — 147
Bibliography — 149
Index — 151

Preface

This is the first of a projected series on the history of Nevada's ghost towns and mining camps. The book covers 175 ghost towns, mining camps, stage stations and historical sites. Some critics may feel that one county's history is not worth a lengthy book, but I believe that every bit of activity—because it is an integral part of the county's history—is essential and should not be left out. I have tried to give a complete history of Nye County, both in photographs and text.

I have sought to cover every site in the county that fits the ghost-town definition of "a shadowy semblance of a former self." All the locations described here, except those within the Las Vegas Bombing and Gunnery Range, were visited by me during the summer of 1979. Since many of the Nye County historical sites are on private property, warning signs must be observed and respected. Please do not tear buildings apart for relics or vandalize the old remains. Take photographs, yes, but leave what still stands alone so that future generations can enjoy our glorious past.

This book is organized as a historical atlas and is designed both for the armchair reader and for the active ghost-town searcher. Though the distance to each town may vary a litte, depending on your vehicle's odometer, every site is clearly marked on the map at the front of the book. Next to the name of the site, I have added in parentheses other names by which it has been known during its existence. Besides the volumes listed in the bibliography I have also used letters and personal interviews in preparing this book. Though I have not included source footnotes, if anyone would like these, please write me care of Dodd, Mead & Company.

Beware while traveling in Nye County. Most of the area is very hot and dry, with water not always readily available. Carry extra water and gasoline. Rattlesnakes abound in the county, so be careful when poking around sites. And look out for deep mine shafts that are hardly noticeable until one is on top of them. I almost drove right into the White Cap shaft before I saw it! Nothing like a 1600-foot fall to wake you up in the morning, or put you to sleep permanently! While visiting these sites, you must also beware of ghost-town fever—once caught, it is practically impossible to lose. I caught it when I was eight years old, and I still have it.

One final note: all photographs in this book that do not have a specific credit are my own.

Good Luck and Happy Hunting,
Shawn Hall

Cambridge, Massachusetts
March 1981

A Short History of Nye County

Nye County was organized in 1864 and was named after the popular Nevada governor J. W. Nye. The first major discoveries in the county were made in 1863 in the Ione area of the Union District. Soon other towns sprang up nearby: Washington, Grantsville, Ophir Canyon. A small courthouse was constructed in Ione at a cost of $800, but it was not until 1874 that a substantial courthouse was built, at Belmont.

Nye County's boundaries constantly shifted during its early years. After a number of disputes, the boundaries were finally settled by surveyors. In 1870 Nye County had a reported population of 1100; by 1875, almost 2100. Growth stopped in the early 1880s and the mines in the county remained fairly dormant until the turn of the century, when Jim Butler made his rich discoveries at Tonopah Springs. This brought renewed interest in the old mines and sent prospectors scurrying over the land searching for new deposits. New towns sprang up at Rhyolite, Manhattan, Round Mountain, Reveille and Johnnie. The teens were the richest years for the county, with Tonopah leading the production figures. Activity slowly declined, then picked up again during World War II. After that war most of the mines closed, although major operations continued for a while at Round Mountain and Manhattan.

Today, rises in mineral prices have led to new mining activity throughout the county. Round Mountain and its mines have been yielding almost $100,000 in gold per week; new mines in nearby Manhattan promise to be equally rich. Molybdenum deposits near Tonopah should last for twenty years or more. Barite deposits are being located throughout the county. It looks as though Nye County will once again be making its mark on national production charts.

The county has a very interesting cross section of history that gives it varied beauty. There are no longer any active railroads, but remains of its four lines—the Bullfrog-Goldfield, Tonopah and Goldfield, Las Vegas and Tonopah, and Tonopah and Tidewater—still make for excellent and interesting exploration. In addition to the ghost towns and present towns, the county has many of the old stage stations that once dotted the landscape. The stage roads are now faint but still traversable, excellent for the person who really wants to go back in time to the era of the stagecoach. Nye County also has many areas of abundant natural beauty. The splendor of the Jefferson Mountains is awe inspiring. Sites such as the Northumberland Cave offer one of the rarer natural wonders a traveler can see. The county's many beautiful canyons are also majestic. Riding up a canyon road for only a few miles leads to a transformation from desert and sagebrush into a land full of aspens, clear and cool water, birds and rocky splendor. The county is one of the most beautiful and varied areas in the state. Anyone visiting Nevada should definitely make a sincere attempt to visit Nye County.

Nye County's Ghost Towns and Mining Camps

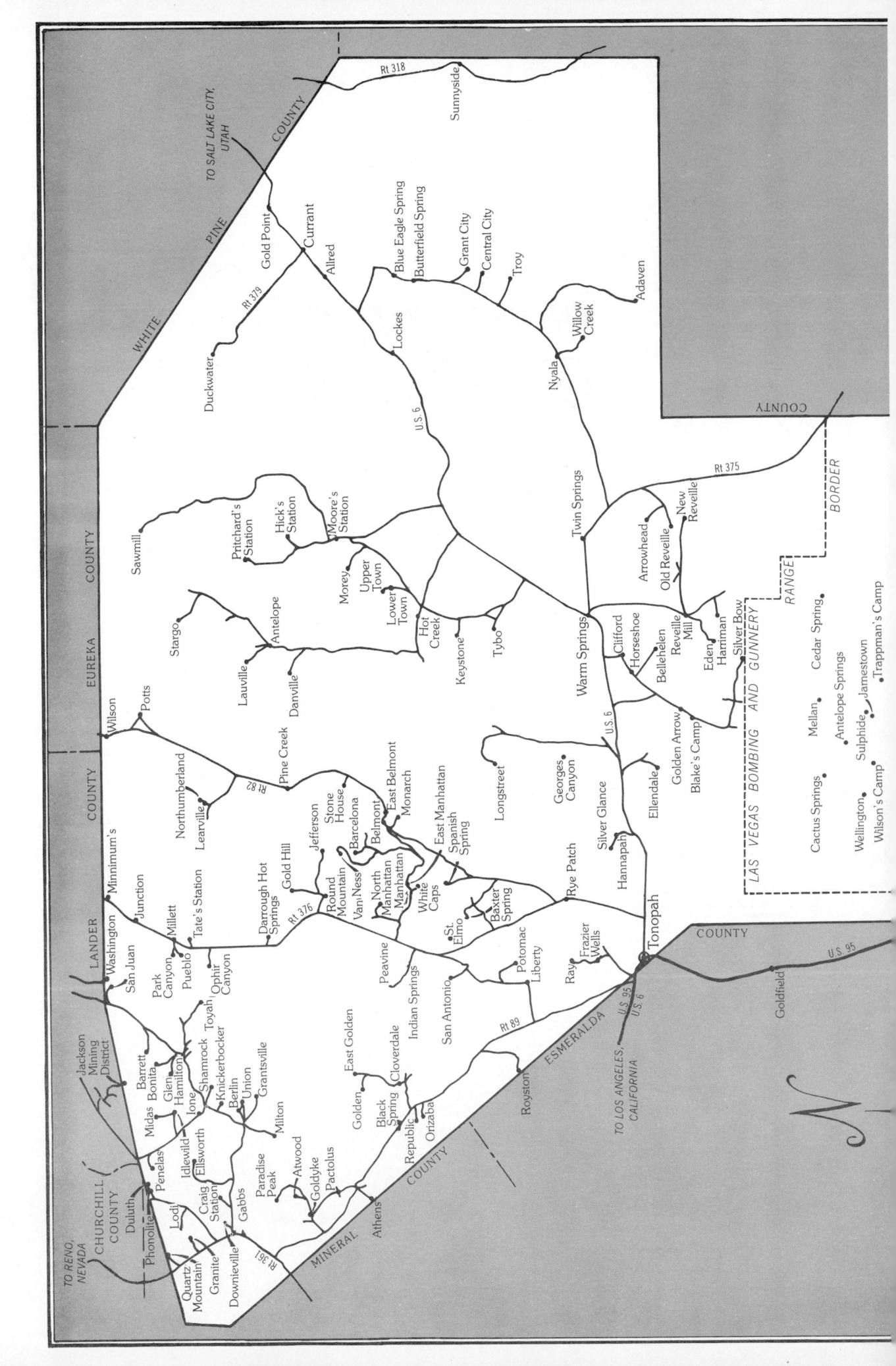

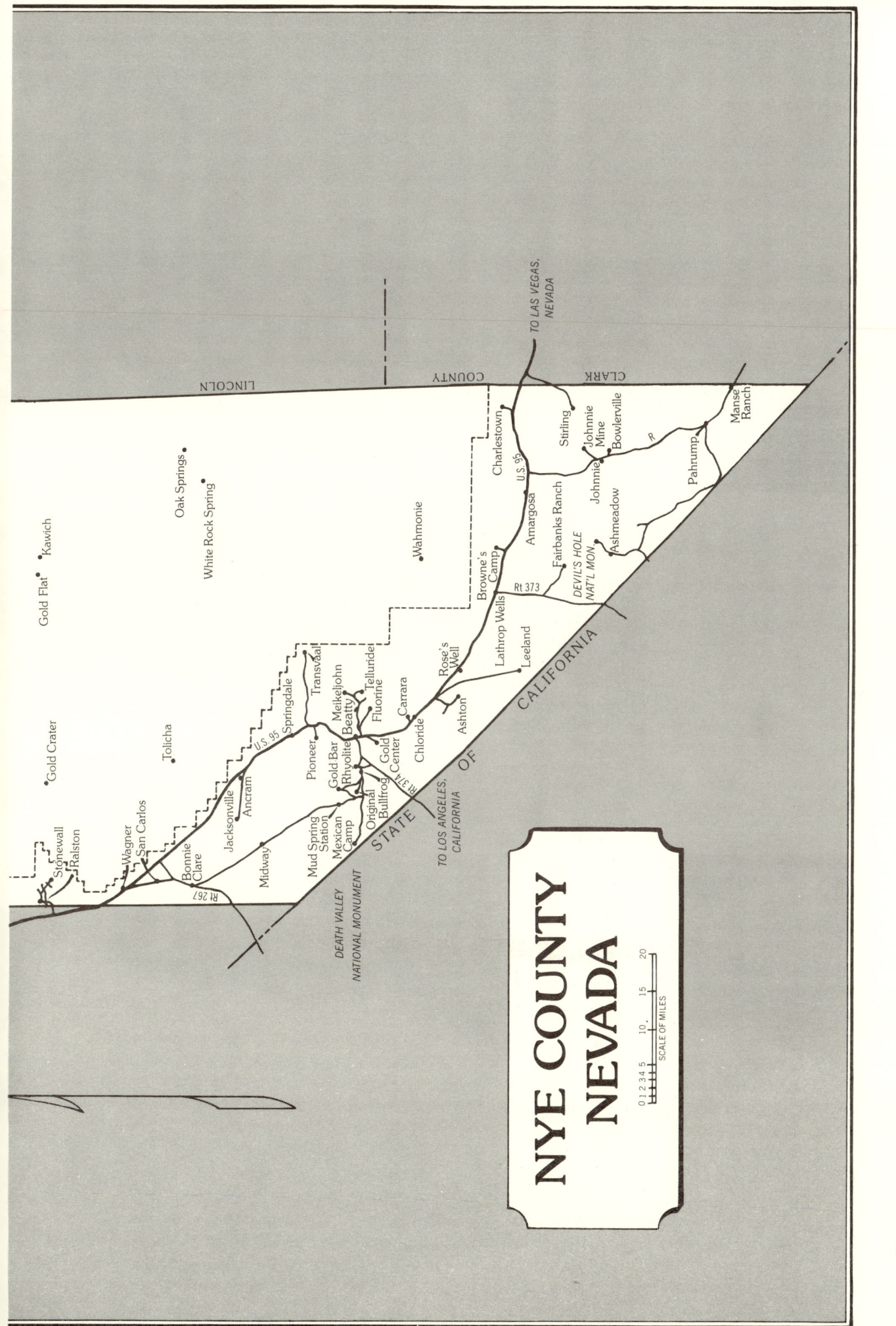

ADAVEN (Sharp)

DIRECTIONS:
From Currant, take US 6 south for 9.8 miles. Exit left and follow for 6 miles. Then exit right and follow for about 24 miles. Exit left and continue on this road for 15 miles to Adaven.

Adaven was originally known as Sharp, after Thomas Sharp, a rancher who settled here in the 1870s. A small settlement formed around his ranch, and the Sharp post office opened on Dec. 14, 1901. The population of Sharp remained fairly constant at twenty-five for the next fifty years. On May 1, 1939, the town was renamed Adaven (*Nevada* spelled backwards). The Adaven post office continued to operate until Nov. 30, 1953. There are still small ranches near Adaven, and a number of older buildings remain. Gasoline and limited food supplies are available in the settlement.

ALLRED

DIRECTIONS:
From Currant, head south on US 6 for 5 miles to Allred.

Allred boasted a small post office from April 17, 1911, until Oct. 31, 1912. Very little is known about the site and nothing remains here.

AMARGOSA (Johnnie Station)

DIRECTIONS:
From Lathrop Wells, head east on US 95 for 16½ miles to Nevada 16. Amargosa is ¼ mile west of this point on the north side of US 95.

Amargosa was a fairly important stop on the Las Vegas and Tonopah Railroad. The railroad station began as a temporary site while tracks were being laid westward toward Rhyolite and Beatty. The railroad siding was set up in the early 1900s and became permanent when strikes at Johnnie created the need for the railroad station. The siding was originally called Johnnie Station until late 1901. In that year a post office was opened and was named Amargosa—Spanish for "bitter water." (While drilling a well at the site, the drillers encountered brackish water, hence the name.) The post office was rescinded in November 1902.

Amargosa continued to slowly grow. When the post office was officially reopened on Dec. 3, 1904, the railroad stop had quite a few buildings, including a store, hotel, restaurant and blacksmith shop. Although the post office closed on March 21, 1905, Amargosa remained a pivotal shipping point for Johnnie and other points west. A daily stage to Johnnie was set up, and Amargosa became a vital supply depot for that town. Amargosa also became a jumping-off point for people heading to the new copper discoveries at Greenwater, California. Amargosa was the closest railroad to the booming town until the Tonopah and Tidewater Railroad was built.

"Alkali Bill" Brong set up an auto stage from Amargosa to Greenwater, charging anywhere from $100 to $200 for the 70-mile trip. Even with the steep price, Brong was never short of passengers who wanted to experience the thrill of being driven across the desert at 50 miles per hour. All of the supplies for booming Greenwater were unloaded at Amargosa and then transferred to stages and mule-drawn wagons for the long trek to Greenwater. In 1907, when the Tonopah and Tidewater Railroad was completed, most shipping activity was taken away from Amargosa.

The town of Johnnie soon became Amargosa's main interest once again. When Johnnie began to decline to 1912, Amargosa quickly faded. By the beginning of 1914 the population was down to 25;

by 1915 the site was completely abandoned. There are no remains at Amargosa. During its existence, the only substantial building was the station. The other buildings, for the most part, consisted mainly of wooden frame tents and some small wooden cabins. Most of these were moved to Gold Center and Bullfrog after Amargosa began to decline. The only ruins of any type at the site consist of the large concrete foundation of the old station. The site is extremely difficult to locate and is not rewarding at all. The only feeling one gets from the site is a sense of accomplishment at even finding the elusive foundation!

ANCRAM

DIRECTIONS:
From Beatty, take US 95 north for 16 miles. Exit left onto a faint road, which is the old Bullfrog-Goldfield Railroad right-of-way. Follow this for 2 miles to Ancram.

Ancram, a water stop on the Bullfrog-Goldfield Railroad, was active from November 1906 to January 1928. In 1910, and for a few years afterward, a road to Ancram was active and the site was used for a while as a passenger stop. Nothing substantial was ever built at Ancram, and today it is indistinguishable from the surrounding desert.

ANTELOPE (Clear Creek) (Crockers Ranch)

DIRECTIONS:
From Hot Creek, continue west through Hot Creek Canyon for 6½ miles. Exit right and follow this road straight through for 20 miles to Antelope.

Antelope was a small stopping place in the Little Fish Lake Valley during the late 1800s. A small ranch had been at the site from the 1870s, but it was not until mining activity in the valley picked up that a regular settlement began. A post office opened here on Feb. 8, 1904. Antelope faded after activity at nearby Danville, Stargo and Lauville was curtailed. The post office closed on July 31, 1908, and soon the Antelope complex returned to ranching.

A small open clay pit was worked in 1944 just to the west of the old ranch. The operation, run by the Coen Companies, Inc., of Los Angeles, employed four men and only lasted for a short while. The ranch was abandoned soon after that and the site slowly deteriorated. Today a number of buildings

The large building served as a boardinghouse in Antelope. In the foreground are the remains of an old wagon.

This decrepit cabin at Antelope was built in the 1860s.

remain at the site. One small boardinghouse, a blacksmith shop and a few old branch-and-clay stables are among the more interesting remains. A number of small dugout stone cabins are located on the side of a small hill, about 200 feet from the main cluster of buildings. The site is definitely worth the trip.

ANTELOPE SPRINGS

DIRECTIONS:
30 miles east-southeast of Goldfield. Off-limits (located inside the Las Vegas Bombing and Gunnery Range).

Initial discoveries of ore at Antelope Springs were made in 1903 by the Bailey brothers, who had earlier made substantial discoveries at Cactus Springs. The brothers staked their claim a mile southwest of Antelope Springs, noted for its main spring that gushed forth over 500 gallons daily to provide the district with a commodity quite rare in the desert. Further discoveries were made by the Jordan brothers in 1906. The Bailey and Jordan brothers were the only inhabitants of Antelope Springs until November 1911, when the first semblance of a camp formed after two newcomers discovered rich ore deposits just south of the springs.

The new discovery was named the Antelope View claim. George Wingfield and the Goldfield Consolidated Mines Company paid $15,000 to the discoverers to lease the claim for a week. The company found rich deposits, but when the week was up, the owners demanded so much for the property that Wingfield and his company left. Even with Wingfield gone, people still continued to come to the area. By the beginning of 1912, there were 150 men working a number of different claim groups in the district. By spring of that year the camp had a dozen wooden buildings, on two separate townsites. A stageline to Goldfield was set up, operating every other day.

In addition to the Antelope View claims, a new claim group was discovered, called the Western Union group. And a newly formed outfit, the Antelope Mines Company, also became active in the district. The company was incorporated in March 1912 as a subsidiary of the National Merger Gold Mines Company. Frank Corehay was president and Frank Howard vice-president. The Antelope Mines Company controlled three claims, all located just north of the camp. One of the claims, the Antelope Mine, had a 300-foot shaft and over 1500 feet of lateral workings. The company never employed more than ten men but still managed to produce a respectable amount of good ore.

There were eight other claim groups in the district. The Antelope View group was the most productive. Its Antelope View Mine, started by Wingfield, had ore that assayed at an average of $200 per ton, with some reaching as much as $600 per ton. The mine had an 85-foot shaft with a 150-foot crosscut tunnel. The Chloride group, located 600 feet southeast of the Antelope View Mine, had a number of exploratory shafts and tunnels ranging from 3 feet to 15 feet; nothing of high value was ever found. The oldest group of claims had been originally located in 1903 by the Bailey brothers. They continued to work their claims until 1912, although no substantial ore deposits were ever found. The other four claim groups—the Auriferous, Good Luck, Reflection and Star of Hope—were worked on a very low level. The ore from these four ranged in value from $6 to $75 per ton.

Difficulty transporting the mined ore to Goldfield hurt Antelope Spring's chances for survival. Even though the ore was extremely rich in some spots, the cost of getting it to mills in Goldfield cut the actual profit margin drastically. After the population peak in 1912, Antelope Springs headed downhill rapidly. Only the richest ore could be sent to Goldfield, and that was quickly running out. By 1913 the population was under fifty; by 1914 the district had been completely abandoned. No revival was ever attempted, and the townsite slowly fell into ruin.

Before being incorporated into the Las Vegas Bombing and Gunnery Range in 1950, Antelope Springs was visited by an old-timer from Tonopah. He found two buildings still standing, with the ruins of a number of others scattered around the site. No present report is possible since the site is now off-limits.

ARROWHEAD (Needles)

DIRECTIONS:
From Warm Springs, head east on Nevada 375 for 19½ miles. Exit right on Reveille Road and follow it for 5½ miles. Exit right and follow this unimproved road for 3½ miles to Arrowhead.

The Arrowhead district was organized in 1919 when fairly substantial silver deposits were discovered in the Reveille range. The camp sprang up rapidly, and soon a small group of buildings was built. A post office opened here on Dec. 24, 1919, and was operated by "Whispering Joe," victim of an avalanche that caused him to lose his voice.

The Arrowhead district was worked by eleven different mining companies during its short existence. Seven of these companies were established during the abortive boom of 1919. The two largest were the Arrowhead Extension Mining Company and the Arrowhead Mining Company, owner of the Arrowhead Mine.

The Arrowhead Extension Mining Company was based in Tonopah, with John Kendall as president and M. J. McVeigh as vice-president and general manager of operations at Arrowhead. The company was incorporated in 1919 with capital of $150,000; a number of stock shares were sold. The mining company purchased over 100 acres south and east of the Arrowhead Mine and a shaft was sunk. The extracted ore brought $65 to $70 a ton. The shaft was eventually sunk 150 feet before the mine closed.

The second major company, the Arrowhead Mining Company, was also based in Tonopah. R. L. Johns was president and Pete Fox was superintendent at the Arrowhead Mine. Incorporated in September 1919 with capital of $150,000, the company purchased four claims, one of which was eventually developed into the Arrowhead Mine. The ore from that mine was quite rich—$100 to $200 a ton. By 1921 the ore value had sunk to $25 a ton. Construction of a small mill was then underway, but the mine closed before it could be completed. Developments in the mine were extensive: before activity was curtailed, the mine's vertical shaft was over 350 feet.

The remaining nine mining companies had limited production. The Arrowhead Annex Mining Company, established in 1919, purchased four claims north of the Arrowhead Mine. A shaft was sunk but never was very successful, and the company soon folded. The Arrowhead Wonder Mines Company was also fairly active in the district. Based in San Francisco, with W. H. French as president, the company had seven claims northeast of Arrowhead and dug two shafts. For a while ore running $110 per ton was extracted. But the veins in the Wonder Mine, thought to be the same as those being worked in the Arrowhead Mine, soon ran out.

The other company of any consequence in the district was the Arrowhead Syndicate Mines Company. It was based in Ely, with C. L. Osterlund as both president and manager. The company was formed in 1919 with backing capital of $150,000. Over 480,000 treasury stock shares were sold; proceeds were used to purchase 80 acres (four claims) south of the Arrowhead Mining Company's property. A shaft was dug, with the help of an 18-h.p. hoist, to a depth of 200 feet. Before the company could get operations really moving, the company ran out of money and was forced to curtail operations in August 1920. Hopes of reopening in 1922 were dropped when necessary capital could not be raised.

Of the remaining four companies that worked the area—Arrowhead Bonanza Mining Company, Arrowhead Esperanza Mines Company, Arrowhead Inspiration Mines Company and Arrowhead Consolidated Mining Company—only Arrowhead Consolidated produced worthwhile amounts of ore.

Activity in the Arrowhead district was fairly short-lived. By 1922 the town was on a sharp decline. The post office closed Sept. 4, 1924, and shortly thereafter the town was completely abandoned. Recently, leaching operations have been taking place in nearby Reveille, and it appears that the ghosts of Arrowhead could again be stirred by the drone of mining machinery. The only building extant at Arrowhead is the blacksmith shop. Extensive mine dumps left from the many companies are in the surrounding hills. Cement foundations and some scattered rubble are the only other remains that mark the site.

ASHMEADOW

DIRECTIONS:
From Pahrump, take State 52 west for 7 miles. Exit right and follow for 20 miles to Ashmeadow.

Ashmeadow, formed in the early 1900s, was a stop for stages heading to the strikes in the Bullfrog district. The Lawrence Kimball stages from Indian Springs served the small town. "Dad" Fairbanks, who ran a ranch just to the north, was responsible for organizing a small tent city at the fertile site. The tent establishments included hotels, restaurants and a saloon.

Abundant clay deposits were discovered around Ashmeadow. Not too much work was done with these until the early teens. The Death Valley Clay Company purchased most of the clay claims and began to process some ore. The mill constructed by the company was very inefficient and was constantly plagued with problems.

The Death Valley and Tonopah and Tidewater Railroad eventually built a narrow-gauge spur line to the clay pits at Ashmeadow. The four-mile line had both Plymouth and Milwaukee locomotives and was directly connected with the T.&T. R.R. at Bradford Siding in California. Arrival of the railroad spur allowed Ashmeadow to continue to grow. In 1901 a wooden falsefront store was moved from Zabriskie, California, to Ashmeadow. By 1923 the town had a steady population of about fifty and a number of substantial buildings, including a few saloons and hotels. The D.V.&T.&T. R.R. officially folded in 1927 but ran sporadically until 1930.

Even though the railroad closed, operations continued at Ashmeadow's clay pits until 1948. Total production was $2.9 million. The best year was 1929, when over $550,000 worth of clay was removed. Limited activity has continued at Ashmeadow since 1948, but for the most part the town has become more agricultural. A number of small ranches are in the area.

ASHTON

DIRECTIONS:
From Beatty, take US 95 south for 12 miles. Make a sharp right at the exit and follow this road for 2 miles. Exit left on a faint road, the old Tonopah and Tidewater Railroad bed. Follow road for 1½ miles to Ashton.

Ashton, a small water stop on the Tonopah and Tidewater Railroad, was never very important and no development ever took place here. Only a watertank and a small wooden shack were built at Ashton, and neither remains today. After the T.&T. R.R. pulled up its rails, not even trains could visit the parched site. The location is indistinguishable from the desert landscape, and the above directions are based on old railroad maps.

ATHENS (Warrior Mine)

DIRECTIONS:
From Black Spring, head north on Nevada 89 for 10.7 miles. Exit left and follow for ½ mile. At fork, bear right and follow for 2 miles to Athens.

The Athens camp grew up around the Warrior Mine and marks the center of the mining area. The Warrior Mine, the principal one in the district, was originally discovered in 1912 by a Civil War veteran who had been grubstaked by a storekeeper named Millett from Manhattan. The mine was purchased by the Warrior Gold Mining Company. During the first few months of production, $20,000 in gold bullion was produced. The mine was sold in 1921 to the Aladdin Divide Mining Company, which began intensive prospecting of the area that uncovered some new ore deposits. Another mining company, the Lucky Boy Divide Mining Company, H. McNamara president, bought the land adjacent to Athens and began active mining exploration during 1922.

The mining activity continued for a few years. Finally the ore became too scarce and operations were shut down. Leasers continued to work the area until 1939; mined ore was sent to the Dayton Consolidated mill in Silver City. No real production or additional activity took place after the leasers gave up in 1939.

Ruins still remain at Athens. The Warrior Mine and a few buildings are still struggling to stand, and the site is covered with rubble. The foundation of a small amalgamation mill, built in 1915, are just east of the Warrior Mine.

ATWOOD (Okey Davis)

DIRECTIONS:
From Gabbs, head south on Nevada 361 for 4 miles. Exit left and follow the Sheep Canyon Road for 9 miles to Atwood.

Atwood was formed in 1901, soon after gold was discovered in the surrounding hills. The camp became the center of the Fairplay mining district, which was organized in June 1903. Two years later a townsite was platted and a Tonopah realty company became chief promoter for the town. A post office opened at the camp on Feb. 6, 1906, and a fairly large hotel also began operations at that time. By the end of 1906, the town had a population of 200. A newspaper, the *Fairplay Prospector,* was published for a short while in 1907.

Atwood's mainstay was the Butler Mine, which had a 280-foot shaft and over 300 feet of drift work. When this mine closed in 1908, most interest in the Atwood area faded. The post office closed Jan. 31, 1908; Atwood was totally abandoned soon after.

There was a revival of the town in the 1920s when a man named Okey Davis discovered rich ore one quarter of a mile south of the old townsite. A small camp of eight buildings was built at the mine and some people moved to Atwood. The mine was operated by the Oatman United Gold Mining Company, which sank a 300-foot shaft on the property. Production from the mine quickly faded, and soon the company folded. As late as 1950, all of the buildings built at the mine were still standing. But today only piles of wooden rubble mark the camp's site. At Atwood, the ruins are even scantier.

BARCELONA

DIRECTIONS:
From Manhattan, head east on Nevada 69, bearing left ¼ mile out of town. Follow this road for 7 miles. Exit left on Silver Creek Road and follow for 8 miles. Remains are scattered from this point on for another mile.

Barcelona, a Mexican silver mining camp, first formed in 1874. The Mexicans made discoveries as early as 1867, but it was not until Castilian grandee Emanuel San Pedro led a Mexican prospecting group into the Spanish Belt district that sincere interest was exhibited in the Barcelona area. During 1874 the Barcelona Mine and a number of other smaller mines were put into operation. A fairly good-size camp formed and soon had a population of almost 175. Quite a few buildings were erected, including an assay office, three boardinghouses and a number of the "usual" business establishments.

Barcelona's boom quickly faltered as the ore faded. By 1877 the town only had a handful of residents. By the next spring the town was deserted. In 1880 some activity was renewed at the site but lasted only a short while. Soon Barcelona was abandoned once again.

There were a number of short bursts of activity throughout the next five decades. The last revival, in 1921, was the largest and most productive. In that year an impressive ten-stamp mill was built at

Ruins of the Barcelona Mine and Mill.

Barcelona. For a while it seemed the town was on the revival trail. But after only a year of activity, the mill was forced to close when ore values plummeted.

The site remained empty until recent years. A new small-scale operation has been reworking the Barcelona mines. The actual town of Barcelona is located about a mile above this new operation. A number of old stone-and-adobe ruins remain at the townsite, along with a few of the old mine shafts. At

Some of the ruins from Barcelona's earlier activity.

the Barcelona Mill site, other stone foundations remain. There are also a few wooden cabins from the 1921 revival. The site is well worth the trip, and fresh water is available.

BARRETT

DIRECTIONS:
From Ione, head north on Nevada 21 for 17 miles. Exit left and follow this road 1½ miles to a fork. Take the left road and follow this for 1¼ miles to Barrett.

Barrett, a small stage stop, was active during the late 1870s and early 1880s. The station was named after J. T. Barrett of Georgia, who ran the station. He came to Nye County in 1869, a few years before he set up the Barrett stage stop. The station was built at the high point of Barrett Canyon and was used to change horses after the hard climb to the summit. There was a solid wood structure along with a few small cabins and a complement of horse stables. A small restaurant operated in the station, and lodging was also available. A post office opened here on May 24, 1882, J. T. Barrett postmaster. The need for stages north diminished, and by 1884 none were running through Barrett. The post office closed on Jan. 23, 1885, and the town was soon abandoned.

Locating the station is extremely difficult. The road ends at the site, but it takes a lot of searching to locate the scattered wooden scraps marking the remote site. The road tends to be very rough and is impassable during wet weather.

BAXTER SPRING (Baxter's) (Cedar Spring)

DIRECTIONS:
From Tonopah, head east on US 6 for 5½ miles. Exit left onto Nevada 376 and follow for 13.3 miles to the junction with Nevada 82. Follow Nevada 82 for 9 miles. Exit left onto road marked by Baxter Spring signs and follow for 6½ miles to Baxter Spring. More ruins are located half a mile past the spring.

Baxter Spring, then known as Cedar Spring, was a stage stop on the line running from San Antonio to Belmont. The small settlement never amounted to much until gold was discovered in 1906 in the hills just west of the stage station.

A small tent camp sprang up almost immediately as the rush to the area began. By spring of 1906 the camp had swelled to a peak population of 400. The

This ruin is one of the few markers of the former boom town of Baxter Spring.

site was renamed Baxter's, or Baxter Spring, after one of the discoverers. Business establishments in the town were mostly in tents and included four saloons, two grocery stores, two general mercantiles, a couple of boardinghouses, a hardware store and a few restaurants. The ore veins were extremely shallow and quickly ran out. By the end of 1906—in just a year—the town was abandoned. A few wooden buildings were built before the veins ran out, but everyone left before more substantial construction took place.

There are some scattered remains. No buildings are standing, but a few partially collapsed ruins can be seen. A number of scattered stone ruins and foundations still remain near the few mines of the district. Nothing at all is left of the old San Antonio–Belmont stage station. The road to the site is rough.

BEATTY

DIRECTIONS:
Located at junction of Nevada 58 and Interstate 95.

The eventual Beatty townsite was first occupied by white men in 1870. The Paiute Indians had been camping at the well-watered site long before a man named Landers built a small ranch there. Landers continued to run his spread until the 1890s. Montillus Murray Beatty, also known as Jim, moved into the abandoned ranch house in March 1896. Beatty, a native of Iowa who had fought for the Union

Beatty's main street, only months after the town formed. The Montgomery Hotel was eventually built on the lot occupied by the Montana Club in his photo. *(Nevada Historical Society)*

November 1905 photo of Beatty titled "The First Snow." The two-story Montgomery Hotel dominates the town. *(Nevada Historical Society)*

during the Civil War, married a Paiute woman not too long before moving to Oasis Valley. His ranch soon became a stop for many tired and thirsty travelers. Beatty and his wife would occasionally travel across Death Valley to stay at their other ranch on Cow Creek.

A small settlement began to form around the ranch during the fall of 1904. As nearby Rhyolite and Bullfrog grew, so did Beatty. In November 1904 Bob Montgomery came to Beatty and staked out the townsite. A post office, with Jim Beatty as postmaster, opened on Jan. 19, 1905. The town had no mining and served as a supply depot for the Bullfrog district. In contrast to other nearby camps, the town had an abundance of water, both from springs and wells. In October 1905 Bob Montgomery completed his $25,000 Montgomery Hotel, which became a landmark in Beatty.

In March 1906 Jim Beatty resigned as postmaster and later that year sold his ranch, along with its many springs, to the Bullfrog Power and Light Company for $10,000. Beatty and his wife moved into the town and resided there in a luxurious house.

During 1906–07 the town of Beatty reached its peak population of 1000. A number of business establishments, including a Porter Brothers store, were opened. Beatty's first railroad arrived in town on Oct. 18, 1906. Four days later the town conducted its first railroad days' celebration. The Las Vegas and Tonopah Railroad had won the race to town; within a year two more railroads joined the L.V.&T. R.R. On April 25, 1907, the Bullfrog-Goldfield Railroad began regular service to Beatty. The second railroad days' celebration cumulated with driving a golden spike into the last rail. The last railroad to arrive in Beatty was "Borax" Smith's Tonopah and Tidewater line, which began service on Oct. 27, 1907.

Beatty had two newspapers, one of which printed only a few issues. The second, the *Beatty Bullfrog Miner*, along with the *Rhyolite Herald*, was the most important paper in the Bullfrog district. The *Beatty Bullfrog Miner*, known earlier as the *Bullfrog Miner*, began publishing in Beatty on May 13, 1905. It was published by C. W. Nicklin, who sold it on Jan. 12, 1907, to Clyde Terrell and Dan McKenna. The two new men had some problems, and on June 15,

1907, they sold the paper back to Nicklin. He continued to publish it but gradually lost interest. On Feb. 22, 1908, Nicklin sold the paper back to Clyde Terrell, who published the paper until it folded on Oct. 24, 1908.

Montgomery's hotel was moved to booming Pioneer in 1908; it burned in that town's fire in May 1909. Jim Beatty, the beloved founder of Beatty, died in 1908. Beatty, along with a friend, had been hauling wood when Beatty fell off the wagon and hit his head. He died the next day, on Dec. 14, at the age of seventy-three. The town named for him now reigns as the sole survivor of the once booming Bullfrog mining district. Long after Rhyolite and Bullfrog had faded, Beatty continued to serve as a supply depot for people still living in the district. Even so, the area has been in a slow, drawn-out decline. The railroads are all gone now, with the L.V.&T. R.R. leaving in the teens, the B.-G. R.R. in 1928 and the T.&T. R.R. in 1940. Today Beatty is a sleepy town of about 100 people. The town is full of history and has some very interesting remains. Food, gas and motels are all available here.

BELLEHELEN

DIRECTIONS:
From Tonopah, head east on US 6 for 34 miles. Exit right and follow this road, bearing left, for 10 miles to faint remains of Bellehelen.

Gold and silver ore was discovered on the west flank of the Kawich range in early 1904. Soon a small camp was formed; a post office opened at the camp on April 27, 1907. In 1907 George Wingfield and his engineers visited the camp to look at the mining properties. They did not find any lasting ore bodies and soon left. The camp folded quickly afterward, and the post office closed on Jan. 19, 1908.

The district remained fairly quiet until early 1909, when the Nevada Bellehelen Mining Company purchased six claims near the old camp. Soon almost 500 people were in the Bellehelen district, feverishly searching all of the side canyons for gold. The company had one tunnel mine well over 600 feet long and dug two shafts of 175 feet and 140 feet. The ore per ton ran from $25 to as high as $165. The values were two thirds silver and one third gold. The company rented a ten-stamp mill in Hawes Canyon, located in the Golden Arrow mining district. The ore from the mines in Bellehelen was shipped to this mill for processing. The tunnel was the big producer of the six claims, but the Never-Sweat and Sciota mines also were fairly consistent producers. Between 1909 and 1911 the Nevada Bellehelen Mining Company removed over $500,000 in gold and silver from the Bellehelen district.

The post office reopened on Oct. 15, 1909. Activity began to decline during late 1910, and by the beginning of 1911 the town had only fifty residents. The post office was shut down on Nov. 15, 1911, and the district fell silent soon after.

1914 photo of the problem-plagued Bellehelen Mill. *(William Metscher)*

Bellehelen was at its peak in the middle teens. The corner of the Bellehelen Mill is visible at right. *(William Metscher)*

The district ended its slumber in 1917 when the Pacific States Mining Company purchased a number of claims near Bellehelen. The company produced over $100,000 before merging with the Tonopah-Kawich Mining Company. The merging companies formed a new company, the Bellehelen Merger Mines Company, incorporated in 1920 with J. W. Oldham as president. The company owned fourteen claims in the Bellehelen district. A new vein, the Midvale, was discovered in 1920 and carried values of $19 to $72 per ton. The company built a 50-ton cyanide mill during late 1922 and early 1923, run by the countercurrent decantation process. Operations were started in May 1923, but the mill was plagued with numerous problems. It was shut down a few months later and was only used a few times after that. The company ceased operations in the district in 1924. They made plans to reopen in 1925, but the plans fell through when financial problems arose.

Another company, the Elgin-Bellehelen Divide Mining Company, became active in the Bellehelen district during the teens. The company was originally known as the Silverfields Ajax Mines Company, but the name was changed in March 1919 during reincorporation. The company purchased a gold and silver mine in the Bellehelen district and immediately began intensive operations. The mine was worked to a depth of 120 feet before operations were stopped. The property was leased out until 1923, when the company left the district to concentrate efforts on their property in Esmeralda County's Divide district.

Three other mining companies worked the district during the 1920s. The Bellehelen Extension Mining Company, incorporated in early 1923, soon had six claims adjacent to the Bellehelen Merger Mines Company's property. Bellehelen Extension had limited production and never realized a large profit. The company folded in 1925 and sold its holdings to the newly formed Bellehelen Development Corporation.

After buying the property, the Bellehelen Development Corporation reopened the three mines, two of which were vertical shafts. The total property covered 120 acres; the best producer was the tunnel mine on the Starlight claim. The ore removed from the Starlight assayed as high as $26 per ton. The company faded during 1926 and by 1927 had folded.

The only other company to work the district was the Bellehelen Consolidated Mines Company, incorporated in April 1924. The company took over six claims in the district but the operation was doomed to failure. Bellehelen Consolidated folded in 1927.

The ruins of Bellehelen are extremely disappointing. Absolutely nothing remains of the camp. Only the ruins of the 50-ton mill mark the site, and even these are not very interesting. The ruins of the Bellehelen ranch are half a mile above the mill ruins. The canyon is filled with wild horses, but the site itself is not worth the trouble involved in finding it.

BELMONT

DIRECTIONS:
From Tonopah, head east on US 6 for 5½ miles. Take Nevada 376 north for 13.3 miles. Exit right onto Nevada 82 for 28 miles to Belmont.

Belmont is the queen of Nye County ghost towns. Its history begins in October 1865 when an Indian discovered a rich deposit of silver in the Toquima Mountains. A small camp called Belmont (meaning beautiful mountains) soon formed. By the beginning of 1866, a full-scale rush had begun. During 1866–67 Belmont was credited with a population as high as 10,000, but better estimates are that about 2000–4000 people were living in the bustling town. The Belmont boom drained the population from many nearby towns, including Nye County seat Ione. As Belmont continued to grow, the residents began to call for a county seat change. In February 1867 Belmont became the new county seat. The town was appropiated $3400 to construct a courthouse; a hugh brick building was started but not totally completed until 1874. A post office opened in Belmont on April 10, 1867, and the town seemed destined for permanence.

Mining in Belmont's early years was very good. Ten major mines were being worked within a year after the first discoveries. The deepest of these was the Belmont Mine, well over 500 feet in the earth. The mine also had about 2000 feet of lateral workings. The full potential of the mine could never be realized because of the exceptionally heavy water flow that continuously hampered mining operations. Other important mines were the Monitor-Belmont, 250 feet; the Arizona, 175 feet; and

Ruins of one of the many saloons once active in Belmont.

wide as the "silver-tongued orator of the West." Fitch was running for a congressional seat and felt that by having his own newspaper he would have an advantage in the election. The first issue of the weekly tabloid came out on June 3, 1868. The paper only lasted until Fitch was successfully elected to office; it folded on April 10, 1869, having served its purpose.

The *Belmont Courier* was first published on Feb. 14, 1874, with John Booth as owner. Booth, along with Andrew Casamayou, put together one of the best liked and most successful newspapers ever published in Nye County. The paper went smoothly until 1875 when Andrew Casamayou died. After his death on December 10, Booth lost most of his

the Green and Oder Mine, which yielded ore valued at $400 per ton.

Six mills were built in and around Belmont during its peak years. The first was a ten-stamp mill built in 1866; it continued to operate until 1869. In 1867 a larger twenty-stamp mill was built. This operated only a short while and was eventually moved to Gold Mountain. The largest mill, the Combination, was built in 1868. It had forty stamps and cost over $225,000 to build. There were also three quartz stamp mills, of five, twenty and thirty stamps. The twenty-stamp mill was the Monitor–Belmont, built by the Belmont Silver Mining Company in 1867. There were also five sawmills in the area, all extremely busy turning out board lumber for buildings in Belmont. The largest of these, owned by men named Crowell and Myers, produced over 4000 board feet of lumber daily.

Newspapers formed an integral part of Belmont. There were three during Belmont's early years: the *Silver Bend Reporter*, the *Mountain Champion* and the *Belmont Courier*. The *Silver Bend Reporter* was the first Belmont newspaper; its initial issue was published on March 30, 1867. The paper was run by Oscar Fairchild, and his brother, M. D., was editor. The paper started out as a weekly but eventually became a semiweekly, published on Wednesdays and Saturdays. Things just did not work out for the paper, however. It folded on July 29, 1868, and was moved to Austin.

The second paper in Belmont was formed completely as a political weapon. The *Mountain Champion* was owned by Thomas Fitch, known far and

The impressive Belmont Court House, which served Nye County from 1867 to 1905, is one of the most famous ghost town structures in Nevada.

Rear view of the courthouse, showing the shattered remains of the jail.

15

The picturesque Cosmopolitan Dance Hall and Saloon in Belmont still struggles to stand but is in a very weak state.

enthusiasm for the paper and finally decided to leave it on Dec. 16, 1876. The paper was never the same. Andrew Maute took over, joined by Sam Donald in 1880. By then Belmont was well on its way to being a ghost town and the paper had a rough time. Donald left in 1889, leaving Maute to keep the struggling paper afloat. The *Belmont Courier* finally folded on March 2, 1901, with this closing statement: "Our last issue—every branch of business in Nye County is dull."

Belmont was not always dull. The town had a number of murders and even a couple of lynchings. The first major conflict occurred as a result of dissension between Irish and Cornish miners. It was April 17, 1867, when the Irish miners marched on the Silver Bend Mining Company's offices. They took the president, R. B. Canfield, placed him on a "rail" and paraded him around town, while stopping at most of the saloons. The group became more and more mean as they drank. One man, Louis Bodrow, a former Austin marshal, dared to confront the mob. John Dignon, one of the parading group, hit Bodrow, and all hell broke loose. In the ensuing gun battle, Bodrow and Dignon were killed, a number of men were injured and Canfield escaped.

The second incident involved the lynching of two men, and it remains a black mark in Belmont's history. The two, Charlies McIntyre and Jack Walker, had been involved in a shooting in May 1874 and both were arrested. They escaped but were soon found hiding in an old mine shaft. That night vigilantes lynched the pair. The man that the pair had killed was known to be no good and the circumstances of the death are unclear. Memory of that night still hangs over the town.

Belmont, after a slowdown from 1868–73, received a big boost when a number of new rich

This 1893 photo was taken after Belmont had begun to decline. The Monitor–Belmont Mill is visible in the far left background. *(William Metscher)*

Later photo taken just before the church in the foreground was moved to Manhattan. *(Western Research Center/University of Wyoming)*

deposits were discovered in the Belmont, Highbridge, Monitor-Belmont and the Quintero mines in 1874. Most of these were located about a mile east of Belmont. A small settlement known as East Belmont formed there. Belmont soon had over 2000 people once again and the outlook seemed good. The mines stayed open until 1887, when declining ore value put a damper on profits and forced close-downs. From 1865 to 1887 the Belmont mines recorded production in excess of $15 million. For the most part the mines remained quiet until about ten years after the turn of the century.

When Jim Butler left his Monitor Valley ranch in May 1900 to head for the strikes in Klondike (Esmeralda County), no one knew his trip would change the state's history. After Butler discovered the rich silver deposits at Tonopah Springs, a huge rush began to that area, emptying many small towns near the site. Almost immediately a strong call went up to transfer the county seat from Belmont to the newly rich Tonopah. By 1903 Belmont only had thirty-six qualified voters and could manage but feeble resistance. In May 1905 the transfer was made. By 1911 Belmont's population had shrunk to less than fifty, and on May 31, 1911, the town lost its post office.

Belmont had a fairly active revival beginning in 1914. The Monitor Belmont Mining Company had acquired almost all of the old mines near Belmont and, in 1915, constructed a huge mill to process the ore. The mill, the Cameron, had ten 1600-pound stamps and a 150-ton flotation system to process ore from the Monitor Belmont's twenty-one claims. The bricks used to construct this mill were taken from the Combination Mill, torn down the year before. The Cameron Mill was also used to rework some tailings from the earlier activity. The company had three major mines (600 feet, 750 feet and 1100 feet), which kept the mill running until 1917. With all this activity, the population of Belmont began to rise slightly. The post office reopened on Sept. 27, 1915. It looked like Belmont was going to get a second chance for survival.

The Monitor Belmont Mining Company left the district after closing the Cameron Mill in 1917. The property was leased to the Nevada Wonder Mining Company in early 1918. Nevada Wonder spent huge amounts of money for exploration that turned out to be fruitless; the company relinquished its lease in 1919. But Belmont was not ready to die yet. A 30-ton cyanide plant opened in 1921 to treat the old tailings. When this was given up, Belmont drifted back to ghostdom. The post office closed on Aug. 31, 1922, and there have been no revivals since. The town still had twenty-eight people in 1945. Soon that figure was down to ten, and that remains fairly consistent even today. The activity from 1914 to 1922 yielded a reported $1 million.

Belmont is the queen of Nye County ghosts—in fact, one of the top three ghosts in the state. The remains at and around Belmont are amazing. There

The gaunt Monitor–Belmont Mill soon after it was shut down and stripped of all machinery. *(Nevada Historical Society)*

Belmont in the 1930s, long after the town became a ghost, seemingly guarded by the gaunt Belmont Courthouse. Even by then most of Belmont was already in ruins. *(MacKay School of Mines/University of Nevada at Reno)*

are picturesque ruins of the three mills. Only a stack and some rubble mark the site of the Monitor–Belmont Mill, located just below the town. The Combination Mill is marked by a huge, pockmarked stack and extensive ruins, including a small brick room that probably housed explosives. The best of the mills is Cameron, whose skeletal brick walls of enormous size are awesome to behold. Both the Combination and Cameron mills are in East Belmont, a mile east of Belmont. The Forest Service has mistakenly labeled the Cameron Mill as the Highbridge Mill. This mistaken identity has also appeared in a few of the more recent books on Nevada. The Highbridge Mill was built in the 1860s and was located on the far side of the mountain behind the Cameron Mill. The mill was high up on the mountain, and today only stone foundations mark the site.

The remains at East Belmont, excluding the mills, are fairly scant. The hillsides are scattered with old

This interesting grave in the Belmont Cemetery is among hundreds of others, most of which are unmarked. Jack Longstreet and his Indian wife are two of the more famous people buried here.

The extensive ruins of Belmont's Combination Mill harbor old nails and other artifacts.

Ruins on the main street of Belmont include the brick-faced former bank and two adjoining saloons.

stone cabins. The one relic that makes East Belmont unique is the horse racetrack. It was known as Monitor Park and operated for a number of years in the 1860s and the 1870s.

Belmont itself is amazing. First there is the beautiful and imposing courthouse, recently taken over by the Nevada Historical Society. The society has protected the building against further deterioration by putting plastic over the windows and locking the doors so vandals cannot get inside. After the old courthouse was abandoned, it was used for many years as a hay storage building for one of the nearby ranches. The cells of the jail, built on the back section of the courthouse, were torn out and used in

The beautiful remains of the Cameron Mill, which had a definite gothic flavor. It was one of the most attractive and expensive mills ever built in Nye County.

19

the Gabbs jail. Gabbs is now planning to build a new jail, and plans are in motion to return the cells to Belmont and restore them to their proper place.

The main street of Belmont contains some of the best remains I have ever seen. In addition to the ruins of a few dozen buildings, there are quite a number of buildings still standing. These include the old bank and the popular Cosmopolitan Dance Hall and Saloon. It was at the Cosmopolitan that the famous actress Lotta Crabtree performed in *Uncle Tom's Cabin*. The very large Belmont Cemetery, just south of the Monitor–Belmont Mill ruins on the east side of the road, includes many wooden headboards along with many fancy gravestones. Jack Longstreet and his Indian bride are both buried here.

Belmont should not be missed. I found myself constantly going back to Belmont for "just one more look." Plan on a day or two to completely tour Belmont and East Belmont. By the way, gas is available here but not on a regular basis.

BERLIN

DIRECTIONS:
From Ione, head south on Nevada 91 for 3 miles. Exit left and follow signs to Berlin (about 2 miles).

The Berlin Mine was discovered in 1895 by State Senator Bell, who immediately sold the mine property to John Stokes of New York. The town was founded in 1897. In 1898 the Nevada Company bought two mills in the Ione area and transferred equipment to Berlin for installation in a new thirty-stamp mill being built here. A post office was opened on July 10, 1900. Berlin kept growing; by 1905 the town had a population of close to 300 people.

Berlin boasted a large store, moved here from Ione in 1900. It served both as a store and a boardinghouse and was one of the most impressive structures in Berlin. In addition to the saloons located in nearby Union Canyon, there were three others closer to Berlin. The Johnson saloon was moved to Ione in 1910; Bob Johnson continued operations here until 1919. The Pucinelli saloon was halfway between Berlin and Union Canyon. During the early years of Berlin's existence, this saloon was the most popular because it was closest to the mine and mill. The Bell saloon was the last one built in Berlin. It was owned by Billie Bell, who had bought the Pucinelli saloon. Bell inherited $3000 and decided to build a new saloon in an excellent location just below town. Bell's enjoyed brisk business until Berlin was abandoned. The Union Canyon town hall was moved to Berlin by Bob Dixon in 1910 to serve as a boardinghouse. A stageline was also running.

In 1907 everything went dead when the mine and mill closed down. A few people did remain, and their persistence was rewarded in late 1909 when the mine and mill were reopened by leasers named Parman and Feenaman. The small revival, which lasted only a year, brought some life back to Berlin. Soon after the Parman and Feenaman operation shut down, Alfred Smith took a lease and constructed a 50-ton cyanide plant just below the mill. The plant was run by only three men. The operation continued on a small scale from 1910 until 1914. The recovery rate of the cyanide processing was just $2.50 a ton.

After the Smith plant closed, there was no more activity in the Berlin area for a number of years. The post office closed on Dec. 18, 1918; Berlin was in its final death throes. The Goldfield Blue Bell Mining Company purchased claims in the Berlin area in the 1920s and the district had a small ray of hope for a while. The company reequipped the Berlin mine with a steam hoist and an air compressor. The operations were never full scale but were of an exploratory nature. The company kept mine superintendent D. S. Johnson at Berlin until 1947. In that year the company dismantled the mill; there has been no mining activity in the area since then. Total production for the district was recorded at $850,000.

There are extensive remains in Berlin. Thirteen buildings are at the site, which has been incorporated into the Berlin-Ichthyosaur Nevada State Park. The state park system has put Berlin in a state of "arrested decay." Among the buildings still remaining are the huge mill, recently restored to working shape by the state; the old assay office, now serving as a ranger's station; and a number of miners' cabins. All three saloons have disappeared, but the building sites are easily found by looking for piles of broken glass. The ruins of five buildings, including the Pucinelli saloon, are half a mile south of town. There is a small cemetery southeast of town; most of the graves are now empty, having

Berlin today is cared for by the state park system. At its peak, houses and saloons covered the now empty land along the path.

Closeup of the Berlin Mine and Mill. The mill has recently been restored by the Nevada State Park System. The building on the left served as a boardinghouse.

This prospector posed in Berlin during its peak. The store behind him was later moved to Ione. *(Western History Research Center/University of Wyoming)*

been moved to different towns after the Berlin collapse. The ghosts of Berlin rest quietly, with only occasional visitors curiously looking over the beautiful old buildings as they head up to the Ichthyosaur fossil site.

Berlin is a definite must for any ghost town lover. Many hours can be spent wandering through the site. There are signs all over erected by the state park system to label and describe the buildings still standing and others that are completely gone.

BLACK SPRING

DIRECTIONS:
From Cloverdale, head south for 1 mile. Exit right and follow this road for 4 miles. Exit right onto Nevada 89 and follow for 3.1 miles to Black Spring.

Black Spring was the scene of fairly heavy mining activity, but not for silver and gold. Diatomaceous earth was the "mineral" mined here. The Nature Products Company, headed by J. M. Fenwick, purchased well over 200 acres of the mineral-bearing earth, which contained a high concentration of silica plus small amounts of iron oxide, alumina and soda. The minerals obtained from the soil were used as a base for Super Dent Tooth Powder and Super Dental Cream. Nothing of consequence remains from the activity in the area, but Black Spring still gives forth a cool stream of water.

BLAKE'S CAMP

DIRECTIONS:
From Golden Arrow, head west for 4 miles to Blake's Camp.

Blake's Camp was an extremely short-lived mining camp formed in June 1905 after gold was discovered in a dry wash west of Golden Arrow. This excitement was the result of discoveries at Golden Arrow and Silver Bow, which brought a flock of prospectors to the area to comb every canyon of the district. Blake's Camp soon had a population of about twenty-five. The gold ore was free gold and was in an area 600 feet long and 2 feet wide. The ore assayed at only $15 per ton, and soon the camp was only a memory.

Not too many buildings were built during the sixteen-month existence of Blake's Camp. A few prospectors made small shelters but nothing substantial. No other deposits were discovered once the vein was finished, and the miners moved back to Golden Arrow. Now the site is marked by only an old corral and a long trench where the vein was. The site is not worth the danger of getting stuck in the many sand traps on the road to the site.

BLUE EAGLE SPRING

DIRECTIONS:
From Currant, take US 6 south for 9.8 miles. Exit left and follow this road for 6 miles. Exit right (south) and follow for 3 miles to Blue Eagle Spring on the right.

A ranch house was built at Blue Eagle Spring in the 1860s. Martin "Pop" Horton, in addition to building his ranch, also constructed a store, a blacksmith shop and a saloon. And Horton ran a station house that served a good many tired travelers. The Blue Eagle Spring ranch became the center of the Blue Eagle ranching district. The store at Horton's ranch remained open until 1910. The ranch has continued to operate to this day. There are still a few original buildings left on the ranch, including the old store and saloon.

BONITA

DIRECTIONS:
From Ione, take Nevada 21 north for 11 miles to Bonita Canyon.

Bonita was an obscure stage station active during the early 1900s. It was a stop on the Ione-Austin stage run. A post office was organized here on Aug. 2, 1907, but was rescinded on March 19, 1908. Soon the stage line stopped running and Bonita faded into the past. Nothing whatsoever remains at the stage station site, and the road to the site is very rough and eventually vanishes. The station was in the canyon, but the exact location is not known.

BONNIE CLARE (Clare) (Clair) (Thorp's Wells) (Thorp) (Montana Station)

DIRECTIONS:
From Beatty, head north on US 95 for 35.4 miles to Scotty's Junction. At the junction take a left onto Nevada 72 and follow this road for 6½ miles. Bonnie Clare is on the right at the base of the mountain.

Mining activity began in the Bonnie Clare district in the 1880s, and a small stamp mill was built at a site known then as Thorp's Wells. The mill handled ore from the three major mines—the Rattlesnake, Hard Luck and Courbat—all located near Gold Mountain, 6 miles to the northwest. The ore was transported to the mill by teams of fifteen to twenty mules. The mill operated into the 20th century and was purchased soon after the turn of the century by the Bonnie Clare Bullfrog Mining Company.

A small camp began to form, and soon a stageline from Bullfrog to Goldfield ran through the camp, now known as Thorp. In 1904 another mill was built, the Bonnie Clare, to treat ore from all over the district. A small post office opened on June 15, 1905. The camp continued to function on a low level until given a big boost in late September 1906 when the Bullfrog-Goldfield Railroad reached Thorp. The B.-G. R.R. station was known as Montana Station. But the residents did not like that name, and when a new townsite was platted in October 1906, the town was renamed Bonnie Clare, after an early settler's daughter.

A number of new properties on Gold Mountain, owned by the Nevada Goldfield Mining Company, began to produce consistently in November 1906. The B.-G. R.R. soon began to work on a spur line to the mines. A second railroad, the Las Vegas and Tonopah Railroad, arrived in August 1907. An impressive two-story wooden depot station was built to serve travelers. Soon after the arrival of the L.V.&T. R.R., Bonnie Clare reached its peak. The town had a population of a little more than 100. Business establishments included saloons, stores

The railroad town of Bonnie Clare, shortly after the rails of the Las Vegas and Tonopah Railroad were laid. *(Nevada Historical Society)*

Ruins of a boardinghouse at Bonnie Clare. An old powder house is just to the right.

and boardinghouses. Bonnie Clare is one of the few towns that had a bona fide train wreck. On October 1, 1907, an open switch caused derailment of a B.-G. R.R. train, killing no one but injuring a number of people.

Although the town was known as Bonnie Clare, the post office did not change its name from Thorp to Bonnie Clare until July 13, 1909. In 1908–09 the combination of Rhyolite's collapse (which slowed railroad traffic) and decline of mining at the Gold Mountain mines put a damper on Bonnie Clare's hopes for the future. The New Bonnie Clare Mining and Milling Company was organized in February 1910 and renovated the old Bonnie Clare mill. Unfortunately the venture proved fruitless and was soon abandoned. By 1911 Bonnie Clare's population had dwindled to less than fifty, and the tailspin continued. The last real activity at Bonnie Clare took place in 1913 when a new mill was built on the old Thorp property. The mill processed ore from the Happy Kelly mine, located just south of the Bonnie Clare townsite.

When the L.V.&T. R.R. and the B.-G. R.R. consolidated in 1914, the B.-G. R.R. right-of-way was abandoned while the L.V.&T. R.R. tracks maintained limited operations through Bonnie Clare. The last real railroad service came in June 1927, when Bonnie Clare was used as a shipping point for all supplies to build Scotty's Castle. After the railroad folded in 1928, Bonnie Clare also quickly folded. Within a short time only the postmaster and a few others were left. When the post office closed on Dec. 31, 1931, the population stood at two. Soon only the empty buildings were left to face the hot days and freezing nights. Ghosts ruled supreme over the crumbling ruins.

During the 1950s the Lippincott mine and a small mill operated at the townsite. Even today the mines are worked off and on. The ruins of Bonnie Clare are quite interesting and are well worth the trip. A

Crumbling adobe and stone building still standing at Bonnie Clare.

The galvanized siding on the Bonnie Clare Mill is left from the last revival. The older sections of the mill are farther up on the side of the mountain.

few complete buildings along with a number of stone ruins remain. Only wooden rubble marks the site of the once imposing depot station. The ruins of the Bonne Clare mill dominate the site and are adjacent to the stone ruins. When in the Bonnie Clare area, be sure to take a side trip to Scotty's Castle, just over the state line.

BOWLERVILLE

DIRECTIONS:
Located 2 miles south of Johnnie.

Bowlerville was a short-lived mining camp that formed around the Bowler mine shortly after the turn of the century. The small camp was named after Fred Bowler, founder of the town. The population never exceeded fifteen, and the camp lasted only 1½ years before totally folding. Nothing substantial was ever built at the site, and not a trace of the camp remains. Only a small tailing pile from the Bowler mine even shows that man was ever here.

BROWNE'S CAMP

DIRECTIONS:
From Lathrop Wells, head east on US 95 for 9 miles. Exit left on a faint dirt road and follow for 2 miles to Browne's Camp.

Browne's Camp was a short-lived mining camp formed in 1907 or 1908. A small tent camp sprung up after some shallow ore deposits were discovered. The camp received supplies from the Chloride stop on the Las Vegas and Tonopah Railroad, just a few miles to the southwest. Browne's Camp disappeared from maps in 1920 before any actual production took place. Nothing remains at the site.

BULLFROG

DIRECTIONS:
From Beatty, take Nevada 58 west for 3.9 miles. Exit right and follow this road for 1½ miles. Exit left and Bullfrog will be ½ mile down this road.

Both Bullfrog and its sister city, Rhyolite, formed soon after initial discoveries were made in the Bullfrog district in August 1904. Frank "Shorty"

Bullfrog's populace, shortly after Harris and Cross made their discoveries. *(Nevada Historical Society)*

All that remains of once prosperous Bullfrog is the old icehouse, and even that will soon be gone. An old rusted-out Buick is to the left of the icehouse.

Harris and Ernest L. Cross made the discoveries in the hills just west of the Bullfrog townsite on August 4. There are different versions as to the origin of the name Bullfrog. Harris's version is that when *he* discovered the ore, which was speckled green, he thought it looked like a bullfrog. Cross's version, and what seems to be the more popular story, is that the name came from an old song he always sang that included the line, "The bulldog on the bank and the bullfrog in the pool."

The tent town of Amargosa City, near the original Bullfrog Mine, was completely moved to the Bullfrog townsite. The town quickly grew, and the population reached close to 1000 during the winter of 1904. In addition to tents, a small number of stone cabins and dugouts were built. Brush and small trees from the nearby hills provided the only source of fuel for the drafty buildings. In early 1905 Rhyolite was formed, and soon fairly fierce competition began between the two towns. Free lots were offered to merchants and potential residents in March 1905. A post office opened on March 21, 1905, and served the 300 permanent residents of Bullfrog. A paper, the *Bullfrog Miner,* began publication on March 31, 1905, with Frank Mannix as editor. It was published in Bullfrog until March 23,

Bullfrog on May 1, 1905, was larger than nearby Rhyolite. Far in the background is the settlement of Original. *(Western History Research Center/University of Wyoming)*

Bullfrog in November 1905, soon after the Bullfrog Hotel had been completed. *(Nevada Historical Society)*

This December 1905 photo of Bullfrog pictures a mule train with the first load of ore from the Denver Mine. Mule trains were the main means of transporting ore until the railroads were completed. *(Nevada Historical Society)*

1906, when operations were transferred to the larger Rhyolite.

May 1905 was the peak of Bullfrog's short existence. H. H. Clark, who earlier was giving Main Street lots away, was now selling them for as much as $1500. A $65,000 water system, an $18,000 two-story hotel and a county jail were all constructed during early 1905. Before construction of the water system, water had to be brought in from the Amargosa River. Former Senator William Stewart, then eighty, moved to Bullfrog in May and built a $20,000 complex that consisted of a one-story, ten-room adobe house and a large law office.

Stewart had a 1200-volume law library in his office, which was believed to be one of the largest in the state. He also owned an entire block on Bullfrog's main street and constantly expressed his opinion that Bullfrog would soon outgrow Rhyolite.

Stewart's hopes were crushed as Rhyolite continued to swell and drain more people from fading Bullfrog. A number of fatal gunfights did not help Bullfrog. Transfer of the *Bullfrog Miner* was a severe blow because it showed that Rhyolite was definitely leaving Bullfrog in the dust. The May 4, 1906, issue of the *Rhyolite Herald* included the headline: *"Verily, The Bullfrog Croaketh."* The article stated that the last mercantile in Bullfrog had closed, moving to Golden Street in Rhyolite. Soon Bullfrog had only a handful of residents. The hotel, Bullfrog's last status symbol, burned on June 25, 1906, a symbolic funeral pyre for the dying town.

By 1907 Bullfrog was practically emptied, with only Stewart and a few others still hoping for a boom. Stewart's confidence in Bullfrog finally faded, and he moved to Washington in May 1908. With Stewart gone and Rhyolite in the midst of its dramatic decline, Bullfrog's last hopes for survival were dashed. The post office struggled into 1909 but finally closed on May 15, 1909. Bullfrog joined the growing ghostly ranks of Nye County.

Today Bullfrog is almost completely flattened. The only visible ruins are those of the old icehouse. These crumbling adobe ruins are not going to last much longer; soon Bullfrog will have rejoined the very earth from which it had so quickly sprung. Some faint ruins of Senator Stewart's house and office still remain but are extremely hard to locate. His library and office sign are now in the Nevada Historical Society museum. At the Bullfrog site Mrs. Earl Gregory runs a small antique and coffee shop. Conversation with her is very rewarding and interesting. Be sure to visit the Bullfrog-Rhyolite cemetery, just south of the Bullfrog townsite.

BUTTERFIELD SPRING

DIRECTIONS:
From Currant, head south on US 6 for 9.8 miles. Exit left and follow this road for 6 miles. Exit right and follow for 6 more miles to Butterfield Spring.

Butterfield Spring has been utilized as a source of cool, refreshing water for centuries. The Indians were the first to use the site, making it a camping spot during their hunting trips. It was not until 1867 that the white man came to the spring. Alexander Beatty, who later made important ore discoveries at Troy, decided to homestead the land; he built a small ranch complex.

Nearby Butterfield Marsh had large deposits of sodium chloride (salt) that was almost 99 percent pure. A lot of this was mined during Tybo's boom for use in its silver mills. After the salt mining was curtailed, no activity other than ranching took place until 1912. In that year the Railroad Valley Company was formed and began exploratory drilling, hoping to find potash salts. Seven test holes, ranging from 745 feet to 1200 feet produced no potash salts. Almost $150,000 was spent on this project; when it failed, the company immediately went bankrupt.

The spring itself makes Butterfield Spring so unique. It is not known how deep the spring is, but the cool, clean water maintains a constant temperature of 54°F. A fish, the chub, lives in the spring and is completely unique because, since it is isolated, it has evolved into a separate strain of chub. Most of the original buildings of the old ranch still remain, including a few sod-type structures.

CACTUS SPRINGS

DIRECTIONS:
Located 10 miles north of Gold Crater, inside the Las Vegas Bombing and Gunnery Range. Off-limits to the public.

The Cactus Springs district was first worked in 1901 when turquoise deposits were discovered by William Petry on Cactus Peak. The largest mine in the district, the Cactus Nevada Silver Mine, was discovered in 1904. Mining activity was limited until 1919, when two mining companies became active in the district. The Cactus Nevada Silver Mines Company was incorporated in 1919, under the control of Joseph Menzel from Rochester, Nevada. The company purchased the seven Bailey claims, which were discovered at the same time Petry made his discoveries. Bailey had sunk a few shallow shafts during his years of ownership and had exposed a large body of silver ore over 2000 feet long and as wide as 6 feet. The ore Bailey removed had assayed at $30 a ton. It was primarily silver but did have traces of gold. The new company extended the richest shaft from 150 feet to 500 feet. Over $280,000 was spent to develop the mines and to bring in new equipment. The mine never returned the investment, and the company folded in 1924.

The second company, the Cactus Consolidated Silver Mines Company, was incorporated in 1919 with J. Kendall of Goldfield as president. The company owned the Cactus View claims, to the northeast of Cactus Springs. No shafts were sunk by the company but ore from surface deposits assayed as high as $900 a ton. The Cactus Leona Silver Corporation was next to try to make a go in Cactus Springs. Cactus Leona bought seven claims in the

This 1950 photo of Cactus Springs was taken shortly before its incorporation into the Las Vegas Bombing and Gunnery Range. *(William Metscher)*

district in 1920. The company spent over $7000 to retimber an old 200-foot incline shaft and to drive a 500-foot tunnel. The two mines followed a 10-foot outcrop of ore that returned almost 60 ounces of silver and $10 in gold per ton. The company gave up in 1924 after the ore ran out, conducting only scant exploratory work over the next few years.

The last company to work the Cactus Springs area was the Gresham Gold Mining Company. It was incorporated in February 1924 and bought seven claims on Cactus Peak, formerly owned by the Kennedy Tellurium Mines Company and the Cactus Range Gold Mining Company. Initial ore shipments assayed over $50 a ton. The company sank a 200-foot shaft along with 150 feet of branching drifts. The mine had a 60-h.p. Fairbanks-Morse hoist and a compressor. The ore body was fairly small, unfortunately, and the company stopped operations in 1927.

Gresham was the last organized mining activity in the Cactus Springs district. There were two smaller claim groups that were owned by prospectors and were worked for a number of years after Gresham left the district. The largest of these two was the Silver Sulphide group, owned by Edith Bailey of San Bernardino, California. Work had begun on these claims in 1920. One claim, the Cactus Silver Mine, turned out to be a profitable investment for Mrs. Bailey. It was eventually sunk to a depth of 165 feet and had over 800 feet of lateral work. The second claim group was the Thompson group, owned by Leonard Thompson. A number of shallow shafts were dug, and one of 230 feet was sunk. These yielded both gold and silver, plus some beautiful turquoise.

Cactus Springs was situated in an excellent area: the springs had a daily flow of 500 gallons, and there was excellent grazing in the area. Unfortunately that did not save the settlement when the ore ran out. Although properties in the district started out very rich, the holdings almost always quickly panned out without substantial financial gain. The small camp never had more than fifty people, for there never was a great deal of interest in the district. Other than a few boardinghouses and a number of small wooden shacks, no other substantial buildings were ever erected. The site was later incorporated into the Las Vegas Bombing and Gunnery Range, isolating the ghosts of Cactus Springs from all human contact.

CANYON

DIRECTIONS:
From Amargosa, head west (north) on US 95 for 15 miles. Canyon was located just past the Skeleton Hills.

Canyon was a small water stop on the Las Vegas and Tonopah Railroad. Built in 1906, Canyon was used by the railroad until the rails were torn up a dozen years later. Nothing of interest remains at the site.

CARRARA

DIRECTIONS:
From Beatty, head south on US 95 for 8.2 miles, then exit left. Ruins of Carrara are ¼ mile off the highway.

Initial activity in the Carrara area in 1904 indicated some very promising marble outcroppings, but they turned out to be too fractured for saleable pieces. Search continued for additional deposits, and in 1911 new ones that were not too fractured were discovered. The American Carrara Marble Company was then formed, with P. V. Perkins as president. The company had strong financial backing from stockholders in the East.

The quarry was located up in the mountains. The townsite was platted on the flat valley next to the Las Vegas and Tonopah Railroad, about 3 miles from the quarry. Perkins began preparing the quarry for mining operations by removing all the topsoil and installing a derrick 65 feet tall with a 60-foot boom, able to handle marble blocks weighing up to 15 tons. Because of the distance from the quarry to the L.V.&T. R.R., work on a 3-mile spur line was started during 1913. Construction went slowly because the desert conditions only allowed the equipment to function properly for two hours in the early morning.

Perkins laid out the Carrara townsite next to the L.V.&T. R.R.. A 9-mile water pipline was built from Carrara to Gold Center, 5½ miles north. Perkins also organized the Carrara Townsite Company and planned a "Townsite Day" on May 8, 1913, to officially dedicate the town. Some buildings were moved to Carrara from Beatty and Rhyolite to help the town look more completed than it really was. "Townsite Day," a gala celebration, included a band from Goldfield and a baseball game.

Shortly a town newspaper, the *Carrara Obelisk,* was founded. The newspaper was diversified: advertising support from Goldfield, publishing done in Salt Lake City, circulation boosted by having all stockholders in the Carrara Marble Company as subscribers.

The railroad to the quarries, completed in early 1914, consisted of two flatcars operated by the Lidgerwood cable system. This system is run by counterbalance: as the loaded car descends from the quarry, it pulls—counterbalances—the empty one up the hill. Both cars ran on the same rail, and there was a turnout at the middle of the railway enabling the two cars to pass each other. A powerhouse was built at the top of the mountain to help protect the building from the numerous landslides that occured during wet weather. Near the L.V.&T. R.R. siding, the marble company built huge saw tables to cut the marble into transportable sizes. Although initial quarrying was begun in 1913, it was not until April 7, 1914, that the first shipment was made. It consisted of six huge blocks of the blue-white marble that were sent to Los Angeles. Soon more shipments left for other areas.

Carrara's peak years were 1915 and 1916. There were then over forty buildings and the population was close to 100. The town's prominence as a marble producer was short-lived, however. The marble tended to be fractured and not pure, and Vermont began producing large amounts of higher quality marble. Then, in late 1916, all electrical power to the town was cut off. This stopped the railroad from operating. The next year, 1917, the *Carrara Obelisk* ceased publication, putting another nail in Carrara's coffin.

After World War I, the L.V.&T. R.R. shut down, essentially cutting off Carrara. There was a small revival during the early 1920s but the operation soon shut down and Carrara slipped into oblivion again. The final blow came in September 1924 when the post office closed. Carrara was now one of the many Nye County ghosts.

Today nothing substantial remains at Carrara. As late as the mid-1960s a few buildings were still partially standing. But now just piles of rubble and faint foundations mark the site. The area is covered with broken glass, china and thousands of old tin cans. The site is recognized by a solitary chimney standing in the middle of the desert. The road to the quarries is still passable for a visit. The buildings a mile to the north were never part of Carrara. They are the remains of the Elizalde Company from the Philippines, which built all the buildings and then abandoned the site in 1936 before production even began.

CEDAR SPRING

DIRECTIONS:
Off-limits in the Las Vegas Bombing and Gunnery Range, 12 miles north of Kawich.

Cedar Spring was a small silver camp that formed soon after the turn of the century. It was located near two good springs, the Jarboe and the Sumner. The camp was still listed on maps as late as 1910, but by then all activity had ceased. No production was ever recorded from the area, and the population never exceeded 15. Because of its location, a present-day status report is impossible.

CENTRAL

DIRECTIONS:
2½ miles west of Manhattan on the south side of Nevada 69.

Central was only one of many small camps that sprang up in the Manhattan district during the early 1900s. It was the largest and best established of these minor camps even though it only lasted for less than a year. Gold was found there in the spring of 1906, and a small tent camp quickly formed. Only a month after the initial discoveries, more permanent wooden buildings were being built, including five saloons, two stores, two hotels, an assay office, a lumberyard and a bakery. Plans were made to build an electric light plant, but after new strikes were made in Manhattan, all attention switched there and the plans were dropped. A post office was established at Central on March 22, 1906, but was rescinded September 19 as the town began its quick collapse. The population of Central, at its peak, was about 100. The entire populace moved to Manhattan in the late summer, soon after Manhattan began its revival. Most of the buildings were moved to Manhattan also, and today only small mine dumps and some scattered wood marks the site of once bustling Central.

CENTRAL CITY (Irwin) (Seymour)

DIRECTIONS:
From Nyala, continue north on the Currant–Nyala Road for 12½ miles. Exit right and follow Irwin Canyon Road for 3 miles to Central City.

The small camp called Central City formed in the early 1870s after prospectors from Troy and Grant City found ore in the canyon. A mining district, called Seymour, was soon formed. The camp quickly faded, but was revived in the early 1880s at the same time as nearby Grant City. The population of the camp reached as high as twenty-five. The site was abandoned by 1883.

The canyon remained empty until 1905, when F. L. Irwin staked a number of claims. Soon a small camp of twenty formed. During its short existence several hundred feet of work was done on a high-grade gold vein. It was quickly worked out, and everyone soon left the canyon area. Interest in the canyon's claims was renewed in the 1930s when two 80-foot shafts, known as the Mayolli claims, were sunk in the area; one had 20 feet of drift work. Ore from the two mines assayed from $8 to $16 per ton. In 1940 a small mill was installed at the camp. The mill consisted of a small crusher, a 4-foot ball mill and a small jig. This activity did not last long, and soon the canyon was empty once more.

Three small cabins still stand at the site, all from the activity in the 1930s. There are also two stone ruins that appear to be from the earlier settlement of Central City. The road to the site is extremely rough and might not be passable.

CHARLESTOWN

DIRECTIONS:
From Lathrop Wells, head east on US 95 for 26½ miles. Exit left, and follow this road for 1¾ miles to Charlestown.

Charlestown was an obscure railroad station and mining camp. The small camp came into existence in 1906 when the Las Vegas and Tonopah Railroad established a station here as construction progressed westward to Rhyolite. Limited mining was done at the site during the early 1900s, but after the L.V.&T. R.R. folded and tore up its rails in 1918, the camp was completely abandoned. Only some wooden rubble from the water tank tower marks the site. Just beyond this are the remains of a small mine, which never produced a large amount of ore.

CHLORIDE

DIRECTIONS:
From Beatty, head south on US 95 for 10 miles to Chloride.

Chloride was a small water stop on the Las Vegas and Tonopah Railroad. Built in 1906, it was in use until the rails were torn up in 1918. The stop also served nearby Carrara during its peak as both supply depot and a shipping point for the Carrara Marble Company. Nothing of interest remains at the site.

CLIFFORD (Helena)

DIRECTIONS:
From Warm Springs, head west on US 6 for 7 miles. Exit left and follow this road for 1½ miles to Clifford.

Contrary to popular belief, the Clifford district was actually discovered in 1905 by an Indian from Tonopah named Johnny Peavine. James and Edward Clifford then staked a few claims, one of which turned out to be the rich Clifford mine. Most of the work was actually done by James Clifford, who worked the prime oxidized ore deposits that lay fairly accessible at a depth of less than 5 feet. The Cliffords sold their claims for $250,000 in 1905. Announcement of the sale stirred up a lot of interest in the district, and Clifford began to boom.

Less than two weeks after the sale, a small tent city had sprung up plus a few saloons. New strikes around the Clifford area soon brought even more people heading to the district. Clifford was close to the Ely stageline; ore mined in the district was shipped 42 miles west to Tonopah. In 1906 Clifford received a big boost when some very important investors began buying large holdings in the district. Among these investors were Hale and Schwab of Pittsburgh, Jack Davis of Goldfield and McCarthy of Tonopah. Their involvement seemed to assure the town's future.

The year 1908 marked Clifford's peak. A post office, called Helena, was opened on Dec. 8 of that year. The town's population reached over 500, with more than 100 houses and numerous tents. The more substantial buildings in Clifford included saloons, a large dance hall, stores and a number of boardinghouses. In 1908 the Clifford Mine and the other claims in the area produced $50,000 in both gold and silver.

The town died soon after as the Clifford Mine slowly ran out of good ore. The post office closed on July 15, 1909, signaling the end of Clifford. The ghosts of Clifford were only occasionally disturbed by leasers who continued to work the area.

In 1925 new operations were started. The Clifford Mine and fourteen claims around the mine were purchased by the Gilbert Clifford Gold Mines Company, which changed its name to the Clifford Gold Mines Company in July 1926. The mine had been under option to the Clifford Silver Mines Company. The new company sank four shafts in the Clifford area, all about 300 feet deep. The four shafts followed a new lode about 50 feet wide. The ore initially removed was worth an average of $50 a ton. Electric power was supplied by a diesel generator, and a Chicago pneumatic compressor was also pressed into service. The ore had to be shipped to Tonopah until the Bellehelen Mill was rehabilitated in 1927. Then ore was sent to that mill for processing, with some shipments assaying as high as $550 a ton. The operation closed in 1929. Except for a small revival near the end of the Depression, the

Clifford Mine in the early teens supported a small camp just below the mine. *(Central Nevada Historical Society)*

district has been quiet ever since. Total production of the district was well over $500,000, with some estimates running as high as $750,000.

Not much remains of once bustling Clifford. The site is marked by the huge tailing pile of the Clifford Mine, clearly visible from US 6. Only one building, of unknown origin, still remains at the site. Some workings of the mine remain, but otherwise nothing substantial is left of the town. Piles of rubble suggest recently collapsed buildings. Clifford is not one of the better ghost towns, but it did play an important part in Nye County's history.

CLOVERDALE

DIRECTIONS:
From Gabbs, head south on Nevada 361 for 5.2 miles. Exit left on Nevada 89 and follow this highway for 30.2 miles. Exit left and follow for 3¾ miles. At four corners, take the left and follow for 1 mile to Cloverdale Ranch.

Cloverdale was a stage station on the Belmont wagon road during the 1860s. The ranch was established during this time and was quite prosperous. In 1872 more stages were routed through Cloverdale. The ranch owners were known to be very hospitable, greeting many a weary traveler as a friend. In 1880 the northward flow of traffic through Cloverdale was heavy enough to conjure up thoughts of building a narrow-gauge railroad from Ledlie. These plans were dropped after it was decided that the project was not financially feasible.

A post office opened at Cloverdale on Sept. 21, 1888, and continued to operate until Oct. 13, 1899. During this period Cloverdale remained quite low-key. In addition to the ranch workers, the only other people at the ranch were overnight travelers. In the early 1900s an auto-stage from Ione to Tonopah ran through Cloverdale. The Cloverdale ranch is still operational, and the buildings on the ranch are very old and interesting.

CRAIG STATION

DIRECTIONS:
From Gabbs, head north on Nevada 361 for 1 mile. Exit right on Nevada 91 and follow for 4.3 miles. Exit left and follow this road for 2 miles to Craig Station.

Craig Station was a short-lived stop on the Ellsworth-Downieville stage run. The stageline eventually went through to Ione but never achieved real importance. Not much is known about the history of the station, which consisted of a small stone building of modest construction along with a small stable. The stage building still stands at the site, marked by tall trees. The site is occupied, so be sure to ask permission before wandering.

CURRANT

DIRECTIONS:
Located on US 6, 114 miles east of Tonopah.

Currant began not as a mining camp but as a farming community. Situated at the top of Railroad Valley, the town became the supply point for the many ranches in the valley. A post office was established in Currant on April 16, 1883, when the small town had a population of around fifty, a couple of stores, one saloon and a number of other buildings. The post office closed on May 5, 1884, but the small settlement continued to serve the needs of the ranchers.

The population remained fairly constant throughout the rest of the century. The post office was reopened on Sept. 19, 1892, and remained open until July 31, 1922. Mining activity came to the Currant area in 1914 when gold ore was discovered on the Shepherd ranch. Soon some small shipments were made. The ore from the property contained not only gold but also traces of lead and copper. A small mine, the Sunrise, was dug in 1916; low-level lead ore was removed, and it also contained small amounts of silver and copper. These small-scale developments never became significant. When the activity stopped, it did not affect Currant at all.

The town continued its sleepy existence for a number of years. The post office reopened once again on Aug. 31, 1926. Historically, nothing of consequence happened in Currant until the late 1930s, when magnesite deposits were discovered in the newly formed Currant Creek mining district. The district encompassed Nye County and White Pine County, location of the major deposits. Small but highly productive claims were in Nye County. The first and largest was the Windous Group, located one quarter mile into White Pine County.

The deposit, discovered in 1939 by Tom Windous, was on land owned by a rancher named Munson. Windous purchased the land from him and then leased the property to the Westvaco Chlorine Products Corporation. The lease ran from November 1940 to February 1942. During that time the company did extensive exploration uncovering a belt of magnesite 500 feet by 100 feet that was worked by the glory-hole method. A number of tunnels and shafts were dug, together containing over 700 feet of workings.

Another major magnesite deposit was the Ala-Mar, formerly known as the Manzoni vein. The deposit, in Nye County, was the largest in the district after the Windous. The deposit, worked by the Ala-Mar Magnesium Company, Inc., consisted of nine claims just south of the county line. Active exploration began in 1940, and soon the ore was being shipped out; a 40-ton shipment was made to the General Electric Company in early 1941. There was quite a bit of development at the site. A small tramline was set up to run from the glory pit to the shipping building, about 300 feet away, where trucks would take the ore for shipment. Three other buildings were also erected including one that served as the compressor house. The Ala-Mar Magnesium Company only produced 500 more tons of ore before folding in 1942.

The Currant post office closed for the last time on Dec. 31, 1943. Today Currant has a population of about sixty-five, most of whom work the small oil wells to the south. Most buildings in Currant are relatively new; there is also a small trailer park for the oil well workers. Extant old ruins consist of a few small wooden cabins and the Currant cemetery a couple of miles north of town. Gas is available in Currant, plus food supplies, a telephone and a small motel.

DANVILLE (Chloride Mining District)

DIRECTIONS:
From Tonopah, take US 6 east for 34 miles. Exit left and follow the Little Fish Lake Valley Road north for 46 miles. Exit left and follow this rough road for 3½ miles to Danville.

The Danville district was organized in 1866 when P. W. Mansfield discovered rich silver ore in the Monitor range. Mansfield was one of a small group of prospectors who ventured into Danville Canyon in hopes of finding a shortcut through the range. His discovery was not developed until 1870, when the district was reorganized. Five mines were started, and soon almost thirty miners were working the area. A freight line was established to Eureka to bring in supplies—at a cost of $25 per ton.

The five principal mines were the Sage Hen, Boston, Eucalyptus, Argonaut and Richmond. In addition to these, over thirty other claims were made along the canyon. The deepest shaft was the Boston, which by 1872 had reached 150 feet. The Eucalyptus mine had the longest tunnel shaft: 125 feet. Initial ore shipments were sent to Austin. After the Morey Mill was built in 1873, ore from the Danville district was shipped there for processing. Some of the ore shipped there assayed as high as $600 per ton. The district was quiet for a while after 1874, but by 1877 the Danville canyon area still had twenty men working in the mines. Most mines closed in 1879; by 1881 only five people were left in camp.

A new silver discovery was made further up in the canyon in early 1883. Soon twenty-five miners were again living in the canyon. A post office opened on Nov. 21, 1883, indicating that the camp might be around for a while. But the revival only lasted a little more than a year, and the post office closed on Sept. 8, 1884. The ghosts, except for an occasional prospector, reigned supreme in Danville from 1886 until 1909.

In 1909 the Boston Mine and the Sage Hen Mine both reopened. Small amounts of ore were removed periodically until 1914. Everyone then gave up on Danville until World War II, when the call for valuable minerals opened up the district once again. However, the ore was of such low grade that operations were curtailed in early 1942. Total production for the Danville district was about $43,000, with the bulk of production in a two-year revival from 1944 to 1946. During those two years $27,000 in silver and gold was extracted from the Danville mines. Most of this activity took place on the Boston claim, which had last been worked in 1934 by the Continental Mines Company of Denver. In 1949 Jack Ekstrom shipped 70 tons from the Boston claim; before the property was abandoned in late 1949, the shaft on the property was over 130 feet deep. After Ekstrom departed Danville, nobody tried to mine the district again.

Danville's remains are quite scant. Since the

The last residents of Danville were photographed in the late 1940s. (MacKay School of Mines/ University of Nevada at Reno)

Present-day photo of some ruins at Danville.

population of the small camp never exceeded thirty-five, few substantial buildings were ever constructed. Two wooden cabins remain and are on occasion used by a Bureau of Land Management survey crew. A few ruins are scattered along the canyon. A fairly substantial stone ruin remains of a building, of undetermined purpose, carefully crafted. Each stone, seemingly sandstone, is exactly cut and fitted; only the walls remain, but even they are impressive. The road to Danville is extremely rocky and also has some dangerous sand traps. Use extreme caution.

DARROUGH HOT SPRINGS (Hot Springs)

DIRECTIONS:
Located ¼ mile off Nevada 376, 8 miles north of the junction with Nevada 92 at Round Mountain.

The hot springs located at Darrough Hot Springs were used by the Indians for many centuries before the white man came to Nevada. John C. Frémont visited the site in 1845 during his fabled exploits. A stage station, the first in the Big Smoky Valley, was built at the springs. James T. Darrough bought the stage station and the hot springs in the early 1880s and gave the area his name.

The station and the immediate grounds remain in the possession of Darrough's descendants. The old stone stage station still stands and is in excellent condition. A small wooden addition has been added to serve as a boardinghouse. The hot springs still run; a pool has been installed, and visitors can swim in the mineralized water for a small fee.

DOWNIEVILLE (Downeyville)

DIRECTIONS:
From Gabbs, take Nevada 361 north for 1 mile. Exit right on Nevada 91 for ½ mile. Exit left and follow for 1 mile to Downieville.

Rich silver and lead deposits were discovered in May 1877 just west of Ellsworth. This pulled many people away from Ellsworth, and soon a new camp sprang up around the site. A large tent city formed, and by 1878 the town had a population of over 200. A number of more substantial buildings were constructed, including stores, saloons, a Wells Fargo office and stageline offices. A supply stage ran from Luning to Downieville on a regular basis.

The town was officially named Downieville in 1879 after the first postmaster, P. Downey, in charge of the post office that opened on March 31, 1879. Downieville thrived for quite a while. The ore from the mines was shipped to mills in Austin and other places. Later, in the mid-1880s, one of the first lead smelters in the state was built in Downieville to process all of the ore from the town mines.

The main mine in the district was the Downieville Mine, dug to a depth of over 500 feet. During its production years from 1878 until 1901, the mine was reputed to have produced from $7 million to $12 million in silver and lead. Downieville continued to grow until the mid-1890s, when the ore

One of the numerous stone foundations still remaining at the Downieville townsite.

became quite low grade. The town struggled into the 20th century but just could not hang on. The post office closed on Oct. 15, 1901, and soon only hot wisps of wind from Gabbs Valley visited Downieville.

The town was revived for a short while in 1923 and 1924. The Downeyville Nevada Mines, Inc., purchased the old Downieville Mine and began to rehabilitate the mine workings. The company was organized early in 1923 with F. P. Allen of Luning as president. The old mine was worked on and off from 1924 to 1927, when the company began operating at a loss. The district has remained silent since 1927.

The ruins of Downieville are fairly extensive, although no complete buildings remain. Over thirty stone buildings are scattered in a small canyon below the remains of the Downieville Mine. The layout of the ruins suggest Downieville had two main roads, parallel to each other. Most of the buildings seem to have been small houses for the miners. In addition to the stone ruins, a number of faint stone foundations abound along the two streets. The interesting stone ruins of the smelter are directly below the Downieville Mine. The ruins at the mine are the best preserved remains at the site. The mine still retains its hoist and engine housing. These were used by the Downeyville Nevada Mines company, which is the reason for their continued existence. The site is extremely desolate but is well worth the trip.

DUCKWATER

DIRECTIONS:
From Currant, take Nevada 20 north for 21.6 miles to Duckwater.

Duckwater was primarily an Indian settlement, although whites did settle here in 1868. The Indians occupied the site long before the Europeans even came to America. A post office opened at the site on Jan. 6, 1873. The small town gradually became predominantly Shoshone, and by the turn of the century the population was over 100. This figure has remained fairly constant since then. The Duckwater post office closed on Jan. 29, 1941, but reopened May 16, 1950, and remains open. The Shoshone Indian Reservation, officially formed in 1940, now has over 3700 acres. A number of older buildings still remain at Duckwater, scattered among newer buildings.

DULUTH

DIRECTIONS:
From Phonolite, continue east for 1 mile to Duluth.

Duluth, a small mining camp, grew up as a suburb of Phonolite. Small ore discoveries were made during March 1907, and a small camp gradually formed east of Phonolite. Two small mining companies, the Big Henry Gold Mining Company and the Duluth Gold Mining Company, became active in the area.

This old sod-type house is the only remaining structure at Duluth.

A post office opened on April 27, 1907, to serve the twenty people in the camp. A newspaper, the *Duluth Tribune,* published once a week and was distributed in Duluth and nearby Phonolite. The interest in Duluth did not last long; by the end of 1907 most people had moved out. The two mining companies folded during late 1907. Except for some minor claim work, no more mining activity took place. The post office closed on Dec. 14, 1907, and the newspaper ceased in 1907. By early 1908 the district was empty.

Ruins at Duluth are scarce. A few dugout cabins remain, but there is nothing else except some faint sunken foundations.

EAST MANHATTAN

DIRECTIONS:
From Manhattan, take Nevada 69 east for 2 miles. Exit right onto a poor road and follow for ¼ mile to East Manhattan. Signs mark the entrance to the road.

The small settlement of East Manhattan sprang up in 1906 soon after Manhattan began booming. The richness of Manhattan prompted much exploration in the area around the town. A few promising ledges were located about 2 miles east of Manhattan, and soon a camp of seventy-five had formed around springs near the budding mines. At its height during the spring of 1906, East Manhattan had two stores, two saloons and a restaurant, all housed in large tents with the exception of one wooden building.

Activity was completely over by the end of 1906, for the ore veins were very shallow and quickly ran out. The tent camp quickly folded, and soon everyone was gone. Not many signs of the settlement remain, but a nice spring marks the site of the camp. Less than one quarter mile east of the spring are the mines, not worked since 1906. The mine was retimbered during the 1950s but no production was recorded. The shaft and hoist house are still in good shape with the original explosive shelter located nearby.

This old mine, still in excellent condition, is among the few signs that East Manhattan ever existed.

EDEN (Gold Belt)

DIRECTIONS:
From Warm Springs, head east on Nevada 375 for 1½ miles. Exit right and follow this road for 13 miles. Exit right and follow this road for 2 miles to the Eden Creek Ranch. Continue past the ranch for 4 miles to Eden.

The Eden district, also called the Gold Belt district, was organized after John Adams discovered silver and gold ore on Feb. 20, 1905, at the head of Eden Creek, then known as Little Mill Creek. Adams worked his find for a number of years before selling the property to Mark G. Bradshaw, who then organized the Eden Creek Mining and Milling Company. The company continued to dig Adams's tunnel mine, which followed the Eden vein for almost 300 feet. The ore from the mine contained 30 ounces of silver and half an ounce of gold per ton. The company employed ten men, but the small camp actually had a population of around twenty-five because many men were prospecting the sides of the canyon for new deposits. The company was reorganized in late 1922; J. W. S. Butler of Sacramento, California, became president. The new management began work on a tunnel that by June 1923 was 1400 feet long, with 1300 feet of drift work.

Another mining company became active in the Eden district in 1925. The Crucible Gold Mining and Milling Company, incorporated in 1925 with capital of $1.5 million, had T. F. Branigan of Tonopah as president. The company, which owned five claims at Eden including the Golden Eagle Mine, operated on an extremely low level. For example, the company spent a mere $1200 in 1925 for operating expenses. Only two men were employed by the company; they worked on two 60-foot tunnels. The ore from the two tunnels was free milling gold ore but only assayed at $14 per ton.

The Southgold Nevada Mines Company, K. M. Terrell president, moved into the district in 1926. Southgold Nevada had a number of claims adjacent to the Crucible Gold Mining and Milling Company's holdings. The main producer for the company was the Southgold Mine, a 400-foot tunnel that had over 1500 feet of lateral workings. There were also a number of other tunnels around the Southgold Mine. The ore from all of these mines assayed at an average of $10 per ton. In 1929 the company built a wash plant at the mouth of Eden Creek. The plant was connected to the tunnel mine by an 1100-foot tramway. The company used this process to extract $50,000 in gold from the ore.

Southgold Nevada took over Crucible Gold Mining and Milling in February 1930. More than thirty-five miners were then working in the district. The company leased some of its property to the Oro Cache Mining and Milling Company, organized in 1929 and run by Harriet Stingley. After a 50-foot shaft was dug, the outlook for valuable ore seemed dim. The company struggled for a few years but finally folded in 1934. Meanwhile, Southgold continued to be active. The company had contemplated building a mill in the early 1930s, but it was not until 1938 that a 35-ton mill in Eden was actually completed. Southgold continued to be active until World War II. After the company left the district, Eden was emptied forever.

The Golden Crown claim group, which included the old Eden Mine, was an important part of the Eden Creek mining district. The claim group was active during the 1920s and 1930s. The Eden Mine had originally been worked in 1906, but hopes for new finds in the mine were quickly dashed and the group was not worked again after 1935. Another group of claims, the Nevada Triumph group, was active in 1926 with seventeen claims. They were owned by George Chubey. When nothing of value was found after a year of work, Chubey left Eden.

Eden's remains are fairly extensive. Four wooden buildings are at the site, plus the scattered ruins of a number of other buildings. The ruins of the tram and the wash plant are easy to find, for they are visible from the road. The Eden Creek Ranch, occupied until recently, is at the mouth of Eden Creek. The site is well worth the trip, but bring extra gas as the site is far from any filling station.

ELLENDALE

DIRECTIONS:
From Tonopah, head east on US 6 for 26 miles. Exit right and follow this road for 2 miles. Take the left fork and continue for 2 more miles. At the next fork take a right and continue for ¾ mile. Bear right at the next fork and follow for ½ mile to Ellendale.

In April 1909 Ellen Clifford Nay, for whom the town was named, discovered a large deposit of float gold in the southern part of Saulsbury Wash. The free gold ore was among the richest ever found in Nevada. The district looked very promising, and the rush to the area was comparable, on a smaller scale, to the rushers at Goldfield and Manhattan after their initial discoveries. Within a matter of weeks, over 400 people were in the district. The first shipments of ore were reportedly assayed at $80,000 a ton; official assay reports list the value at $4100 per ton,

Ellendale is pictured in its infancy in this 1909 photo. *(Nevada Historical Society)*

still an impressive figure. The test load consisted of 5 tons of ore that returned almost 205 ounces of gold and 145 ounces of silver per ton. The complete shipment was worth over $20,000. District production in 1909 was over $50,000.

The Ellendale townsite was immediately laid out and almost all of the lots were sold during the first two months. Many wooden buildings were built, including a number of saloons and a few boardinghouses for the miners. The value and amount of gold seemed to suggest that Ellendale was here to stay. A railroad was planned to Tonopah, and a group of surveyors even mapped out a route for the railroad bed. A telegraph line to Tonopha was constructed in late 1909; a telegraph line was a luxury few towns had. Two weekly newspapers, the *Lode* and the *Ellendale Star,* began publishing. They were printed in Tonopah and brought to Ellendale by wagon. Neither of the papers lasted into 1910.

Ellendale received a bitter blow when, in late 1909, newspapers in Rhyolite and Tonopah called the Ellendale riches a swindle. This stopped the flow of people to the district, but Ellendale still survived. In 1910, with mainly leasers working the district, another $20,000 in gold and silver was produced. The original claims played out in 1911, but some smaller ore bodies were discovered and limited production continued through 1912. The production total for the district from 1909 to 1912 was just over $1 million.

After 1912 the district belonged almost entirely to the ghosts. Some activity took place in 1929 when the Raymond Van Ness Mining Company discovered a barium ore deposit that contained almost 700,000 tons; after a few shipments the company left the district. The last activity in Ellendale took place in 1938 and 1939. The Gilbert brothers reopened the old Ellendale Mine and took out $10,000 in gold and silver before the vein they were following panned out. Since then, the only inhabitants of the town have been the wind and desert animals.

Hardly anything remains at Ellendale. For many years only one building stood at the site, and it finally succumbed in the late 1960s. Apparently the

Almost every town, including Ellendale, had its own version of the famous Northern Saloon. This photo was taken by E. W. Smith on June 11, 1909. *(Nevada Historical Society)*

sides of the building gave out and the roof fell down, because the roof is still completely intact. The sites of the saloons are easy to locate just by looking for broken beer bottles. The only other markers of the site are the depressions in the sand where other buildings once stood. Mine ruins and tailing piles are in the hills surrounding the site. The road to Ellendale tends to be very sandy and should not be attempted without a four-wheel-drive vehicle.

ELLSWORTH (Upper Weston) (Summit City) (Mammoth)

DIRECTIONS:
From Gabbs, head north on Nevada 361 for 1 mile. Exit right and take Nevada 91 east for 8 miles. Exit left and follow Ellsworth Canyon Road for 6 miles to Ellsworth.

Indians discovered a large silver ledge in the hills west of Ione in 1863. The next year the Mammoth mining district was organized by Sam McKeon and A. T. Hatch. Soon two small camps formed next to the mines in Ellsworth Canyon. The two, called Ellsworth and Upper Weston (Summit City), were less than one quarter mile apart. Both enlarged until they were considered one, and the joint settlement was called Ellsworth.

A post office opened on March 7, 1866. The town grew quite slowly through the late 1860s but started booming in 1870 after a steam-powered ten-stamp mill was built. Soon Ellsworth had a population of over 200. A number of businesses began to flourish, and a stage and freight line to Wadsworth was established at a shipping cost of $50 per ton.

Principal mines in the district were the Morning Call, General Lee, Peoria, Lisbon, Silver Wave and Mount Vernon. The latter was the deepest of the six at 180 feet. The ore from the mines assayed at an average of $100 per ton. A new mine, the Esta Buena, was established in the early 1880s by Don Manuel San Pedro of Grantsville. The ore from this mine sometimes assayed as high as $1000 per ton.

Ellsworth's ore became increasingly low grade. In 1872 the mill only functioned periodically; by 1874 it had closed and only twenty people were left in Ellsworth. The town struggled through 1884, but after the post office closed on Dec. 29, 1884, Ellsworth slowly passed away.

The district remained dead until 1923 when the Tonopah-Brohilco Mines Corporation began working twenty claims in the Mammoth district. The company, incorporated on Jan. 29, 1923, as a reorganization of the Brohilco Silver Corporation, had George Porter as president and Victor Keith as superintendent. There were two rich claim groups among the twenty—the Silver Leaf and the Black Reef group. They produced ore that assayed at an average of $25 per ton. The company did not make the grade, however, and folded in 1925.

The last company to work the Mammoth district was the Return Mining Company. It owned a 240-foot shaft mine that yielded ore assaying at $35 per ton, with values in both silver and gold. The company brought in a used twelve-stamp mill and also built a small cyanide concentration mill. Return Mining was active in the district from 1924 until early 1926. After the company left, the district fell silent. It was not until 1928 that mining activity returned when Donald Benton of Salt Lake City, Utah, purchased the old Flagstaff Mine and a number of adjacent claims. Benton organized the mine and claims into the Eary group. Mining operations were begun, producing ore that assayed at an average of $55 per ton. Benton maintained control of the group until 1933. In that year he sold the property to J. L. Corlett, who had been operating a small mill in Lower Ellsworth. Corlett did not have as much luck as Benton did but still realized a fair profit. Corlett's departure in 1944 signaled the end of mining in the Ellsworth district.

The ruins of Ellsworth include five wooden buildings, four of which are still inhabited. In addition there are a number of older stone buildings about half a mile below the wooden buildings. These include the remains of the steam-powered stamp mill. The many old stone foundations scattered around the mill ruins make for interesting exploration. The road to Ellsworth, although graded, has some treacherous sand traps. Beware.

FAIRBANKS RANCH

DIRECTIONS:
From Lathrop Wells, take Nevada 29 south for 5½ miles. Exit left and follow this road for 6½ miles to Fairbanks Spring, site of Fairbanks Ranch.

Fairbanks Ranch was a well-known travelers' stop during the 1890s and early 1900s. The ranch, run by R. J. "Dad" Fairbanks, was a stopping place for the numerous freight stages that passed through the area on their way to Bullfrog and Rhyolite. Fairbanks was active in freighting construction supplies to build both the Tonopah and Tidewater Railroad and the San Pedro, Los Angeles and Salt Lake Railroad.

The ranch was also a stopover for the many prospectors heading to the new booms in the Bullfrog mining district. Most were coming from the fading towns of Ivanpah and Manvel, to the south. The road from Amargosa to Greenwater also passed through Fairbanks Ranch. A man named Kimball set up a stageline from Johnnie to Fairbanks Ranch in the early 1900s that continued until 1909. After completion of the railroads, the ranch lost most of its transient visitors; Fairbanks left the ranch soon after. Today only scattered wooden rubble remains at the ranch site. But the spring continues to flow.

FLUORINE

DIRECTIONS:
From Beatty, head south on US 95 for 1½ miles. Exit left onto Fluorspar Canyon Road and follow it for 1 mile. Take the right fork and follow this road for 2½ miles to Fluorine.

Fluorine, a fair-sized mining camp at the base of Bare Mountain, formed in 1905 soon after high-value ore was discovered on the slopes of Bare Mountain. The nearby camps of Telluride and Meikeljohn were also active during this period. Fluroine reached its peak in 1907 and continued strongly until 1910. During this time a spur line of the Tonopah and Tidewater Railroad to Fluorine was contemplated, but plans fell through after the town began to decline. A post office opened at the camp on May 26, 1908. The camp was already beginning to falter, and the post office was closed on July 15, 1909.

A number of people and mining companies were active in the Fluorine area during its heyday. One of the three earliest and best producers at Fluorine was the Vidano group, located east of the camp. The group contained a number of claims, including one with a 140-foot shaft. The ore assayed at an average of $10 per ton. Three buildings were built at the mine site. The other two key mines were the Panama and the Old Diamond Queen, both on the east slope of Bare Mountain. The Panama Mine was the larger, with a depth of 200 feet and over 100 feet of lateral work.

Another major claim was the Bull Moose, active since 1909 but most productive from 1913 to 1915. The claim was originally owned by the Carrara Mining, Milling and Leasing Syndicate, which did not do much work on the property but did build a ten-stamp mill there before selling to the Bull Moose Mining and Milling Company. Bull Moose only worked the claim for a short while before selling the claim and mill to Jules Baird in 1915 for $156,000. Baird continued work in the one tunnel mine on the property and also dug two new 50-foot shafts. He employed five men, but the ore just was not rich enough. Baird gave up in early 1916.

Some cinnabar ore was taken out of Bare Mountain by J. B. Kiernon and A. A. Turner in 1908. However, the deposits were shallow and the claims were never developed. There were two other minor operators at Fluroine. The first was the Kismet Mining Company, which worked the Lonsway property. After sinking two small shafts with dismal assay results, the company gave up and left the district. The only other significant development took place on the Decillion claim. A 50-foot shaft was dug, but the ore was poor and the claim was soon abandoned.

Fluorine had completely died out by 1916. There is hardly a trace of the townsite now, although a few mines have recently been reopened and with limited production.

FRAZIER WELLS (Frazier Springs)

DIRECTIONS:
From Tonopah, head west on US 95 for 1.3 miles. Exit right on a tar road and follow for 4 miles. Exit left onto a dirt road and follow this rough road for 2¾ miles to Frazier Wells.

Frazier Wells was a small stage stop for travelers heading to the mining boom at Ray, a couple miles north. A small camp of ten formed at the wells during 1901, shortly after Judge L. O. Ray had made his discoveries at Ray. A few small business establishments, including a saloon and a small food store, were active in Frazier Wells in tents. When Ray ceased to exist around 1903, the tents in Frazier Wells were quickly folded and soon the camp was as empty as Ray. Only a few tall trees mark Frazier Wells. In the summer of 1979 the springs had dried up completely. The spot is an excellent resting

This desolate site was once the stage stop of Frazier Wells. The springs are by the tree at the left and the station was just past the snarl of barbed wire in the foreground.

point, for it is the only shade for miles around. The road to the site tends to be extremely rough.

GEORGES CANYON (Fresno)

DIRECTIONS:
From Stone Cabin, head west for 1 mile. Bear left and continue on for 2 miles to Georges Canyon.

Limited activity took place in Georges Canyon from 1903 to 1931. Charles Ira Farcher discovered gold and silver ore in the canyon in 1903. The ore assayed as high as $300 per ton. Work was soon begun on a mine, named the Clipper. Farcher continued to work the mine for many years, and in 1929 he built a two-stamp mill nearby. A small tent camp of ten formed near the mine and mill and was named Fresno. Farcher stopped work on the mine in 1931 after it had produced over $12,000 in gold and silver. When operations were curtailed, the shaft was 180 feet deep.

Joe Clifford, who at that time ran the Stone Cabin ranch, also did some mining work in Georges Canyon. Clifford owned the Little Joe claim, whose ore assayed at $20 per ton. When work was stopped on the claim after a few years, the shaft was almost 90 feet deep.

There are few remains left to show that there was activity in the canyon. Absolutely nothing remains of the Fresno camp, and only the ruins of the Clipper Mine mark the site. I could not locate the Clifford Mine, but maybe someone else will have better luck.

GLEN HAMILTON

DIRECTIONS:
From Ione, head north on Nevada 21 for 9 miles. Exit left and follow for ¼ mile. Exit left again and follow for 2 miles to Glen Hamilton.

Glen Hamilton was a small stage stop on the Ione-Austin stage run. There was a post office here from May 18 to Oct. 15, 1866. Only a small log structure was built at the site, along with a small corral. Today nothing at all remains and the site location is approximate.

GOLD BAR

DIRECTIONS:
From Bullfrog, continue westward for another mile. Take a right at the fork and continue for ½ mile. Take another right at the fork and follow this road for 3½ miles to Gold Bar.

Gold Bar was a small mining camp in the rich Bullfrog mining district. The camp was the most

The Homestake Mine and Mill as it was in May 1908.
(Nevada Historical Society)

important of those that sprang up in the early 1900s west of Bullfrog. The mainstay of the camp was the Homestake Mine, which had ore averaging $30 per ton and sometimes as high as $150. An impressive ten-stamp mill was built at the site. The crushed ore was shipped on the Las Vegas and Tonopah Railroad, a few miles to the south.

A camp of over fifty grew around the mine and mill, and a number of fairly substantial buildings were erected. By early 1908, however, the ore had begun to fade. The mill closed in May 1908, and soon work on the mine also stopped. The mine was over 500 feet deep when operations ceased and had almost 5000 feet of lateral tunnels. Only a few ruins mark the site. There is quite a bit of scattered rubble but little else. The mill foundation is easy to locate, and the partially collapsed Homestake shaft is just above the mill ruins.

GOLD CENTER

DIRECTIONS:
From Beatty, head south on US 95 for 2½ miles. Exit right and follow this road for ½ mile to Gold Center.

Gold Center was an important terminus for three railroads during the early 1900s. The townsite, platted in late 1904, was an important water source for nearby Bullfrog and Rhyolite, both then beginning to flourish. Even though the Amargosa River was barely a few feet wide, it was the only water supply within miles and was highly treasured. The origin of Gold Center's name is a mystery of sorts,

for when the town formed in 1904 it was the center of nothing and did not have any gold. A post office opened on Jan. 21, 1905, but the town was not really put on the map until 1906.

In June 1906 the Las Vegas and Tonopah Railroad reached Gold Center. A railroad yard set up by W. C. Bryan included a number of station buildings, switches, turntables and a 2000-foot sidetrack. The yard was located on the 116.1 mile marker for the L.V.&T. R.R. This yard was used by the L.V.&T. R.R. until the railroad reached Rhyolite. In 1907, when the yards were completed at Rhyolite, those at Gold Center were abandoned. The first freight train pulled into Gold Center on Oct. 7, 1906; on board was Governor Sparks. The first passenger train, loaded to capacity, came just five days later.

The Tonopah and Tidewater Railroad, after much delay, reached Gold Center in late 1906 and was eventually continued to Goldfield. The Bullfrog-Goldfield Railroad also ran through Gold Center. After being abandoned in 1914, the railroad's right-of-way was incorporated into the T.&T. R.R. Gold Center reached its peak in 1907; the town had a post office, hotel, bank, brokerage firms, a few mercantiles and a score of saloons. A newspaper, the *Gold Center News,* which began publication in September 1906, reached peak circulation of just over 100 during early 1907 but folded late that year. The most imposing and unique building was the Gold Center Ice and Brewing Company's combination brewery-icehouse. The company built this

This combination ice plant and brewery made the town of Gold Center unique in Nye County history. The products of the plant were highly regarded and always commanded a high price. *(Nevada Historical Society)*

structure in 1907 and was soon supplying many of the saloons in Gold Center and Rhyolite. The company did not last too long, however. The brewery was closed in late 1908 or early 1909.

The only mining activity in the Gold Center area was done by the Gold Center Water and Mills Company from 1907 to 1909. The company sank a number of shafts and dug a few tunnels, but no worthwhile ore was discovered. The company did build a thirty-ton concentration mill to serve the district, but not too many mining companies wanted to send their ore to Gold Center and the mill soon closed.

When nearby Rhyolite began to decline in late 1908, Gold Center also faded. The post office closed on Nov. 30, 1910. By the beginning of 1911, the population was down to twenty-five. The town struggled to survive, but when the L.V.&T. R.R. tore up its rails in 1918–19, the end came. The remains of Gold Center are very scant: the stone foundations of the brewery and the mill are all that remain. Scattered wood boards give a general idea where the town was located. The harsh desert climate has almost completely erased all signs of the once bustling railroad town. The nearby Gold Center Ranch was formed after the death of Gold Center.

GOLD CRATER

DIRECTIONS:
Inside the Las Vegas Bombing and Gunnery Range, 10 miles east of Stonewall Mountain. Off-limits to the public.

Discoveries on Pahute Mesa in May 1904 led to establishment of the Gold Crater mining camp. By September 1904 over 200 miners had flocked to the booming camp, but most soon left. During the short boom over 300 lots were sold in the townsite, most during a two-week period. For the most part these sold for $50 each, a low price compared to other towns and thus attractive to speculators. But the town never developed enough for them to capitalize on their investments.

During the height of the Gold Crater excitement, a water pipeline was planned from Stonewall Mountain, 10 miles to the east. But the boom subsided before the pipeline could be built. The water supply was acquired from two wells located some distance from town and also from tanks on Pahute Mesa. The town was almost empty during the winter of 1904, with only a few hardy souls willing to stay the chilling winter. The following year only leasers came back to work the sites in Gold Crater. They sank new shafts and continued limited development of the mining district. The ore taken out of Gold Crater during this period ran from $40 to $240 a ton. It was laced with heavy values of gold and smaller amounts of silver. The leasers left Gold Crater soon after 1905, and the district remained fairly quiet until 1914.

In 1914 the Gold Prince Mining and Leasing Company was incorporated, with capital of $500,000. The company was based in Grand Island, Nebraska, with Dr. A. Farnsworth as president. It purchased the property of the defunct Gold Crater Construction and Mining Company and built a 25-ton amalgamation and concentration mill. The gold ore removed from the mines by the Gold Prince company was low in value, running only $15 per ton. Operations continued, however. A 12-h.p. hoist was installed, but the ore became steadily lower in value. The mine closed when the shaft was over 265 feet deep; despite the depth, only a small amount of gold and silver was ever removed. The operation never reopened, and soon Gold Crater belonged to the ghosts. Now only the rumble of Air Force jets and the shaking of atomic testing disturb the ghosts.

GOLDEN

DIRECTIONS:
From Cloverdale, continue north for 1 mile. Take the right fork and follow it 4½ miles. Exit left and follow this road for 3 miles to Golden.

Gold was discovered here by Indians in 1902, but no real activity took place until January 1906 when a rich free-gold vein was discovered. A small camp formed at the site; it looked as if the gold would last for a while. A post office opened Feb. 26, 1906, to serve about fifty people living at the camp. The ore was not consistently high grade, and when large deposits at Manhattan and Round Mountain were discovered, most of the people in Golden moved to these new strikes.

A small number of people stayed behind and continued to work both the small mines and the Cloverdale placers, located just east of the camp. The post office closed Dec. 14, 1907, but the camp continued its meager existence for a number of years before finally succumbing. In 1910 there were still thirty people living in Golden, but by 1913 the site was abandoned.

There has been a lot of activity in the Golden area since 1913. In the 1920s Barney Francisco staked ten claims just north of the townsite. A shaft was sunk on one of the claims and was called the East Golden Mine. Francisco built a homemade tube mill at the mine, but it was a failure. He leased the mine in 1941 and the leasers built a Huntington mill, complete with crushing plates and a concentrating table. Assays from the mine ran from $20 to $30 per ton.

The Cloverdale placers were reworked in 1931. A company sank twenty-six shallow shafts, ranging from 20 feet to 50 feet, in an effort to locate substantial deposits, but the search was fruitless. In the early 1950s a group of claims, named the West Golden claims, were worked but never recorded any production.

Only a partially collapsed wooden cabin marks Golden today. The headshaft and another cabin still remain at the East Golden Mine; the shaft has almost completely collapsed. Only scattered shallow shafts mark the site of the Cloverdale placers.

GOLDEN ARROW

DIRECTIONS:
From Tonopah, head east on US 6 for 34 miles. Exit left and follow this road and the signs for 12 miles to Golden Arrow.

Discoveries by the Page brothers in September 1905 prompted a small rush to the Golden Arrow area. A townsite was laid out in 1906 by the Golden Arrow Mining Company. Soon, four mining companies, along with many individual claim workers, were in the district. By 1907 the town had a number of wooden buildings, including a two-story hotel and a few stores and saloons. Water was obtained from a spring on the Longstreet Ranch, 7 miles to the northeast. A railroad, being planned from Tonopah to Ely, was supposed to run through Golden Arrow, but the idea was forfeited when Golden Arrow faded before the plans were put into motion.

The largest of the four mining companies working the district was the Golden Arrow Mining Company. The company owned seven claims here, five of which had shafts. The shafts were from 50 feet to 150 feet deep and the ore, carrying values in both gold and silver, assayed as high as $100 per ton. Another important company was the Cotter Mines Company, which owned thirteen claims and controlled the deepest shaft in the district, the Gold Bar, which eventually reached 500 feet. The ore from the mine assayed at an average of $25 per ton; a number of ore shipments were sent to the West End Mill in Tonopah. The Kawich Consolidated Company controlled twenty-six claims in Golden Arrow and, in acreage, was the largest company in the district. Their main producer was the Mascot Mine, which had ore assaying from $25 to $55 per ton. The only other mining company here was the Golden Arrow Mohawk Mining Company, which owned six claims. The company had a 500-foot tunnel that produced silver and gold ore assaying at an average of $20 per ton. There were eleven other mines, four over 100 feet deep: the Geneva, 200 feet; Crescent, 125 feet; Black Dog, 115 feet; and Bunker Hill, 100 feet. They were not large producers and for the most part were independently owned.

Unfortunately for Golden Arrow, the town was more of a real estate promotion that a real town. The ore did not last long enough for an established town to form. Golden Arrow was practically emptied by 1909, although a short revival in 1911 saw forty-five people back in the district. After that rejuvenation ended in 1912, Golden Arrow was left to the ghosts, with the gaunt remains of the hotel

This photo shows one of the many active mines near Golden Arrow during the boom of 1908. *(William Metscher)*

standing as a lonely sentinel. World War II saw some limited activity in Golden Arrow. The Cliffords, from Stone Cabin ranch, worked the Jeep group from 1941 to 1946 during the winter ranching slowdown, digging a 100-foot shaft. Before the Cliffords stopped working the Jeep group in November 1946, they had mined almost $5000 worth of gold and silver.

The mines remained quiet until very recently. Within the last few years a new mining company has been reprocessing the old tailing piles with a cyanide leaching system. This is the same company working the old camps of Reveille and Keystone. Unfortunately, the company had an initial disregard for history and flattened most of the ruins at Golden Arrow. There are a number of mine ruins in the area and few wooden buildings, but they might not be there for long.

GOLD FLAT (Nixon)

DIRECTIONS:
In the Las Vegas Bombing and Gunnery Range, 3 miles west of Quartzite Mountain. Off-limits to the public.

Gold Flat was another of the many flash-in-the-pan towns located around Pahute Mesa. All of these camps formed just after the turn of the century as a result of the excitement at Gold Crater. The small camp was originally known as Nixon, after one of its founders. A few months later, in February 1905, the name was changed to Gold Flat in an attempt to show how rich the camp was. Unfortunately the name had more gold than did the surrounding hills. Gold Flat soon ceased to exist. Since the camp never consisted of more than tents, it is doubtful that anything is left today.

GOLD HILL

DIRECTIONS:
From Round Mountain, take dirt road north for 4 miles to the Gold Hill Mine and Mill.

Gold Hill was never a settlement or town but was a small mining complex 4 miles north of Round Mountain. The mine at Gold Hill had been worked periodically after the turn of the century. Intensive mining operations began in 1927, when the Gold Hill Mining Company purchased the Nonpareil group of claims, which included the Gold Hill Mine.

The company had been incorporated on Nov. 7, 1927, with backing capital of $1 million. The company built a small stamp mill with cyanide tanks the following year. The Gold Hill company was reorganized in April 1929 and was renamed the Gold Hill Development Company. In 1930 the company was once again reorganized and renamed, becoming the Gold Hill Consolidated Mines Company; P. H. Murray of Visalia, California, was president and W. H. Farris of Round Mountain was mine superintendent. Equipment at the mine included a 15-h.p. Fairbanks-Morse hoist and a two-drill compressor. The company worked the area until late 1930.

Another company, the Gold Zone Divide Mining Company, was also active near Gold Hill during the early 1930s. The company was originally called the Tonopah Gold Zone Mining Company but underwent a name change when reorganized and incorporated in February 1918. In late 1929 the company purchased the mines near Gold Hill that were controlled by the Divide Mining Company. The company sank a shaft in 1930 and found fairly decent gold ore, but the depth of the ore was shallow. The Gold Zone company left the Round Mountain district in 1933 to concentrate on its holdings in the Divide district.

In 1930 a $770,000 mill was built on the property near Gold Hill that the Tonopah Mining Company and the Tonopah-Belmont Development Company had purchased in 1929. The two companies operated the mill until 1933, when the ore values from the 500-foot Gold Hill Mine began to fall. In 1934 T. F. Cole bought the mill and the surrounding property; he died in 1938 before any real plans were put into operation. The Gold Hill area was operated periodically after his death but not to any great extent. Production from 1930 to 1942 for the Gold Hill Mine and Mill and other nearby operations was just under $1 million. The mine hoist still remains, along with foundations of the mill.

GOLD POINT

DIRECTIONS:
From Currant, head north on US 6 for 9 miles.

Gold Point was not so much a town but rather a general ranching area north of Currant. There are a number of abandoned ranches. The most impressive is the old Fisher ranch, where a number of older

Old falsefront mercantile store on US highway 6 at Gold Point.

buildings still remain; the unique building is a very nice falsefront of unknown purpose. Three small mines are northwest of the Fisher ranch. These were never producers and were most likely individual efforts by prospectors. The Gold Point area is well worth the trip just to see the old falsefront.

GOLDYKE (Tom Burns Camp)

DIRECTIONS:
From Gabbs, head south on Nevada 361 for 2 miles. Exit left and follow this road for 10 miles to Goldyke.

Goldyke, a small mining camp, sprang up after discoveries in nearby Atwood sent prospectors searching the mountains and canyons around that booming camp. These prospectors discovered gold a mile southeast of Atwood in January 1906, and Goldyke quickly formed. A post office opened on Jan. 9, 1906. Soon a newspaper, the *Goldyke Daily Sun,* began publication. During 1907 an auto-stage from Goldyke to Luning was organized and was soon in full swing. The main mine at Goldyke was a 140-foot shaft. A five-stamp amalgamation and gravity concentration mill was built at the mine. The veins were quite shallow, and Goldyke quickly faded. The post office closed on Oct. 15, 1910, and Goldyke followed into oblivion.

There was some scant activity in the 1940s when the Jim group of claims, located one quarter mile from Goldyke, were worked by Tom Burns. A few buildings formed around the claims, but soon this activity also faded. The remains at Goldyke are very scant: there is one building, barely standing, and the ruins of the five-stamp mill. Other than that, only scattered debris marks the site.

GRANT CITY

DIRECTIONS:
From Currant, head south on US 6 for 9.8 miles. Exit left and follow this road for 6 miles. Exit right and follow this road for 10 miles. Exit left and follow Grant Canyon Road for 3½ miles to Grant City.

After discoveries were made in the Grant Range in 1867, the Grant mining district was organized on Oct. 27, 1868. A small townsite, Grant City, was platted soon after. The street system was laid out and a number of small stone cabins were built. By the summer of 1869, Grant City had a population of over 100 and a number of businesses, including a saloon and a blacksmith shop.

The two veins that supported the camp were the Meridian and the Blue Eagle, with ore that assayed as high as $300 per ton. A test shipment of ore sent to Austin in 1869 returned $500 to $600 per ton, but this rich lode was destined to run out quickly. By 1870 the town was sinking rapidly and soon was emptied. There was a small revival during the early 1880s—twenty-five people came back—but in 1884 the town was left to the ghosts and the cries of coyotes echoed through the crumbling ruins.

Grant City's remains are located amidst a small stand of trees. There are a few stone ruins left from the 1860s. Wooden remains in the canyon are probably from the revival of the 1880s or from the 1940s, when some Los Angeles people used the area as a summer lodge. The site, while small, is interesting and worth the trip. There is a small spring and the water is excellent.

GRANTSVILLE

DIRECTIONS:
From Ione, take Nevada 91 south for 6.4 miles. Exit left and follow this road for 1½ miles. At four corners, take a right and follow this road 4 miles to Grantsville.

Gold was discovered in Grantsville canyon in 1863 by P. A. Havens, already well known for his discoveries around the Ione area. Havens immediately organized the site into a mining district and laid out the groundwork for a good-size town, which he named after Ulysses S. Grant. Havens sold lots in the town for between $50 and $500; soon about fifty people were residing in the picturesque canyon. But Havens's rich claim was quickly worked out and the growing camp faded, becoming a ghost town for the next ten years.

The camp was reborn in September 1877 when the Alexander Company came to Grantsville at the suggestion of Manuel San Pedro, an original inhabitant of the town. The company bought a number of claims in the canyon and built a twenty-stamp mill, enlarged three years later to forty stamps. The company made some very good discoveries, and the population of Grantsville soon swelled to almost 1000.

The first newspaper, The *Grantsville Sun*, "dawned" on Oct. 19, 1878. It was run by D. L. Sayre but did not last long, folding in June 1879. Its successor was the *Grantsville Bonanza*, which started publication on Dec. 11, 1880, with men named Maute and Donald as publishers. This paper struggled through 1884 but finally folded due to lack of public interest.

A post office was opened on Feb. 3, 1879; mail was delivered three times a week. Three stagelines—to Eureka, Wadsworth and Austin—were set up. By 1881 the town had over forty business establishments, including ten merchandise stores, five saloons, two assay offices, an express office and a bank. A school was built by the Odd Fellows with a reported capacity of sixty students; the small brick building is one of the few buildings still standing in Grantsville.

There were fourteen major silver mines in Grantsville canyon. The best producer was the Alexander Mine, with a 1200-foot shaft and a 500-foot incline shaft. The Brooklyn Mine was another steady producer for the Alexander Company. The canyon mines produced over $1 million in gold and silver before 1885, when the district was temporarily abandoned.

Grantsville was the scene of a number of murders. The first occured on Aug. 10, 1880, when Thomas Burn shot and killed Thomas Mack, who was sleeping. Both men had been drinking together, and no motive for the killing was ever mentioned. Burn was sent to the state prison. The second and third murders took place in March 1881 when Mattias Salmon shot and killed a popular Grantsville resident, S. Merrill, for no apparent reason. Salmon was thrown into the Grantsville jail, actually an old

When this photo of Grantsville was taken in the 1880s, the town was near its peak. *(Nevada Historical Society)*

The old Grantsville one-room schoolhouse is in bad shape and probably will not last much longer.

This solid little stone cabin in Grantsville seems like it will last forever. But the relentlessly harsh Nevada climate will eventually bring the walls down.

abandoned tunnel shaft. An angry group of Grantsville citizens broke in, dragged the luckless Salmon to the stamp mill and lynched him from the crossbeams. The death was later ruled justifiable homicide.

Grantsville was slowly fading during the 1880s. By 1884 the population had diminished to 400. The camp kept functioning, but only barely. Grantsville was stubborn and reluctant to die. Every time the town seemed to be on its last leg, a new revival would keep it going for a little while longer. Luck ran out in 1901: the Grantsville post office closed on October 31. By then only a handful of people remained in the dying town. A small revival between 1921 and 1923 brought some activity back to Grantsville. The Webster Mines Corporation, based in Wilmington, Delaware, bought the old Alexander Mine and renamed it the Webster Mine. The company soon gave up its efforts, and the district remained silent for four years. The company kept control of the property and leased the mine in 1927 to William Hooten and associates, then in 1928 to the Stabler family of Los Angeles. The company remodeled the stamp mill, changing it to ten stamps and adding a rod mill and two flotation cells of 50-ton capacity driven by a distillate engine. The finished concentrate contained over 200 ounces of silver and was comprised of almost 30 percent lead.

The district was quiet until 1939, when a man named Barrows purchased the Silver Palace Mines and began operations. A 50-ton flotation mill was built near the mines during the fall of 1939. The mines produced over $100,000 for Barrows before he closed down in 1940. The last mining activity in the Grantsville district was in 1945–47. The Alexander and Brooklyn Mines Company reworked some mines and obtained $50,000 in lead concentrates for the war effort. After the company left the district in 1947, Grantsville was abandoned once more, this time becoming a permanent member of the ghostly register.

The ruins of Grantsville, some of the best in Nye County, range from the solid brick schoolhouse to small stone cabins. The schoolhouse still stands sturdily although it has been heavily vandalized. The main streets are easy to locate, for long rows of foundations mark the once booming business area. Only one building still remains in this district, and it appears to have been one of the blacksmith shops. A few more recent wooden cabins are north of what used to be the center of Grantsville. A large spring,

Grantsville's mine office building still stands. An old safe with its door blown off, possibly from this building, lies in the streambed just below town.

coming from a pipe, runs freely through the ruins; the drinking quality of the water is questionable, for it has a high mineral content.

The ruins of the stamp mill are just below the brick schoolhouse. A few buildings remain in front of the mill. The brick building served as an assay office. An old bulldozer, left from the World War II revival, is slowly rusting in front of the mill. An interesting aspect of my exploration was discovery of an old safe, with its door blown off, about half a mile below the mill. There was no clue as to the origin of the safe.

Plan to spend a day in Grantsville. The ruins are so extensive and so intriguing that it would be an injustice to hurry through them. By poking around the many foundations, it is fairly easy to determine the sort of establishment housed in each. I rate this ghost town in the top ten of Nye County, definitely a must.

HANNAPAH (Silverzone) (Volcano) (Bannock)

DIRECTIONS:
From Tonopah, head east on US 6 for 18 miles. Exit left and follow this road for 1½ miles to Hannapah.

Initial discoveries were made in the Hannapah area in 1902. Soon work began on the Hannapah Mine and by 1905 a small camp had formed nearby. The district was explored further during the next few years. A townsite was platted in early 1906, and on Feb. 6, 1906, real estate promoters hosted a huge barbecue to attract potential customers to the new Hannapah district. The people liked the barbecue but not the townsite; very few lots were sold. By 1907, after only limited mining production, the district and the townsite were abandoned.

In 1915 a short boom followed silver discoveries in the southern part of the Hannapah mining district. This small settlement was called Volcano; the boom soon ended and so did Volcano. The district was revived once again in 1915 when the Hannapah Mine reopened. Fredrick Browne, who owned the mine, claimed that over $150,000 in ore had been exposed when the mine was retimbered. The mine was known to be rich, but earlier operations had removed the easily mined richer ore and further exploration of the property was thought to be unprofitable. Browne proved this assumption incorrect; the Hannapah Mine produced from 1919 until early 1921.

Two other mining companies were active in the district during the 1919 revival. One was the Silverzone Mohawk Company owned by William Gray and J. J. Clark, both from Tonopah. They also owned the Silverzone Mines Company, which worked property in Silver Glance, one quarter mile west of Hannapah. The Silverzone Mohawk Company sank a new 80-foot shaft that yielded ore assayed at an average of $30 per ton. The company leased to Charles Spilman the old Tripod shaft, originally worked to a small extent in 1905. Ore removed from the shaft assayed as high as $80 per ton.

The second active company was the Hannapah Divide Extension Mines Company, incorporated in December 1919 with W. R. Porter as president. The company owned nine claims in the Hannapah district, now known as the Silverzone district. Old shafts were reopened in 1919 and small shipments of silver ore were sent to mills in Tonopah during 1920.

By 1921 the district was dead once again, except for one claim that remained active through 1922. Ben Richardson, who had bought a number of claims, found one to be quite rich and thus began exploratory work in 1922. He was unsuccessful, but the Hannapah Extension Mines Company decided to gamble. They purchased the claim from Richardson in 1922. The company lost the gamble when the ore turned out to be quite poor in quality. Richardson continued to work his other claims, finding a vein rich enough to warrant digging a shaft well over 300 feet deep. Richardson built a small Straub mill, with ore house, to process ore from his mine. He continued to work the mine until 1935, when the ore ran out and he left the district.

The last revival in the Hannapah district took place in 1927, when three companies became active here. In that year the World Exploration Company of Fort Worth, Texas, purchased the Hannapah Extension Mines Company, which had been idle since 1922, and began limited activity that lasted until 1929. Financial problems then forced the company into bankruptcy. The second company in the district was the Appache Hannapah Mines Company, incorporated in 1927 with Walter Lynch of Alhambra, California, as president. The

The headframe and tailing pile of the old Hannapah Mine.

Looking south from the Hannapah Mine. This is all that remains of the town.

A combination outhouse/rootcellar remains behind one of the few buildings left at the Hannapah townsite.

company owned four claims in the district: the Helen, the Helen No. 1, the Silver Horde and the Dickey Bill. These had values in both gold and silver, with the highest values being in silver. In 1928 the company sank a new 300-foot shaft. An electric line was strung from Tonopah to power the electric mine hoists. The venture proved fruitless and the company folded in 1929.

The last company to work the district was the Hannapah Silver Star Mining Company, organized in early 1928 with Russell Boardmen as president. The company owned seven claims in the Hannapah district, all adjacent to the Hannapah Extension Mine. Activity continued, without much profit, until early 1929. When the company folded, the Hannapah district joined the long list of Nye County ghosts.

Very little remains of Hannapah. Careful search will reveal the original site. One wooden building still remains, just below the Hannapah Mine. There are also a few other wooden ruins along with the complete workings of two mines, including the mine hoists and engine housings. Exercise extreme caution, for unmarked shafts are located throughout the site and are well hidden.

HARRIMAN

DIRECTIONS:
From Eden, travel 2 miles south to Harriman.

Harriman was formed following exploration caused by the discoveries at Eden Creek, 2 miles to the north. There were six major claims at Harriman, all purchased by the Nevada Gold Sight Mining Company in 1907 and 1908. The company dug three tunnels, which had over 1400 feet of workings. The gold ore mined from the tunnels was valued from $10 to $25 per ton.

The camp never grew to any size; peak population was less than twenty-five. The mining company built a few wooden boardinghouses, but that was the extent of construction. Needed supplies were brought in from Eden. The camp did have an ample supply of wood, used both for heating during the cold nights and for support beams in the tunnels. Water, a commodity valued everywhere in dry Nye County, was quite abundant. Unfortunately, the ore was not as plentiful as the wood and water and became increasingly harder to find. By the end of 1910, the Nevada Gold Sight Mining Company was operating in the red; it folded in early 1911. There were still five prospectors digging around Harriman in 1911, but by 1912 the site belonged only to the ghosts.

The remains of Harriman are very scant. Only the ruins of one boardinghouse marks the site. Fairly large tailing dumps are on the sides of the canyon, with many small "prospector holes" pockmarking most of the area. Harriman is quite difficult to reach, not because of the roads but because of its distance from a filling station. If you plan to visit the site, be sure to bring extra gas.

HICK'S HOT SPRINGS

DIRECTIONS:
From Beatty, head north on US 95 for 5.3 miles to Hick's Hot Springs.

Hick's Hot Springs came into existence in January 1907 when the Bullfrog-Goldfield Railroad set up a grading camp here. The site was later a water stop until the B.-G. R.R. closed in 1928. It is still an active area, with a number of hot spring resort-type setups.

HICK'S STATION

DIRECTIONS:
From Warm Springs, head north on US 6 for 20.9 miles. Exit left and follow this road for 2½ miles. Take the right fork and continue for 7 miles. At the four-way junction, take a right and continue for 5 miles. At the end of the road take a left onto a new road and continue for 8 miles. Take the left fork and continue for 1 mile. Bear right at the fork and follow for 8 miles to Hick's Station.

Hick's Station was a former stop on the Warm Springs–Eureka stage route. The station was not as carefully constructed as nearby Pritchard's and Moore's stations. The advantage of Hick's Station was that it had an abundance of water, although the Shoshone Indians called the springs *sapiaua*, which means scum water.

A number of buildings still remain. A small ranch operated here after the stage run stopped; the site is clearly marked "no trespassing," so closer examination was not possible. A small pond at the site hosts a number of wild ducks. The last half mile before the site is extremely treacherous. I became stuck in a 100-foot sandbar located in a gully just before the site and it took eight hours of jacking the truck up and down to escape.

HORSESHOE

DIRECTIONS:
From Tonopah, head east on US 6 for 35 miles. Exit right and follow for 1½ miles. Take a right at the fork and follow straight through for 5 miles. At the end of the road, take a left and follow for 1¼ miles to Horseshoe.

Horseshoe, a small offshoot camp of Clifford, formed in 1908. It had two major mines, the Lawrence Mine and the Original Horseshoe Mine. The Lawrence Mine was over 200 feet deep and had 750 feet of lateral work. The Original Horseshoe Mine was a much smaller mine; after rich initial silver discoveries, the ore quickly faded and the mine was abandoned. The camp died in 1911, and nothing at all remains.

HOT CREEK

DIRECTIONS:
From Warm Springs, take US 6 north for 20.9 miles. Exit left and follow for 2½ miles. Take a left at the fork and follow for 9 miles to Hot Creek Ranch. Remains are on the ranch.

The Hot Creek mining district was organized in 1866 after discovery of ore in a number of canyons in the Hot Creek range. In early 1867 a small town formed along Hot Creek and was named after the creek, which had received its name because steam often rose from the creek in the morning. The town grew very fast, and by the summer of 1867 contained a number of small stone buildings. On August 7 it was awarded a post office. Hot Creek peaked in 1868, with a population of over 300.

Business establishments included a number of saloons, a hotel, a blacksmith shop, a restaurant and an assay office. Two stamp mills, located to the north in Carrolton and Lower Town, were built in 1867 to process ore from the Hot Creek mines.

Hot Creek began its decline in late 1868 after new strikes in White Pine County lured away most of the 300 residents. The town continued to function at a low level until the summer of 1877, when Henry Allen contracted with Tybo Consolidated Company to build fifteen brick kilns. The purpose of the kilns was to supply charcoal for the lead smelters in Tybo. The kilns, which were built in two nearby canyons, were completed in September 1877, and over 600,000 bricks were used in their construction. These kilns were an average of 25 feet in diameter, and each had a capacity of 1400 bushels of charcoal.

A minor mining revival took place in 1880, and a small ten-stamp mill was built at the site. The mill only operated for a year before it was dismantled. The post office closed on March 13, 1881, and the town was soon abandoned. Total production for the Hot Creek district from 1867 to 1881 was just over $1 million.

The district remained quiet until early 1897, when new ore discoveries prompted the return of some people. The post office reopened on May 5, 1897, and continued in operation until Jan. 26, 1912. The Hot Creek Syndicate Trust took control of most mines and had thirty-two claims in nearby Rattlesnake Canyon. Hot Creek's population in 1910 was still twenty-five, but after the Syndicate folded in 1911 the town rejoined the ghosts.

The Hot Creek Ranch Company took over the property and organized a large ranch, which has been a savior for the town's buildings. The ranch owners have taken care of the remaining buildings and still use some of them. One of the most impressive structures is a stone building that served as a hotel. It was a victim of a fire but was restored during the revival of the early 1900s. The remains of the charcoal kilns, north of Hot Creek, are well worth the trip; they are unique and are some of the very few located in Nye County. A number of other ruins are higher up in Hot Creek Canyon. For the most part these are only old homesteads that were not connected with the mining activity here.

IDLEWILD

DIRECTIONS:
Located 4 miles north of Ione in Idlewild Canyon.

Idlewild Canyon was the site of a small offshoot camp of Midas. Only a handful of prospectors ever resided here, and no actual mining took place at the site. Historically, little is known about the settlement. Recently the Idlewild Canyon area has been used by the Boy Scouts of America as one of their outing places. A large old log structure of unknown purpose still remains at the site, but nothing else is left. Fresh spring water is available.

INDIAN SPRING

DIRECTIONS:
Located inside the Las Vegas Bombing and Gunnery Range, 10 miles southeast of Kawich. Off-limits to the public.

Indian Spring, a small mining camp, formed at the base of Wheelbarrow Peak. The camp was active during the early 1900s but never achieved prominence. No more than fifteen residents lived here, most in tents although a few stone cabins were built. The camp was completely abandoned in 1910 after the two small mines on Wheelbarrow Peak closed. A present report is not possible because the site is off-limits.

This old log structure of unknown use is all that remains at the Idlewild townsite.

INDIAN SPRINGS

DIRECTIONS:
From Manhattan, head west on Nevada 69 for 6.8 miles. At the junction with Nevada 376, exit left (south) and follow for 2.8 miles. Exit right and follow for 2 miles to Indian Springs.

The small camp of Indian Springs formed in 1865 around a mill just to the north of San Antonio. A ten-stamp Pioneer mill was built here in 1865–66 to treat the extremely high-value ore coming out of the nearby San Antonio Mountains. There was a population of ten at one time. When ore values declined and the Pioneer mill was shut down and moved to Northumberland in 1868, Indian Springs ceased to exist. Today only scant rubble marks the site.

IONE (Ione City)

DIRECTIONS:
From Gabbs, head north on Nevada 361 for 1 mile to Nevada 91. Take a right and follow for 22.1 miles to Ione.

Ione formed in November 1863 soon after initial silver discoveries were made in the Union district by P. A. Havens. At first the camp had only a handful of residents, but within a few months there were over fifty buildings and more people. By January 1864 the populus of Ione was demanding that a new county be formed because of the richness of the Ione area. The state government consented in January 1864; an official county government was organized on April 26 of that year. The town was allotted $800 to build a county courthouse; present-day residents say it is the small wooden cabin still standing today. By the spring of 1864, the town had a post office, more than 100 buildings and a population of 600.

Two newspapers began publication in Ione in 1864. The *Nye County News*, which printed its first issue on June 25, was organized by Henry DeGrout and Joseph Eckley. The *News* ran into problems and folded after about a month. It was reborn on July 1, 1865, with Eckley now the sole proprietor. Despite glowing promises, the paper ran into more problems and finally ceased operations for good in May 1867. The second paper, the *Advertiser*, was extremely short-lived; it was first published on Sept. 17, 1864, and expired on October 29 of the same year.

Most of the mining in the Union district was located miles from Ione. But a five-stamp mill, the

Ione on Independence Day, 1897, included a store, formerly of Berlin, and a number of falsefronted buildings, of which only a few remain. *(Nevada Historical Society)*

Operating a hand windlass illustrates the hard work involved in a small-scale operation. This photo was taken near Ione in the 1930s. *(MacKay School of Mines/University of Nevada at Reno)*

Present-day view of one of the better falsefronts still in Ione.

Pioneer, was constructed at the town. The mill never turned a real profit and closed in 1866. New strikes at Belmont in 1867 lured away many of Ione's residents. A bitter blow was dealt to the town in February 1867 when the county seat was moved to Belmont. Ione began a quick slide, its population sinking to 175 by 1868. The town experienced many ups and downs during the next decade. In the 1870s, Ione had a few good years of production, but Belmont remained the focus of attention and Ione's population continued to shrink. By 1880 the population stood at twenty-five with only a few business establishments still functioning. This figure remained fairly constant for many years. The post office closed in 1882, and it was not until the early teens that a revival brought back some people. The post office reopened on July 16, 1912, then closed again on April 30, 1914. When production became more consistent in the district, the post office reopened yet again, on Dec. 18, 1918; it remained open until 1959.

The new mining involved mercury. During the early excitement about gold and silver, the rust-colored cinnabar ore had been overlooked. Most mining was done by the Mercury Mining Company, which had its principal properties in nearby Shamrock Canyon. The company produced over 11,000 flasks of mercury, each weighing 75 pounds. A large mill was built on the edge of Ione but was never used consistently. Mercury mining continued into the 1930s. After that activity ceased there was only sporadic mining, but Ione clung to life. In 1945 its population was still at forty-five. When the post office closed on April 30, 1959, only a handful of residents were left. Total production for Ione and the immediate area ranged from $500,000 to $1 million.

The mill built for mercury was torn down in 1950; only its foundations now remain. Today the little town quietly sleeps, awaiting another revival and discovery of that elusive "rich" lode. Ione still retains its flavor, with an abundance of old and very interesting old buildings. Among the better ones are the old schoolhouse and a few falsefront stores. A number of very old stone cabins are also left. Gas and limited grocery supplies are available at Ione's one remaining store. This quaint town is a definite must for any ghost-town buff.

JACKSON MINING DISTRICT (Gold Park) (Barnes Park)

DIRECTIONS:
From Ione, head northwest out of town for 12 miles toward Penelas. Exit right (sharp) and follow for 10½ miles. Exit right again and follow for 1½ miles. Exit right and follow for ½ mile. Then try a left and follow for another ½ mile. Go right at the fork and follow for 5 miles to the Jackson mining district.

The Jackson mining district is on the Lander-Nye County border but is included here because major mines in the district were located in Nye County.

The first discovery of ore in the Gold Park Basin was made in 1864 by prospector Thomas Barnes. Shortly afterward a small mining district was formed, named the North Union mining district. In 1878 the district was reorganized and was renamed the Jackson mining district. By that year there were three principal mines and seventeen other sites. The three principal mines—the San Francisco, Arctic and North Star—all had vertical shafts just over 50 feet deep.

In 1880 another group of prospectors, led by Frank Bradley, found more ore deposits. Soon operations in the Gold Park Basin stepped up. By 1893 the district had three large claims and a mill, all of which were purchased then by the Nevada Mining Company. The company built a new stamp mill, which continued operations until the teens. The property was bought in 1919 by Robert B. Todd, who organized the Star of the West Mining Company. Todd built a new 50-ton amalgamation and concentration mill, completed in 1921.

The Star of the West Mining Company was originally incorporated in Delaware in 1919 with capital of $1 million. By the end of 1921, the mining company owned fifteen mining claims and three mills in the Gold Park Basin. It also owned over 4000 feet of workings and the 50-ton mill. Shortly after 1921, however, activity in the Gold Park Basin was curtailed when the quality of the gold and silver ore declined. Total production of the Jackson mining district easily exceeded $1 million.

The district was in an excellent spot, with an abundance of water and wood in the surrounding mountains. The district was not only known for its silver and gold but also for its semiprecious stones, including geodes, agates and other jeweler gems. No buildings remain in Gold Park Basin, but evidence of activity is still visible. Tailing piles are throughout the basin, and mill foundations make for interesting exploration.

JACKSONVILLE

DIRECTIONS:
From Ancram, continue westward on the unimproved road for about 5 miles to Jacksonville.

Jacksonville, a water stop on the Bullfrog-Goldfield Railroad, was active from November 1906 to January 1928. The water stop was in the middle of the hot, dry Sarcobatus Flat. The steam engines were in constant danger of overheating, and the need for water led to establishment of a number of water stops similar to Jacksonville throughout Sarcobatus Flat. The water at the Jacksonville stop came from two nearby wells, the Tonopah and the Seattle. When the B.-G. R.R. folded in January 1928, Jacksonville's service was no longer needed and the site soon passed into ghosthood. Nothing at all remains.

JAMESTOWN

DIRECTIONS:
Located inside the Las Vegas Bombing and Gunnery Range, 12 miles south of Antelope Springs. Off-limits to the public.

Jamestown was short-lived. The mining camp was formed in early 1908 after gold was discovered on Pahute Mesa. Soon close to 100 prospectors had flocked to Jamestown. A post office opened on June 15, 1908. The Golden Chariot Mining Company was organized in Jamestown in 1908 and began intensive operations. The company, with Carl Feutsh as president, owned a number of claims in the district. Many of the claims were copper producers, but there were a few gold mines. The richest of the gold lodes was Golden Chariot No. 1. It was over 300 feet deep and had initial assays of $200 per ton. Other gold mines included the Franz Hammel Mine (240 feet deep, with 400-foot lateral workings) plus the Mohawk, Daisy and Last Chance mines, owned by Engrace LaBarthe. The deepest LaBarthe mine was 200 feet.

Consistent production lasted only into 1910. The post office closed on Aug. 31 of that year and the town continued to slip downhill. The Golden Chariot Mining Company folded in late 1910, and by 1911 the town had emptied. A number of buildings were built in Jamestown, but not much is known about their origin. A visitor to the site in the 1930s reported three buildings still standing, including the old post office. Now the site is inside the Las Vegas Bombing and Gunnery Range, and only the occasional rumble of Air Force jets disturbs the ghosts of Jamestown.

JEFFERSON

DIRECTIONS:
From Round Mountain, head north out of town for 1 mile. At the fork take a right and follow this road for 1½ miles to a point overlooking a small canyon with a stream. Head downroad into the canyon but do not cross the stream. Continue straight (east), parallel to the stream, for 4 miles to Jefferson. There are a few stream crossings but none are very deep. Ruins of Jefferson are scattered along the canyon for ¾ mile.

The initial silver ore discovery was made in Jefferson Canyon in early 1866. More substantial discoveries were made in 1871, when a test load of silver ore sent to Austin returned over $28,000 in silver. In 1873 two men, John Johnson and Robert Fergerson, discovered rich silver ore, and the Green Isle mining district was formed. Two principal mines, the Prussian and the South Prussian (also known as the Jefferson), started operations. Another mine, the Sierra Nevada Mine, was discovered by C. J. Kanrobat and also became a fairly consistent producer. A large ten-stamp mill was built at the Jefferson Mine in 1874; a smaller mill was built at the Prussian Mine in the same year. The Prussian Mine, which had a 250-foot shaft, constantly had water trouble that hampered operations.

It was not until completion of the two stamp mills that interest in the Jefferson area increased. By the end of the summer of 1874, the town contained two separate sections. The main city district was three quarters of a mile above the mining and milling area. It contained a post office (which opened in October 1874), two general merchandise stores, a Wells Fargo office, hotels, a school and other "necessary establishments." During 1874 a toll road was constructed over rugged Jefferson Mountain to Belmont. Supplies for the booming town were transported by a mule team daily from Wadsworth, well to the northwest of Jefferson.

Jefferson's peak years were 1875 and 1876; production then was almost $1.5 million. During the boom years over 120 claims were filed, but most turned out to be merely granite deposits. The population of Jefferson was a little over 800. Soon after, in 1876, production slowed and the mill at the Jefferson Mine closed. In 1878 the Prussian Mine mill followed suit. The post office closed in January 1879, sounding the death knell for the town. Between 1877 and 1882 only 40 tons of ore were removed from the claims, and reportedly only four miners remained at the camp to continue operations.

A revival was attempted in 1908 after attempts in 1883, 1885 and 1890 had been unsuccessful. The mines and mills were all purchased by a group of New York businessmen for $350,000. The group built a new 100-ton mill, which was used to treat the huge mounds of ore that had been pushed aside in the hurry to get at the richer ore. This operation did not last too long, and soon Jefferson belonged to the ghosts again.

The Sierra Nevada property was purchased in 1917 by Charles H. Stoneham of New York Giant fame. Production was started to help satisfy the demand for metal in World War I. The mill built in 1908 was reequipped for flotation. Despite low-grade ore, it opened for operations; it closed in 1918. Late that year the old Kanrohat Mine properties were purchased by S. H. Brady, who organized the Jefferson Gold and Silver Mining Company. The huge 100-ton mill was reopened and a cyanide settling tank was added. The Kanrohat Mine was further developed to a depth of over 1000 feet. New ore was discovered, but the size of the deposits was fairly small. The main source of revenue for the mining company came from reprocessing over 60,000 tons of ore in the old tailing dumps. During the short revival fifteen men were employed by the mining company. The company ran out of capital and folded in early 1919. Jefferson was empty once more.

Remains of Upper Jefferson include buildings shown here and others in the area to the left of the photo.

The old post office in Upper Jefferson.

This remain in Lower Jefferson shows the great care used in construction. Judging from relics found buried inside, the building was either a mine office or an assay office.

A last-gasp effort at reviving the district took place in 1928 when the Elsa Mining Company reopened the mill and installed new equipment, but the same fate was in store. The revival failed almost as soon as it had begun. Jefferson was laid to rest forever after the failure.

The Jefferson ruins are extensive and extremely interesting. The lower section of the town contains ruins of the mills and quite a number of smaller buildings in various stages of decay. There are also acres of old dumps that will delight any type of collector— broken glass, pieces of china and old tin cans litter the site. In the upper section of Jefferson more substantial ruins remain, most remnants of the later revival attempts. Many buildings still stand in relatively good condition. The road from the lower section to the upper section is impassable, for Jefferson Creek now flows down the middle of the road. Even four-wheel travel is impossible, but a short hike is well rewarded.

JETT (Argentore) (Silver Point)

DIRECTIONS:
From Round Mountain, head west on Nevada 92 for 2.7 miles. At junction with 376, take a left and follow for 1½ miles. Exit right (signs at road are for the Round Mountain Airport). Follow this road for 6½ miles to Jeff, located in scenic Jett Canyon. Later activity took place at the mouth of Jett Canyon.

The Jett mining district was discovered by John Davenport during 1875. The next year the district was officially organized but did not really become active until 1880, when over 100 claims were made in Jett Canyon. There were three major mines inside the canyon: the Centennial, Seventy-Six and Idlewild. The Centennial was easily the richest, with ore assaying between $100 and $300 a ton. The other two mines had relatively low-grade ore that contained no gold and only small amounts of silver. The Centennial mine had a vertical shaft of 190 feet while the Idlewild had a 200-foot tunnel.

This is the only structure left at the site of Jett.

The remains of the Jett Mine in breathtakingly beautiful Jett Canyon.

In response to the activity in 1880, a post office was opened on March 16, 1880. Soon the camp contained a sawmill, butcher shops and cabins for the miners. The ore mined at Jett was shipped north to Eureka for smelting. Supplies were freighted in from Austin, 60 miles north, at a cost of $30 a ton. Activity slowed in the district during 1881, and on April 21, 1881, the post office shut down. A short revival started by a New York firm warranted reopening the post office in 1890. The excitement faded as quickly as the ore did, and the post office closed for good on March 25, 1891.

The district remained dormant until the early 1920s, when a rich vein was discovered near the mouth of Jett Canyon. A new settlement was started at the mouth of the canyon, 2 miles from the original site. The new vein, named the Gilbraltar, was discovered by the New York–based Gibraltar Silver Hill Mining Company. The vein contained fairly high quantities of silver, lead and zinc along with antimony. These new discoveries gave rise to a settlement with a huge boardinghouse and a number of cabins.

Unfortunately the vein was relatively short. Activity slowly stopped until, by 1925, the district was completely abandoned. A cabin and the workings of the Centennial Mine still remain amid breathtaking scenery. The canyon is extremely beautiful and remains nice and cool. It is hard to believe that just a few miles away from this beautiful canyon is desert valley bleakness. Nothing remains of the settlement at the mouth of Jett Canyon, marked only by some faint foundations and wood scraps.

Johnnie (Montgomery)

DIRECTIONS:
From Pahrump, follow Nevada 16 north for 16 miles to Johnnie, located on the west side of the highway.

Johnnie was formed in 1891 soon after prospectors discovered gold at the Johnnie Mine site, a few miles northeast of the townsite. (A separate section on the Johnnie Mine and the history of that site follows. This section deals specifically with Johnnie.) The Congress and Johnnie mines were the mainstays of Johnnie. The Congress, also known as the Chispa, was just west of the Johnnie townsite and was also discovered in 1891. A small rush soon developed, with most people coming from fading mining camps in the north. By May 1891 over 100 men and women were living at the camp, then known as Montgomery for the Montgomery brothers, who were in the prospecting group that discovered ore in the Johnnie district. A post office named Montgomery opened on Aug. 7, 1891, to serve the booming district. Supplies were brought in from

Daggett, 150 miles away, via the Sante Fe Railroad. Water for the camp was brought by donkey from Horseshutem Springs, 4 miles east across Pahrump Valley. The veins turned out to be quite shallow and the camp quickly emptied. The Montgomery post office closed on March 17, 1894, and a ghostly silence fell over the camp.

A Utah mining company bought the Congress Mine in early 1898. Soon more than fifty people were back at the camp. A post office, named Johnnie, opened on June 28, 1898. There were a number of labor disputes at the Congress Mine during the next few years including one where the leasers and the mine owner had a major disagreement that did not end until two men lay dead. During the dispute the one-stamp mill and a cookhouse were burned, the mine office was dynamited and the safe was looted. This revival lasted only until mid-1899. The post office closed on April 1, 1899. Johnnie was once again a ghost.

Soon after discoveries were made in Goldfield and Bullfrog in 1904, some prospectors drifted down to the Johnnie area. New discoveries in 1905 prompted reopening the Congress Mine, and initial work on a number of new claims also began. The post office was back in service on May 27, 1905, remaining in operation until Dec. 31, 1914. A new townsite was platted at the old site in May 1905, and the lots sold very quickly. By early 1907 almost 350 people were living in Johnnie. In addition to utilizing structures left from earlier activity, several new stores were built along with saloons, hotels and restaurants. A daily stage was organized to Amargosa, on the Las Vegas and Tonopah Railroad; the fare was $3. The Johnnie Consolidated Mining Company purchased the Congress Mine in 1908 and worked it until 1914. Activity faded in that year and the town's population dropped from 100 to less than 15. After the post office closed, Johnnie went downhill, only to be rescued once again by new discoveries in late 1915.

Placer gold was discovered around the townsite, and soon Johnnie was showing some of its old vim and vigor. The post office reopened on April 14, 1916, as Johnnie began its last and longest revival. The Eureka Johnnie Gold Mining Company became active here in 1921. The company sank four shafts, the deepest 130 feet; the four had total workings of 900 feet. A small two-stamp mill was built, and ore processed by the mill assayed at about $10 per ton. The company continued to work the district until 1925, when financial woes forced it to fold. Johnnie did not fold, though, for the placer gold operations were rich enough to keep people in town. The post office closed Nov. 6, 1935, but a handful of people still remained. New activity in the late 1930s at the Johnnie Mine drew most of the people from the town, and the site was soon empty.

The whole site—160 acres—was purchased lock, stock and barrel by Matt Kusic after World War II. He sold it to Al Padgett, who in turn sold it to Deke Lowe, the present owner. Lowe has revived the camp, not as a mining venture but as a secluded home for a number of people, including Fred S. Cook, a well-known Nevada historian, and Kathie Milone, an interviewer on a Las Vegas TV station.

There are numerous remains at the site, including a few wooden cabins slated for restoration to house people who want to move back to Johnnie. A number of trailers are on the site until more suitable buildings are repaired or erected. Lowe plans to bring power to the town, via a line from Pahrump and proposes to build a water pipeline from Horseshutem Springs, the source of water for Johnnie's earlier settlers. It is always encouraging to see a desolate ghost town being reclaimed and protected from the harsh desert and rampaging vandals.

JOHNNIE MINE (Labbe Camp)

DIRECTIONS:
From Pahrump, head north on Nevada 16 for 17 miles. Exit right and follow for 1½ miles to Johnnie Mine.

The Johnnie Mine was discovered in 1891 by five prospectors searching for the lost Breyfogle ledge. The rich Johnnie Mine that they discovered is believed by many to be the lost ledge. The mine was named after Ashmeadow Johnnie, an Indian from Pahrump Valley. Another mine, the Crown Point Globe, was also discovered in 1891. Discoverer Ed Oldfield built a one-stamp Kendall mill at the site.

In 1908 a sixteen-stamp Nissen mill was constructed at the Johnnie Mine. The mine and mill continued to operate until 1914. Production for the Johnnie Mine from 1910 to 1914 was close to $4 million. The mine and mill changed hands in 1916 but was only operated intermittently until 1919, when A. P. Johnson of Los Angeles bought the property. The mine was reopened and eventually dug to a depth of 1100 feet, plus over 12,000 feet of lateral workings. The owners installed distillate engines, a 40-h.p. hoist and a ten-drill compressor. The sixteen-stamp mill, which had a capacity of 80 tons, was reopened. Ten men were employed in both the mine and the mill. Johnson and his associates continued to work the Johnnie Mine until 1924.

The Crown Point Globe Mine contained rich pockets of gold ore. The value per ton was erratic; one shipment of 150 tons yielded almost 14,000 ounces of gold. The mine was dug to a depth of 200 feet and had over 500 feet of drift tunnels. The mine still retains most of its original machinery, including the old 1891 hoist. The Crown Point Globe Mine is also known as the Overfield Mine; it was owned and worked for a number of years by the Overfield Mining Company of Chicago.

The Johnnie Mine was the scene of extensive activity beginning in 1937. A regular camp formed here, including a store, pool hall and other establishments. A post office opened on Sept. 14, 1937, and remained open until July 1, 1942. Water for the active camp was obtained from nearby Grapevine Springs via a 4-inch pipeline. The camp was also known as Labbe Camp, after Charles Labbe, one of the principal owners of the mine and mill. Production was stopped in 1942; the property was later purchased by George and Judy Warner. Production for the district from 1934 to 1942 was in the neighborhood of $25,000.

The ruins at Johnnie Mine are fairly extensive. The sixteen-stamp mill has been preserved very well and is ready for use if the mine ever reopens. A number of buildings remain at the site. A talk with current owner George Warner is very rewarding—and be sure to ask his permission to look around the site. About a mile north of the Johnnie Mine is a small group of wooden buildings probably built during the activity of the 1930s. Total production for the Johnnie Mine and the Crown Point Globe Mine was reported to be as high as $20 million, but this figure seems exaggerated. Still, the mines have a very impressive production record. Be sure to pack plenty of water because the Pahrump Valley area tends to be extremely hot and dry.

JUNCTION

DIRECTIONS:
From Round Mountain, head west on Nevada 92 for 2.7 miles. Exit right (north) on Nevada 376 for 27 miles to Junction.

Junction was the main post office for the northern part of Smoky Valley. The Junction post office opened March 20, 1873, at the old Lognoz Ranch on the Austin–Belmont stageline. The post office closed July 31, 1906, after most mining activity in the surrounding area had stopped. A ranch is still active here. A few old buildings remain on the ranch as relics of the early activity at Junction.

KAWICH (Gold Reed)

DIRECTIONS:
Located 70 miles southeast of Tonopah, inside the Las Vegas Bombing and Gunnery Range. Off-limits to the public.

Initial discoveries of gold ore in the Kawich Mountains were made in December 1904 by a small group of prospectors from Tonopah. A rush to the area occurred during early 1905, when as many as 450 people were living here. The camp was named after Chief Kawich, a Shoshone, whose name meant "mountain" in Shoshone. By April 1905 the tent camp had a number of saloons and stores. Water, which was scarce in Kawich, was brought in from Cliff Spring, 12 miles to the east. A post office opened April 10, 1905, and was officially named Kawich, although a number of residents called the camp Gold Reed after mine superintendent O. K. Reed. By 1906, however, the camp was known only as Kawich. A stageline was set up between Kawich and Tonopah at a cost of $10 for a round-trip ticket.

The Gold Reed Mining Company became active in the district in early 1905 and began work on three mines: the Chief Kawich, Gold Reed and Diamond No. 2. The two largest mines, Chief Kawich and Gold Reed, were both over 150 feet deep. Diamond No. 2, even though only 100 feet deep, proved to have the richest ore, although the amount was limited. The gold occurred in thin pyrite veins that assayed at an average of $35 per ton; the ore value from the other two mines rarely broke $10 a ton. The district's ore became even lower in grade as spring 1905 progressed, and by the end of the summer only ten people were still working the mines. The Gold Reed Mining Company struggled

Kawich in 1905, shortly after being formed, included small mines on the slope of Kawich Peak.
(United States Geological Survey)

into early 1907 but finally folded after failing to find higher value ore to help finance continuing operations.

Kawich was on a downhill slide after only nine months of existence. The downhill trend continued until the district was totally abandoned in 1908. The post office operated until June 15, 1908; the postmaster was one of only three people still living in town. It was not until the 1940s that anyone came back to the Kawich district. Albert and Robert Martel reopened the Gold Reed Mine and dug it to a depth of 300 feet. They found nothing of value and soon left the district. No other large-scale revivals ever took place in the Kawich district, and a good many people wondered why any activity at all had taken place. The site is now inside the Las Vegas Bombing and Gunnery Range, isolating Kawich from visitors. I highly doubt that anyone would want to visit the desolate site anyway.

KEYSTONE

DIRECTIONS:
From Warm Springs, head north on US 6 for 8 miles. Exit left and follow this road for 3½ miles. Bear right at the fork and follow for 6½ miles. Exit left and follow for 2 miles to Keystone.

Keystone was a small but active camp dating from the 1860s. The town quickly grew to two-saloon size and had a population of fifty. The Keystone Mine was the mainstay of the town, and a fairly large mill was built adjacent to it during the late 19th century. A post office opened at Keystone on Jan. 26, 1912, and stayed open until March 12, 1927. After the post office closed, Keystone was very quickly left to the ghosts. Recently new cyanide

This cabin at Keystone was occupied until quite recently and still retains the old furnishings put in by the person who lived there many years ago.

leaching operations have been started up, bringing some new life to the ghostly town. A number of old stone buildings are left here, but the ruins of the old mill were flattened to make it easier for the leaching crews. The site is well worth the trip. Fresh spring water is available.

KNICKERBOCKER

DIRECTIONS:
From Ione, head south on Nevada 91 for 1¾ miles. Exit left and follow for 1½ miles to Knickerbocker.

Knickerbocker was a small milling camp that formed around the impressive Knickerbocker Mill. The mill was built in the summer of 1865 with money from Eastern backers. By the time the mill was completed in early 1866, over $130,000 had been spent on construction. The mill, consisting of twenty stamps and six roasting furnaces, operated from 1866 until 1875. It was the principal processor of Grantsville's ore until a mill was built there in 1869. During the mill's operating years, as many as twenty-five people resided nearby.

After the mill closed in 1875 the canyon quickly emptied; no other activity ever took place here. In 1898 the mill and its contents were purchased by the Nevada Company, and all of the machinery was moved to booming Berlin to be used in a new thirty-stamp mill.

Today the beautiful rock ruins of the mill dominate the old camp. The rock walls reveal that the mill was extremely large and elegant. A few small stone cabins also remain in the canyon. The workmanship of both the mill and the cabins is extremely intricate and shows the great care used in building them, something not often seen in the hustle and bustle of a mining camp. A trip to the site is well rewarded, but be careful: rattlesnakes abound in the ruins.

LAUVILLE

DIRECTIONS:
From Antelope (Clear Creek Ranch), head south for 3 miles. Exit right onto a poor dirt road parallel to Wattles Creek and follow this for 2½ miles to Lauville.

Lauville was a small and extremely short-lived mining camp active during the early 20th century. Lauville, along with nearby Antelope and Stargo, never achieved significant size: peak population was only around fifteen. A few stone cabins were built here to accompany a few flimsy tents. Lauville

The majestic Knickerbocker Mill was one of the most carefully constructed mills in Nye County, as is evident from the fine stonework.

disappeared from all maps in 1912, and no activity has been recorded since. Nothing much remains except a few piles of stones left from the cabins. Fresh water is available from nearby springs.

LEARVILLE (Searville) (Learnville)

DIRECTIONS:
Located ½ mile south of Northumberland.

Little is known about this small camp that sprang up in 1868. A number of name variations appear, but *Learville* is the name on postal cancellations. Learville formed around a ten-stamp mill built by the Quintero Company in the summer of 1868. The mill employed ten men, most of whom resided in nearby Northumberland. A few small stone cabins were built near the mill, but none remain today. The mill itself was never a success, and after numerous problems it finally shut down for good in 1870. The camp supported a post office from Dec. 3, 1868, until March 19, 1869. Only the faint remains of the mill mark the obscure site in Northumberland Canyon.

LEELAND

DIRECTIONS:
From Beatty, head south on US 95 for 12 miles. Exit right and follow for 9 miles. At the fork exit right and follow for 1½ miles to Leeland.

Leeland, a small railroad station on the Tonopah and Tidewater Railroad, was established in 1906 at the 144-mile marker on the T.&T. R.R. The station became an important shipping point for Lee, California, which boomed 5 miles to the west in 1906. Regular train service through Leeland began on Oct. 15, 1907. As Lee continued to grow, so did Leeland; by 1911 twenty-five people were living at the station.

A post office opened at Leeland on Nov. 23, 1911, and the town reached its peak the following year. After Lee folded, Leeland began to fade. The post office closed on Nov. 14, 1914, and the town slowly sank into oblivion although the site was still used as a water stop. When the T.&T. R.R. tore up its rails in the early 1940s, Leeland was left to the ghosts.

Absolutely nothing remains at the site. The only way to locate Leeland is to follow the old T.&T. R.R. right-of-way to a point where the road to Lee used to run; the station site was here. Lack of remains, the difficulty of location and remoteness of the site make Leeland not worth the travel effort.

LIBERTY

DIRECTIONS:
From Tonopah, head west on US 95 for 1.1 miles. Exit right on Nevada 89 for 12.3 miles. Exit right and follow for 3½ miles. Exit right again and follow for 3 miles to Liberty.

Liberty was just a mine rather than a mining camp, although a small group of workers did reside here. The mine was originally located in 1867. A small mill was built next to it in 1868. The mine was worked until 1874; by the time it closed, the shaft was over 700 feet deep and had over 10,000 feet of lateral workings. During its seven years of activity, the Liberty Mine's total production was close to $112,000. The ore was primarily silver, with small traces of gold.

The mine remained quiet for many years. Eventually the Tonopah Liberty Mining Company purchased the property and reopened the mine in 1910. Soon after, a 125-ton mill was constructed. The company operated the mine from 1910 to 1912 and produced almost $500,000 in silver and lead. Declining ore values cut heavily into production profits, and the company sold the mine plus twenty-two nearby claims to the Liberty Group.

The Liberty Group, headed by James Lindsay of Philadelphia, discovered a new ore body that assayed 60 ounces of silver and small traces of lead. This ore body turned out to be quite small, and soon the activity ended. No other activity has taken place at the site since then, although Anaconda Mining Company has begun intensive operations about a mile north of the Liberty Mine. Only the stone foundations of the mill and the collapsing shaft mark the site of Liberty. Today some extensive new mining operations are taking place near the old Liberty Mines. The Anaconda project promises to be one of the richest new finds in Nevada; over 600 men will eventually be working the mine here.

LOCKES (Ostorside)

DIRECTIONS:
Located 21½ miles south of Currant, on US 6.

Lockes, first known as Ostorside, was a ranching settlement that was later developed into a service station and food store. The Lockes Ranch was owned and run by Eugene and Sarah Locke until the late 1960s. The site was the only place to get gas and food between Currant and Warm Springs. Now the beautiful green, serene site is slowly eroding away. A number of buildings remain, and the site is worth a stop.

LODI (Bob) (Marble) (Lodi Tanks)

DIRECTIONS:
From Gabbs, head north on Nevada 361 for 3½ miles. Exit right on Lodi Valley Road for 7 miles. At Lodi Tanks, exit left and follow this road for 2 miles to Lodi.

The Lodi district formed around the Illinois Mine, discovered by Henry Welch and John Kirkpatrick in 1874. The district was officially organized on May 14 of the following year. A 1000-foot shaft was sunk at the Illinois Mine, and a ten-ton smelter was erected. By 1878 Lodi had a population of over 100. Businesses included a store and a blacksmith shop; a boardinghouse and cabins were also built. A freight line was established from Lodi to Wadsworth, 100 miles northwest, with shipping costs at $45 a ton. The Illinois Mine closed in 1880 after producing $400,000. The silver ore that had been removed assayed as high as $500 a ton, but the deposits were not consistent. More than twenty-five claims were made in the Lodi district by the end of 1881, but only six people remained to work the claims.

The district remained very quiet until 1905, when new discoveries were made here. Two separate settlements developed. The settlement at the Illinois Mine was called Bob. A new settlement, at Lodi Tanks, was selected as the new Lodi townsite. A post office called Marble opened March 2, 1906.

The Lodi Mines Company, J. I. Bart owner, was organized with mine offices in Luning, Nevada. The company owned twenty-two claims in the district, including the Illinois Mine. It was worked to a depth of 1060 feet, with over 4000 feet of drift work. The company leased some of the claims to companies such as Rural Mines, Inc., United Lodi Mines Company and Illinois Nevada Mines Corporation.

This panorama of Lodi Valley from the ruins of a Lodi mill includes Phonolite in the mountains to the left and Lodi Wells at the center of the photo.

This auxiliary shaft of the Illinois Mine is almost 1000 feet deep. A cold blast of air whistles from the shaft.

The curious object to the right of the main shaft of the Illinois Mine is an old steam engine modified to power the mine's hoist.

This used to be the center of Lodi. At left are the hotel ruins and in the foreground are ruins of the saloon.

The townsite at Lodi Tanks developed rapidly during the first few years of the revival. Water was plentiful. Soon a number of saloons, a few mercantile companies and some corrals were constructed. The Illinois Mine was starting to be a very steady producer, and in June 1909 a new 100-ton smelter was built to help handle the extra amounts of ore. Mining operations faltered in 1914 when water began to fill the mine. The town struggled to survive, but the post office closed on Dec. 15, 1917, and Lodi never was the same. An experimental concentrator was built in 1919 but was soon abandoned.

The Illinois Nevada Mines Corporation purchased the Illinois Mine in 1921. Two men working for the company, Hughes and Hatterly, made a rich gold discovery just south of the Illinois Mine. A 40-h.p. hoist was installed, and soon the mine was producing again. Only the higher levels of the mine were worked; most of the ore came from the 200-foot and 300-foot levels. The company also built a water pipeline from Marble Canyon, 6 miles from Lodi, across Lodi Valley. The fresh water flowed by gravity, and there was a constant supply. From the Illinois Mine, the water pipeline is still visible all the way across the valley.

Activity by the Illinois Nevada Mines Corporation ended in 1928. Except for a slight revival during 1940, the district never reopened. Remains at Lodi Tanks include a number of brick foundations, the metal water tanks and the corrals. At the Bob site the ruins are much more extensive. There are two mines, both with complete workings. One building still stands, apparently the blacksmith shop. A huge pile of wooden rubble marks the boardinghouse; its demise appears to have been quite recent. An abundance of stone foundations from the earlier operations are scattered in a small arroyo just below the Illinois Mine. The ruins of the smelter are just to the left of the road heading into Lodi. There are also extensive dumps that make exciting digging. Lodi is a very interesting site and should not be missed.

LONGSTREET

DIRECTIONS:
From Tonopah, head east on US 6 for 18 miles. Exit left on Stone Cabin Road and follow for 5½ miles to Stone Cabin Ranch. Take a left and follow this road for 1 mile. Take a right at the fork and follow this road for 9¼ miles to Longstreet.

Longstreet, a small camp, was formed by Jack Longstreet after he discovered gold and silver ore here in the early 1900s. Jack Longstreet's shady reputation hindered development of the camp; skeptics felt this was another of his numerous schemes.

Jack Longstreet, married to an Indian squaw, had killed a number of men and had carved notches into the handles of his guns. He wore his hair extremely long, supposedly because "everyone else did it" but actually because in his youth his ear had been notched when he was caught rustling cattle.

The small camp never had more than fifteen people working the tunnels and vertical shafts in the canyon. The camp did not even last one year, and no substantial buildings were erected.

The district remained silent until 1929, when the Golden Lion Mining Company purchased the Longstreet Mine and began fairly intensive operations. The company developed the mine to a depth of 300 feet and installed two diesel engines and a seven-drill compressor. A 100-ton cyanide mill was built in 1929; sporadic prodcution took place until 1931. These two years of activity produced $10,000 in gold and silver for the Golden Lion company. The mill was removed in late 1931, months after it had closed. Since then, Longstreet has been a complete ghost.

The remains here are not very interesting because the camp never really matured. All that is left are the mine hoists and the rubble of the cyanide mill. The road to Longstreet is extremely rough and rocky, demanding four-wheel drive transportation. The reward of reaching Longstreet is not worth the effort to get here.

LOWER TOWN

DIRECTIONS:
Located in lower Six-Mile Canyon, 5 miles northeast of Hot Creek.

Lower Town was a very small camp that formed in 1867 after a five-stamp mill was built here. The mill shut down after only a few months and the camp was quickly abandoned. Only faint foundations of the mill mark the site. No roads go directly here, and it is a long hike to reach the site.

MANHATTAN

DIRECTIONS:
From Tonopah, head east on US 6 for 5½ miles. Take Nevada 376 north for 33.7 miles. Exit right on Nevada 69 for 6.8 miles to Manhattan.

The Manhattan district was active long before the town of Manhattan even formed. George Nicholl discovered silver-rich ore here in 1866. Following the discovery, over fifty claims were located in the area. Two mines, the Mohawk and the Black Hawk, were developed during the next three years. The Mohawk Mine had a 100-foot horizontal tunnel, and the Black Hawk Mine had a 60-foot vertical shaft. The ore mined at these and other claims was sent to mills in Belmont. The ore averaged close to $100 a ton, with some reaching as high as $2500 a ton. Activity was good enough that a freight line was set up from Austin to Manhattan Gulch, at a cost of $60 a ton. By 1869 activity was slowing; by the beginning of that winter, the district was totally abandoned. Manhattan remained silent for almost forty years until major discoveries were made in 1905.

The initial rediscovery was made by a cowpuncher from Seyler Ranch in Big Smoky Valley. John C. Humphrey and three others from the ranch were traveling from Belmont through Manhattan Gulch. They stopped to eat lunch. Humphrey finished first and wandered away. He found an outcropping only 100 feet from the lunchsite. The four cowpunchers managed to break off a few

The old Catholic Church in Manhattan was moved here from Belmont soon after the turn of the century.

There are many interesting gravestones in the Manhattan Cemetery.

pieces of the ore; the subsequent assay report showed the value of the rocks to be over $3000. With this discovery, Manhattan literally sprang up. A new ledge assaying as high as $10,000 a ton was discovered, focusing even more interest on Manhattan. The turning point for the booming camp came when mining promoter Humboldt Gates, known for only investing in sure successes, began investing heavily in some of the new claims in the area.

Property speculation went wild during the boom. Lots were selling as high as $1900. Soon the gulch was filled with saloons, hotels, assay offices and a few schools. Telegraph and telephone service was also brought in, and an electric power substation was built. A post office opened Dec. 25, 1905. At that time the town already had three banks and a Wells Fargo express office. Two newspapers started circulation during January 1906. The *Manhattan Mail* was the first, making its appearance on January 10. It was published every Wednesday, by Haworth and Anderson. By 1909 they had leased the *Mail* to Frank F. Garside. He left in 1910 to start another paper, the *Manhattan Post*. The *Mail* stopped circulation for three weeks before another publisher was found. The replacement, Roy Mighels, was soon replaced; a number of others followed. The right combination was never found, and the paper folded on June 24, 1911. The second newspaper in Manhattan was the *Manhattan News,* which started publication during January 1906 and folded July 7, 1907.

Manhattan was served by three other newspapers during the early part of the century. The *Manhattan Times* did not even last a year, starting on July 6, 1907, and folding December 7. The *Manhattan Post* was started by ex-*Mail* publisher Frank Garside on Oct. 25, 1910. After the *Manhattan Mail* folded in 1911, the *Post* was the only paper left. It continued publication until May 30, 1914. The last paper to serve Manhattan was the *Manhattan Magnet,* started on March 23, 1917, by William M. Godwaldt. The paper, nicknamed "Queen of the Tocquimas," enjoyed five years of publication. But the collateral backing the paper failed, and the *Magnet* was forced to fold on Sept. 30, 1922. From then on Manhattan had to rely on Tonopah for newspapers.

Two very dramatic events took place in April 1906. The first was the shocking murder of Manhattan sheriff Thomas W. Logan. Exact circumstances of the murder are not known. The killer was Walter

Numerous falsefronted structures were built in Manhattan.

The once impressive Associated Milling Company's mill lies in ruins on the outskirts of Manhattan.

C. Barieu, described as a low-down gambler and a fiend. The setting for the murder was the Jewel Saloon, where Barieu and another gambler got into a wild fight. Sheriff Logan was summoned and was able to stop the conflict. But as Logan was leaving Barieu pulled out his gun and shot him four times, missing with a fifth shot.

Another account, carried by the *DeLamar Lode* on April 17, said that Barieu hit a woman. Logan threw Barieu out of the saloon. Barieu then shot at Logan through a side window in the saloon but missed. Logan ran out of the establishment and then Barieu fired the four shots, mortally wounding the sheriff. Even mortally wounded, Logan supposedly disarmed Barieu and knocked him unconscious. And there are other versions, probably none completely accurate. Sheriff Logan was extremely popular, and his friends organized the largest funeral Nevada had witnessed up to that time. It was held in the Odd Fellows and Eagle lodges at Tonopah. Barieu never was convicted of Logan's murder; the case was well publicized and eventually resulted in Barieu's acquittal.

Manhattan had only one week to recover from the Logan tragedy before a much worse disaster struck. The San Francisco earthquake of April 1906 jolted Manhattan almost as much as it did San Francisco. Much of the mining activity in the Manhattan district was backed by San Francisco financiers, who withdrew their support to help rebuild San Francisco. Manhattan's banks closed, and many mining companies with excellent potential were also forced to close. The population quickly dropped to a few hundred. New discoveries in September 1906 and June 1907 kept the town barely alive.

The old Manhattan schoolhouse is in excellent condition.

The eastern part of Manhattan in the 1920s. *(Western History Research Center/University of Wyoming)*

The town's perseverance paid off when, in 1909, rich placer deposits were discovered on the edge of Big Smoky Valley, a few miles below Manhattan. This discovery revitalized the town to some extent. Activity was boosted again in 1912 when a rich new lode was discovered at the bottom of the already rich White Caps Mine. A 75-ton mill was constructed. The population of Manhattan rose to almost 1000 during the next two years. After the mid-1920s production declined and most operations shut down.

During Manhattan's lengthy production period, many different mining companies were active in the district. The most important was the White Caps Mining Company. (This company has a separate section in this book.) The Manhattan Consolidated Mine Development Company was another major force in the district. It was based in Tonopah, with mine offices in Manhattan. The company, incorporated in 1913 with capital of $1 million, issued 1,350,000 shares of stock at $1 a share and was listed on the San Francisco stock exchange. J. H. Miller was president, with M. N. Page mine superintendent. Manhattan Consolidated engaged in extensive litigation with White Caps Mining Company, finally resolved in 1917. The company's property consisted of five claims that covered about 82 acres. There was a shaft over 600 feet deep and more than 4000 feet of workings. Ore removed from the property assayed from $18 to $30 a ton. The mine had a 50-h.p. hoist and a six-drill compressor.

Another major company was Union Amalgamated Mining Company, which resulted from a merger between Manhattan Amalgamated, Litigation Hill Merger Company and Manhattan Earl. Union Amalgamated was based in Manhattan, with C. F. Wittenburg as president. The company owned six claims on Litigation Hill, which produced over $200,000 in gold and silver. The ore ran from $15 to $25 a ton. In addition to the six claims, the company also owned the Manhattan Milling and Ore Company's ten-stamp mill. Union Amalgamated reorganized in November 1917, with Wittenburg still president. Its new name was Manhattan Union Amalgamated Mines Syndicate. The change did not help much: the mill was closed in 1918, and in July 1919 the company folded.

Two other mining companies were important factors in Manhattan's mineral production. Manhattan Big Four Mining Company incorporated early in 1906 and had sixty claims in the district. A 500-foot shaft was dug, but the high-grade ore was soon

1915 view of Manhattan from Mustang Hill. *(United States Geological Survey)*

gone and was replaced by extremely low-grade ore. The company owned a 100-ton mill that closed in 1913, with a short reopening in 1917. The other company was the reorganized Manhattan Red Top Mining Company, based in San Francisco. Originally known as the Red Top Mining Company before reorganization in October 1912, the company owned sixty acres of claims in the district, including a 200-foot vertical shaft. A 40-h.p. hoist was installed along with a compressor, drills and other new mining equipment. The company was forced to shut down in March 1918 because of heavy water seepage into the shaft.

Numerous smaller companies also worked the district. Some of these, like the Original Mining Company, lasted for many years but just never hit the big ore bodies. Others, like the Zanzibar Mining Company, Mammoth Gold Mining Company and the Manhattan Dexter Mining Company, were backed by very wealthy businessmen who could bankroll extensive operations. But the value of the ore was so low that the companies folded.

Some companies succumbed before they even became established. They were formed prior to determining whether it was feasible to try to recover the ore. Examples of such companies include Manhattan Mustang Mining Company, Manhattan Sunrise Mining Company, Manhattan Copper Mining and Milling Company and Wolftone Extension Mining Company.

In 1939 a 3000-ton dredge was built in lower Manhattan Gulch. An artificial pond was constructed, with water piped in from Peavine Creek. The dredge, owned by the Manhattan Gold Dredging Company, operated until 1946. The operation recovered almost $4.6 million on a huge volume of processed ore: one cubic yard of ore only yielded 21 cents of pure mineral.

Total production of the Manhattan district is now well over $12 million. After dredging operations ceased in 1946, Manhattan began once more to slip

Manhattan's main street, 1907. *(Central Nevada Historical Society)*

The major group of the Manhattan Mines was booming when this photo was taken in the teens. *(Western History Research/University of Wyoming)*

into ghost town status. The town now has only a few dozen people. The post office and saloons remain open. The old concrete electric power substation serves as a curio shop for Manhattan-area souvenirs; the shop owners are extremely friendly. Gasoline, some groceries and a phone are all available in Manhattan.

The remains at Manhattan are extensive and very interesting. In addition to numerous cabins and small houses, there is the old stone post office along with a number of falsefront buildings. The Catholic church in Manhattan, moved from Belmont in 1908, recently received restoration funds from the Nevada Historical Society. A visit to the Manhattan cemetery, located half a mile west of town, is a must.

New mining activity has started up again recently. This is a surface operation involving cyanide leaching. In the summer of 1979 the operation was just getting into full swing. A company named Argus Resources started deep mining operations in the spring of 1980 and has reopened the 650-foot shaft on Litigation Hill. The shaft is presently filled with water up to the 400-foot level, but the Sierra Pacific Power Company plans to bring power to the mine site that will allow it to be pumped dry and dug even deeper. Argus Resources has also purchased seven other mines, including the White Caps Mine. Rich

Panorama view of Manhattan, taken on Feb. 18, 1906. *(Nevada Historical Society)*

The center of the Manhattan business district, winter of 1909. *(William Metscher)*

Close-up of Manhattan's business district near its peak. Notice the tents on the hillside. *(Nevada Historical Society)*

This 1907 view of Manhattan's main street, soon after electric power came to town, shows one of the first automobiles in Nye County. *(Nevada Historical Society)*

The Manhattan Dredge, active during the 1930s and 1940s, floated on water piped in from Peavine Creek, across Smoky Valley. *(William Metscher)*

The bleak remains of dredging operations in Manhattan dominate this photo. The large concrete structure to the right is the power station, and the impressive mill on the left is the Associated Milling Company's mill. The western edge of Manhattan is just visible at the end of the road. *(MacKay School of Mines/University of Nevada at Reno)*

ore may again flow from the Manhattan mines. With this new lease on life, hopefully this beautiful little town will never become a complete ghost.

MANSE RANCH (White's Ranch) (Yount's Ranch)

DIRECTIONS:
From Pahrump, head south on Nevada 16 for 6½ miles to Manse Ranch.

Manse Ranch was founded in 1875 by Joseph Yount and his family after Indians had killed their horses and they were forced to settle down. A large spring was at the ranch site, and soon Yount had a 160-acre spread. In addition to the famous orchard, Yount also raised chickens and milking cows. The Manse Ranch, also known as Yount's Ranch, was the only stopping place for prospectors traveling from Las Vegas to mining camps in the West. Everyone was welcome here, and all visitors were well fed. By the beginning of the 1890s, the ranch included a large house plus storerooms, corrals, stables and barns.

A post office opened at the ranch on July 15, 1891, to serve all of Pahrump Valley. In 1905 the ranch was purchased by Harsha White. He and Nehemiah Clark operated a sawmill in Clark Canyon, 10 miles east on the northwest side of Mt. Charleston. The sawmill, which supplied wood for the railroad ties being laid to Bullfrog and Rhyolite, continued to operate until 1915. Regular stages from Ivanpah to Bullfrog stopped at Manse Ranch for water and food. The population of Manse Ranch and the immediate area was fifty in 1911, and this figure remained fairly constant for quite a while. The post office closed on March 31, 1914, but the ranch continued to function. The stagelines stopped in the teens and the ranch became solely an agricultural enterprise. The ranch is still in use but has been incorporated into a more recent dairy farm adjacent to the old Manse Ranch.

MEIKELJOHN

DIRECTIONS:
From Beatty, head south on US 95 for 1 mile. Exit left and follow for another mile. Bear left and continue for 6½ miles. Exit left and follow for 2 miles to Meikeljohn.

Meikeljohn, a short-lived camp, formed during the same period as nearby Telluride and Fluorine. The camp was named after George D. Meikeljohn, a popular politician of that time. The camp lasted only a few months, and nothing of value was ever found. Meikeljohn never progressed beyond the tent camp stage, and the prospectors took everything with them when the camp died. Nothing at all remains.

MELLAN

DIRECTIONS:
Located inside the Las Vegas Bombing and Gunnery Range, 34 air miles east of Goldfield. Off-limits to the public.

Mellan was a very small mining camp that never was a big producer and yet managed to last more than ten years. Mellan began in October 1930 when Jess and Hazel Mellan discovered small gold pockets in the nearby mountains. The ore assayed from $17 to $25 per ton. A group of about fifteen people formed a camp near the discovery site.

The Mellan Gold Mines group gained control of most of the claims and began work on two shafts. During this time Mellan reached its peak population of twenty-five. The Mellan Group continued to work the mines until World War II. By then the shafts were 400 feet and 100 feet deep and had almost 700 feet of lateral work apiece. Total production for the Mellan district was only about $5000. Minor activity took place after the war but by 1950 the camp was abandoned. Victor Kral reported in the 1950s that the camp still had several standing buildings, headframes and hoist houses, and an ore bin. Now Mellan is incorporated into the Las Vegas Bombing and Gunnery Range and no reports on the camp's present condition are possible.

MEXICAN CAMP

DIRECTIONS:
From Bullfrog, continue west for 6½ miles, ignoring all roads exiting to the right. At a fork at 6½ miles, take a right and follow this road for 4½ miles to Mexican Camp.

Mexican Camp was a small, short-lived mining camp that sprang up during the early 1900s. The camp was a result of frantic exploration following gold discoveries in nearby Rhyolite and Bullfrog. Almost overnight a small tent camp formed. Peak population was about twenty-five. The gold faded quickly, and Mexican Camp was abandoned only three months after being formed. Nothing remains of the site except some shallow test-mining holes.

MIDAS

DIRECTIONS:
From Idlewild, continue north for 2 miles to Midas.

The small mining camp of Midas existed from the 1880s until the turn of the century. The camp sprang up soon after nearby Ione became active. Midas had a post office from 1882 until Jan. 15, 1903. The town reached its peak population of about seventy-five just before the turn of the century. Midas hung onto life and still had a population of twenty-five in 1910. But the town died soon after, for the limited mining could not support the residents. Today only scattered rubble marks the site. Fresh water is available from nearby Midas Spring.

MIDWAY

DIRECTIONS:
From Bonnie Clare, head back down to Nevada 72. Continue across Nevada 72 and follow this poor road for 1¼ miles. Take the right fork and follow for approximately 8 miles to Midway.

Midway was a small water stop on the Las Vegas and Tonopah Railroad. The stop was used from August 1907 until early 1914. Soon after the railway was abandoned, the water stop was dismantled. Today nothing remains at the site.

MILLETT

DIRECTIONS:
From Round Mountain, head west on Nevada 92 for 2.7 miles. Exit right (north) on Nevada 376 and follow for 21½ miles to Millett Ranch, on the east side of the highway.

In 1873 Charles Scheel built a small ranch on the eastern slope of the Toiyabe. He ran the ranch until

1896, when Albion Bradbury Millett bought the property and gave it his name. Millett had owned the Twin River Ranch, but after marrying Scheel's widow he moved to her ranch.

Millett remained just a ranch until 1905, when prospectors flooded the North Twin River mining district after major strikes in Round Mountain and Manhattan. In early 1906 rich ore was discovered in Park Canyon, just west of Millett. Soon a small townsite was platted next to the ranch. By June 1906 Millett and the surrounding camps in the district had over 300 gold-hungry people. On May 3, 1906, a post office was established to serve the entire North Twin River mining district. Mrs. Millett opened a large general merchandise store in 1906. Also built during the 1906 rush was the impressive Lakeview Hotel, a two-story structure noted for its comfortable rooms. Soon a number of saloons, a blacksmith shop, a wagon repair shop and other buildings were also erected.

Most of the ore mined in the district was shipped through Millett to Austin, and soon Millett became a very important shipping center for the Toiyabe and Tocquima range mines. Unfortunately most of the mines faded quickly, and by 1911 the population of Millett was down to fifty. By 1916 the mining district was dead, but the Millett post office, located in the general store, was kept open until July 3, 1930.

The remains of Millett are now on the George Frawley ranch. Dugouts mark the sites of the many buildings. The original Scheel ranch house also remains, along with the crumbling stone walls of the Millett general store. Be sure to ask permission before exploring.

MILTON

DIRECTIONS:
From Ione, head south on Nevada 91 for 6.4 miles. At the point where Nevada 91 heads west, continue straight and follow this road for 3½ miles to Milton.

Milton was a small vegetable ranch run by a man named Milton. He raised vegetables and sold them in Grantsville and Berlin during the 1880s. A small antimony mine was worked in Milton Canyon during the 1930s and 1940s. The mine and a number of surrounding claims were owned by E. Berryman. Operations were not very successful and were finally given up by Berryman, who took a big loss on his venture. At the Milton ranch site, a trailer and one wooden structure still remain. At the antimony mine, nothing remains.

This wooden building is all that remains at obscure Milton. Not much is known about the settlement, but the name appeared on maps as early as 1881.

MINNIMUM'S (Baumann's)

DIRECTIONS:
Located ¼ mile east of Nevada 376, 34 miles north of Round Mountain.

Minnimum's station was formed in early 1862 as part of the Belmont-Austin stageline. It became more important during the 1880s and 1890s when mining activity increased in the Toiyabe Mountains. Some mining was done directly west of the station, and a number of prospectors resided in Minnimum's while working claims in the mountains. The station never really boomed, but its peak population was over twenty-five—not bad for a stage stop. After the turn of the century, the station began to become obsolete and was eventually abandoned in the early teens.

The remains at Minnimum's are beautiful. A few old stone cabins, with brush-and-mud roofs, still stand at the site. Stone foundations are also here, scattered near the still-standing cabins. The site is a definite must, not because it has a lot of ruins but because of the quality of the few it does have.

A few stone cabins in good shape still stand at Minnimum's Station site.

Another of the picturesque remains at Minnimum's, with the beautiful Toiyabe Mountains as a backdrop.

MONARCH

DIRECTIONS:
From Tonopah, head east on US 6 for 5½ miles. Exit left on Nevada 376 and follow for 13.3 miles. Exit right and follow Nevada 82 for 25 miles. Exit right and follow this road southeast for 4 miles to Monarch.

Monarch resulted from one of the biggest promotional scams in Nye County. The town was the brainchild of the Reverend Benjamin Blanchard, who platted the townsite during the summer of 1906. He also had ranch estates and mining claims platted. Blanchard began a tremendous promotion campaign, including advertisments in Tonopah and Virginia City newspapers and personal travel all over the western part of the country. He ended up selling over 2300 lots to the unsuspecting public.

By October 1906 the townsite had a population of 150 and contained a number of stores and shops along with three boardinghouses and two hotels. Almost all of these buildings were transported to Monarch from other camps in Nye County. A paper, the *Monarch Tribune,* began publication on August 18, 1906. During its one-month existence it acted as a propoganda medium for Blanchard. Freight and stage lines were set up to the town, and the telephone and telegraph company began to put up a service line. The Western Pacific Railroad even entertained thoughts of having a spur line to Monarch. An official order to establish a post office was given on October 15, but soon thereafter Monarch's bubble burst.

By the end of October Blanchard had sold 2400 town and ranch lots. After collecting over $75,000 from the trusting people, he left town with the money—and also left behind more than $73,000 in debts. Blanchard left under the guise of going back East to ascertain why the Eastern financial backers had not sent funds. Once out of town, Blanchard disappeared with all of the money. Within weeks Monarch was well on its way to ghosthood. By November 1906 only a handful of people were left, most acting as watchmen for the empty buildings. The post office was rescinded on March 25, 1907, putting the final nail in Monarch's coffin. The ruins at Monarch are extremely scarce: a few outhouses and some scattered wood boards.

MOORE'S STATION

DIRECTIONS:
From Warm Springs, head north on US 6 for 24 miles. Exit left and follow this road for 15 miles to Moore's Station.

Moore's Station was a stage stop on the Tybo and Eureka stage run. The Shoshone Indians had visited the site long before the stageline began. They called the springs at the site *dzicava,* meaning dried juniper water. The station was established in the mid-1870s, soon after two brothers settled there and established a small ranch. The two men dug a small reservoir, brought in a number of fruit trees and established one of the earliest orchards in Nevada. After the stage stopped running, Moore's Station lost its importance.

The station house and the ranch have been used as recently as the early 1970s. The remains of Moore's Station are extremely impressive. The stage house is still in excellent condition although that status could change since no one is living here. A number of sod-type buildings and a few stone

These old ranch buildings remain at Moore's Station.

Moore's Station, the author's favorite, includes this sturdy structure at the center of a small ranching complex and orchard. The building was occupied until the early 1970s.

remains are also at the site. Two stone buildings, one for storage and one for a garage, are both in excellent condition. A few small stone dugouts also remain, along with the sod ranch buildings. The orchard is in poor condition. Running water is still available at the site. Moore's Station is a personal favorite of this author.

MOREY

DIRECTIONS:
From Warm Springs, head north on US 6 for 20.9 miles. Exit left and follow for 3 miles. Take the right fork and follow for 7¾ miles. At a point where another road intersects, continue straight for 3½ miles. Go left at the fork and follow for 3 miles to Morey.

During 1865 a large group of prospectors from Austin came to southeastern Nevada. One of this group, T. J. Barnes, discovered rich ore only six miles from Moore's Station. The Morey mining district was organized the following year by S. A. Curtis, John Emerson and William Muncey. Although the ore find was favorably reported in the *Reese River Reveille* in 1867, the Morey camp did not actually form until 1869. The district gradually grew, and on Nov. 15, 1872, a post office was opened.

A ten-stamp mill was built in 1873 by the Morey Mining Company but only functioned for a month before it was closed down. Ore was then sent to mills in Tybo and Belmont. Morey's population during 1873 was as high as ninety-five. In addition to its own post office, Morey also contained a store, a blacksmith shop, a livery stable, an express office and a boardinghouse. A daily stageline ran to Belmont and Eureka. Supplies for the camp were brought in from Eureka at a cost of $35 per ton.

The mill reopened from April to December 1880, producing $81,000 in gold and silver. There were seven major mines in the district along with thirty-five other claims. The seven mines were the Little Giant, Black Diamond, Monterey, American Eagle, Bay State, Cedar and Keyser. The deepest shaft mine was the American Eagle, which reached 370 feet. The longest tunnel mine was the Bay State, which had a length of 1100 feet. Activity in the district slowed after 1876, but there still was enough to maintain the post office. A good-sized revival began during the early 1880s and lasted until 1891. Three new mines were established: the Magnolia, Mount Airy and Black Hawk. The ore from these operations was sent to Eureka by freight wagon.

Weak activity in the district continued through 1905. After the post office closed on April 15, 1905, the district was almost totally abandoned. By 1909 Morey was completely empty. The Morey Mining Company still maintained their claims and staged a small revival in 1921 when two new properties, the Smuggler and the Airshaft, were discovered. The revival lasted two years, and by 1925 Morey was a ghost for good. The mines have been tested once in a while since then but with no sustained activity. Total production for the Morey mining district was a little over $475,000. Only ruins of stone cabins and wooden mine hoists mark the site of almost vanished Morey.

MUD SPRING STATION

DIRECTIONS:
From Beatty, head north on US 95 for 11 miles. Exit left and follow this road for 10 miles. Exit left and follow for 5 miles to Mud Spring Station.

Mud Spring Station was a water stop for the Las Vegas and Tonopah Railroad. The stop was on top of Mud Spring Summit, where trains needed to replenish their water supply after the steep grade coming out from Rhyolite and the Amargosa Flats. A pipeline from springs on the nearby hillside kept the tank full of cool water to soothe the strained boilers of overworked engines. The stop was abandoned when the L.V.&T. R.R. stopped running in 1914. Nothing marks the site except a small group of green trees.

The large Northumberland Mill, during its peak production period in the 1930s. The mining camp was just out of the photo to the left. *(MacKay School of Mines/University of Nevada at Reno)*

NORTH MANHATTAN

DIRECTIONS:
From Manhattan, head west on Nevada 69 for 3½ miles. Exit right and follow this road for another 3½ miles. Exit right and follow for 2 miles to North Manhattan.

North Manhattan, an extremely short-lived mining camp, formed in early 1905 and was abandoned late that summer. The camp was high up in Bald Mountain Canyon near some small gold veins. A tent camp of twenty quickly materialized, but the veins played out just as quickly and the canyon was soon abandoned. No additional activity ever took place here. Only small tailing piles mark the site.

This small group of cabins is just south of the mill ruins. Small springs are near the cabin on the left.

NORTHUMBERLAND (Monitor) (Bartlett)

DIRECTIONS:
From Belmont, continue north on Nevada 82 for 24 miles. Exit left and follow this road for 6 miles. Exit right and follow for 1½ miles to Northumberland.

Rich silver ore was discovered on the eastern slope of the Tocquimas in 1866 by a man named Logan. The Northumberland mining district was organized that year, named for the English county north of the Humber River; possibly Logan was from that area of England. A small camp formed in 1868 when a small ten-stamp mill was moved to Northumberland from Indian Springs, run by the Quintero Company. The ore did not last, however, and by 1870 the district was abandoned.

This boardinghouse from the last Northumberland revival has survived.

77

Only wooden supports remain of the small tramway used to transport tailings from the Northumberland Mill to the mouth of Northumberland Canyon.

In forty short years the once proud Northumberland Mill has almost completely disappeared.

In 1875 discovery of two new mines, the Monitor and the Blue Bell, revived the camp. The name was changed from Northumberland to Monitor; the camp was also known as Bartlett for a while before the name was changed back to Northumberland in 1879. By then the population was about fifty and the town included an unofficial post office, a store, a boardinghouse, and a number of saloons. A freight line to Austin was set up at a cost of $20 per ton. In 1879 a new ten-stamp mill was built, but it only functioned for three months before closing. Activity in the district once again slowed, and by 1881 Northumberland was again abandoned.

Another revival took place in 1885 and 1886. Sixty people began working the district. An official post office opened Feb 24, 1885, but mining activity quickly faded and the post office closed July 16, 1886. The district remained quiet until 1908, when new silver discoveries prompted a spurt of activity. A new 100-ton cyanide and concentration mill was built and remained in partial operation until 1917. The district became fairly quiet, with only leasers periodically working the area. The Northumberland Mining Company bought the mill and a number of claims in 1939 and began intensive operations. With machinery brought in from Weepah, the company enlarged the mill to a capacity of 325 tons. The company produced well over $1 million in both silver and gold before closing in 1942. No activity has occurred in Northumberland since 1942, but quite a lot of surface mining has been done recently at the mouth of Northumberland Canyon.

The remains of Northumberland are fairly extensive. A number of wood buildings remain, apparently left from the Northumberland Mining Company's activities. There are a few stone ruins from the earlier activity, but these are hard to locate. The most impressive ruin is the huge 325-ton mill; the huge concrete foundations are amazing. Only forty years ago this was an operating mill, but the harsh elements have made this once impressive structure nothing more than a pile of rubble. Another point of interest are the wooden supports of a tramway that ran from the mill to a flat meadow lower in the canyon. These are located for 1½ miles on the side of the canyon, where the tram transported the large volume of tailings away from the mill so they would not clog up the canyon. The end of the tramway is marked by a huge, absolutely staggering tailing pile. The Northumberland cave is on top of the hill behind the pile. At the mouth of Northumberland Canyon are the ruins of an old chlorination mill used from 1870 until 1880. The drive through Northumberland Canyon is extremely scenic. The townsite itself is also well worth the trip. When exploring, be on guard for rattlesnakes, especially in the mill ruins.

NYALA (Mormon Well) (Polygamy Well) (Sharp Ranch)

DIRECTIONS:
From Warm Springs, head east on Nevada 375 for 15.9 miles Exit left onto the Currant–Nyala road and follow for 22.1 miles to Nyala (Sharp Ranch).

Nyala was a small ranching settlement that also served as a rest stop for weary travelers. A well was

The complete population of Nyala posed for his photo in 1914. The tents to the left contained a mercantile store and the post office. *(Central Nevada Historical Society)*

dug at the site in the early 1900s to provide water for horse teams traveling through the hot, dry Railroad Valley. The well was known both as Mormon Well and Polygamy Well. In 1913 a regular settlement began to form at the well site when Herman and Alvena Reischke moved here and set up a small ranch plus a small boardinghouse, a general store and a small restaurant. A post office opened on Feb. 5, 1914, and the settlement was renamed Nyala. Alvena Reischke suggested the name Nyala after seeing a photograph of the East African antelope and thinking the animal so beautiful that it deserved to be the name of their little settlement. The Reischkes continued to work the Nyala Ranch complex until August 1917, when they sold out entirely to men named Goodman and Crosby. The new owners ran the ranch until the 1920s. In that year, George Sharp, who had been buying most of the ranches in Railroad Valley, purchased the Nyala complex. Sharp and his wife, Mary, kept the ranch in operation but closed the store and the restaurant.

George Sharp died in 1933 during a trip into the desert, and the Nyala Ranch was left to his eldest son. The post office closed on Jan. 15, 1936, but the ranch continued to be a consistent cattle producer. The ranch is still in the Sharp family. Most of the original buildings are still in use along with some newer ones.

OAK SPRINGS

DIRECTIONS:
Located inside the Las Vegas Bombing and Gunnery Range, 42 miles east of Tolicha. Off-limits to the public.

The Oak Springs area was the scene of limited activity during the summer of 1905. A number of claims were opened up and small amounts of gold, silver, copper and chrysocolla were taken out. The mining quickly ended, the area was not active again until 1911 when the Oak Springs Copper Company began operations. The company, based in Provo, Utah, with E. B. K. Ferguson as president, was organized on May 20, 1911, in Utah. Its initial capital was $50,000; stock shares were printed and sold for 5 cents each. The company purchased the Washoe claims numbers 1 through 7, with the most productive being claims 4 and 6. Oak Springs Copper worked the site extensively for 1½ years and shipped out a fair amount of copper ore. The claims ran dry in early 1913 and the company pulled out of the district.

Oak Springs remained fairly quiet until 1917, when a new claim, the Horshoe, was opened up. Soon small amounts of silver-laced copper ore was being shipped. The claim was worked until the early 1920s. The district was dormant until 1938, when the Goldfield Consolidated Mines Company initiated exploratory work here but found no substantial ore deposits and soon left. The Tamney tungsten property, owned by V. A. Tamney, began to produce tungsten concentrate in 1938; $9000 in tungsten concentrate was extracted before Tamney left in 1940. There also was a small "turquoise" mine at Oak Springs. The mineral actually was a blue chrysocolla, easily mistaken for turquoise. A few hundred pounds of the pure mineral were sold by the mine owners as turquoise. Since 1940, no mining activity has taken place in the district.

The Oak Springs mining district was never short of water. In addition to Oak Springs, there were a number of other nearby springs. A fairly good wood supply was also available on nearby Oak Springs Butte. The ore mined at Oak Springs had to be transported all the way to Caliente, the nearest shipping point. Because of the cost of getting the ore to the railroad, Oak Springs never really developed into a good producer; the ore was not rich enough to offset shipping costs and still leave a profit. Oak Springs is off-limits inside the Las Vegas Bombing and Gunnery Range and thus no current report on the site is possible.

OPHIR CANYON (Twin River) (Toiyabe City) (Ophir City)

DIRECTIONS:
From Round Mountain, head west on Nevada 92 for 2.7 miles. At the junction of Nevada 376, take a right (north). Follow 376 for 16 miles. Exit left and follow for 2½ miles to Ophir Canyon.

Initial discoveries in Ophir Canyon took place in 1863 when a Frenchman named Boulrand discovered silver. Further discoveries were made in 1864 by Joseph Patty, G. H. Willard and John Murphy, for whom the Murphy Mine was named. The Twin River Mining Company was organized in 1864 and immediately purchased the Murphy Mine. The next year the company constructed a $200,000 twenty-stamp mill, which included the first Stetefeldt furnace ever built. The mill also had eight roasting furnaces and eight amalgamating pans.

An $8000 wagon road was built from the stage road in the middle of Big Smoky Valley. The expense for the road was higher than normal because of the need to build nine bridges over creeks that flowed near Ophir Canyon. By 1867 almost 400 people were living in the canyon. Buildings here included a church, a number of saloons, a few stores, a school and fraternal lodges. A post office opened on June 18, 1867, was called Twin River, although the town was known as Toiyabe City to its residents. A thrice weekly freight line to Austin was also set up, at a shipping cost of $25 per ton.

The Twin River Mining Company ran into trouble because of the extremely tough rock in which the silver was imbedded. On occasion the Murphy shaft was extended as little as 10 feet after workers labored all day and all night. The company also had to spend large sums each month to sharpen the 18,000 drills used to penetrate the rock. The mine and mill produced $700,000 before declaring bankruptcy in late 1868. Although the mine did produce extremely well, the company was never able to pay any dividend because of the cost of removing the ore. An example is the 1867 production record for the Murphy Mine: $427,000 in gold and silver, with extracting costs of $326,000.

When the Twin River Mining Company left in 1868, the town was practically abandoned, although the post office remained open. The Cambridge Silver Mining Company purchased the former Twin River operations in 1869 and began exploring the holdings. The Murphy Mine was reopened in 1872 after a rich new ore body was discovered in the lowest level of the 500-foot shaft. The *Reese River Reveille* commented on the discovery, reporting that "the Murphy Mine will soon rank among the most permanent and best paying mines in eastern Nevada." Operations were begun in earnest in 1874, and the mine continued to produce steadily into the 1890s. The town—now known as Ophir Canyon or Ophir City—never exceeded a population of 100 after its peak in 1867. Between 1863 and 1893 over 100 claims were made in the canyon, and four shafts were sunk. Total production for the district during this period was slightly over $3 million. In early 1893 costs of mining the tough ore began to be more than the value of the ore; by the beginning of 1894, the mines had closed. The post office shut down Dec. 5, 1893, signaling the end of Ophir Canyon.

This photo of the Murphy Mine and Mill in Ophir Canyon was taken soon after the mill closed. *(Central Nevada Historical Society)*

Another shot of the Murphy Mine and Mill, thirty years later. Hardly a trace remains today. *(MacKay School of Mines/University of Nevada at Reno)*

This is one of the few buildings still at the Ophir Canyon townsite.

The canyon remained quiet until 1917, when the Nevada Ophir Mining Company purchased eight claims in Ophir Canyon, including the Murphy Mine. The company was incorporated in Utah in 1917, with Walter Trent as president and a man named Harrington as mine superintendent. Claims included shaft mines of 500 feet (the Murphy Mine) and 300 feet. The Murphy Mine had branching tunnels every 100 feet, including one on the sixth level that was well over 700 feet long. Nevada Ophir built a small stamp mill in 1918, which operated until 1923. The company suspended all operations in Ophir Canyon in 1923, then reopened again the next year. A small cyanide mill was built, but the venture proved unprofitable. The company folded in 1925.

There has been extremely limited activity in Ophir Canyon since 1925 by small independent groups. After Nevada Ophir Mining Company folded, only one other mining company ventured into the district. The Ophir Canyon Mining Company was formed in 1935 and tried to make a profit for the next two years. After successive losing years, it folded in 1937. Presently a small operation is working a small mine near the entrance of Ophir Canyon.

The best remains in Ophir Canyon are the Murphy Mine and Mill, located up in the canyon. The walls of the mill and a few nearby buildings still remain, along with the headworks of the mine. Other remains include ruins of the later stamp mill, some structures and the headworks of a few mines. A number of stone ruins are on the north side of the canyon. A small, recently rehabilitated graveyard at the mouth of Ophir Canyon contains many unmarked graves along with a few forlornly marked. The remains are not very rewarding, and a visit to the town is not as interesting as its history.

ORIGINAL (Orion) (Amargosa)

DIRECTIONS:
From Bullfrog, continue westward for 1½ miles. Bear left and continue for 1 mile. Bear right and continue for ¾ mile to Original.

Original was a small settlement located near the Original Bullfrog Mine. It was here that excitement over the Bullfrog district began when Frank "Shorty" Harris and Ernest L. Cross made their discoveries on Aug. 4, 1904. A small camp formed at the site, also known as Orion, but most of the people lived in Bullfrog. The Las Vegas and Tonopah Railroad established a stop, called Original, just south of the Original Bullfrog Mine.

Once Bullfrog and Rhyolite began to boom, the tent camp of Orion was gradually moved to more suitable locations in nearby booming towns. Both Harris and Cross sold their shares of the Bullfrog Mine soon after the discovery. Cross sold his half for $25,000; Harris got drunk and sold his share for a mule and $500. The Original Bullfrog Mines Syndicate controlled the mine and continued to operate it until the Panic of 1907 forced the mine to close. An attempt to reopen the mine in 1917 by the Reorganized Original Bullfrog Mines Syndicate never got off the ground. The property was sold at a tax sale in 1918 and remained out of operation until 1924, when it was worked by a few leasers.

The property was purchased in 1926 by the newly formed New Original Bullfrog Mines Company. The company leased the mine to the Bullfrog Mines Company. When that company folded in November 1927, the New Original company reclaimed control of the mine. In January 1928 the Nevada Operating Company took a twenty-year lease on the mine, did some work and built a four-mile water pipeline from Indian Springs. The company folded in 1929 and the New Original Bullfrog Mines Company regained control.

The New Original Bullfrog Mines Company left the district and two men, J. Burmeister and W. S. Ballinger, both from Auburn, California, began to work the mine in the early 1930s. They renamed it the Burmball Mine and set to work retimbering the 220-foot shaft. By time they finished working the mine in the late 1930s, it was 250 feet deep and had 2400 feet of lateral work.

The mine has been worked periodically since the 1930s, but no recorded production has taken place. Absolutely no ruins remain at the Orion site, for the camp never progressed beyond the tent-camp stage. There are some scant remains at the mine, including the hoist and one dilapitated building. The site is very hard to reach and is not worth the effort.

ORIZABA

DIRECTIONS:
From Black Spring, head south on Nevada 89 for 4½ miles. Exit right and follow for 1 mile to Orizaba.

Gold and silver ore was discovered in the western part of the Cloverdale district in 1911. The property came under the control of the Diamondfield Black Butte Reorganized Mining Company, based in Goldfield. The company was incorporated in 1905, then reincorporated in 1910 with capital of $2 million. The Diamondfield company sold their claims to the Orizaba Mining and Development Company but maintained a financial interest with the company. The new company was incorporated in 1915 with capital of $1 million.

Initial discoveries in 1911 consisted of six claims covering 120 acres. The ore had quantities of gold,

This 1909 photo shows the Orizaba Mine before it was fully developed. *(William Metscher)*

silver, lead and copper. By October 1915 over 1500 tons of rich ore were uncovered in the Orizaba Mine; another 1200 tons of lower grade ore in the tailing piles were also processed. During the next two years, the Mine Selections Company gained control over all stock and assets of the Orizaba Mining and Development Company, becoming the new owners of the property. By 1918 the holdings of the Mines Selection Company had expanded to nine claims extending over nearly 180 acres. The district continued to improve its production for a while, but by late 1918 only an estimated $18,000 in ore remained in the mine veins.

Modern equipment was brought in by freight wagons from Millers, but the ore was rapidly fading. Six months later the area was almost completely deserted as the once rich ore disappeared. The mine was last worked in 1949 by Hubert Welch, but he gave up in less than a year. Total production for the district was close to $128,000. This might seem quite low, but silver, the mainstay of the Orizaba ore, was only worth 60 cents an ounce during the mine's peak activity.

Fairly extensive ruins still remain. In addition to ruins of the two larger mines, three structures are still struggling to stand against increasing odds. A quarry is located a quarter mile past Orizaba.

PACTOLUS

DIRECTIONS:
From Gabbs, head south on Nevada 361 for 5 miles. Exit left and follow Nevada 89 for 16.4 miles. Exit left and follow this road for 2¾ miles to Pactolus.

Pactolus was an extremely minor and short-lived gold mining camp. Initial discoveries of high-grade gold were made in 1903, prompting a small camp of twenty. In August 1904 a post office was awarded to Pactolus, but it was rescinded in December of that year after interest in the camp had faded. Most of the patented claims around Pactolus were owned by Sam Eva of San Francisco. The only major mine was the Doctor Mine, which had several shipments of $75-per-ton ore during 1905–07. The shipments became smaller and smaller, until the mine was finally closed.

The camp quickly emptied after the Doctor Mine ceased operations. In the 1920s new discoveries brought over thirty men back to the camp. A number of new buildings were built, the old ones being used for firewood. This activity turned out to be very limited; there is no recorded production. No other activity has taken place here since. Only one dilapidated building marks the site.

PARADISE PEAK (Jim Graham's Camp)

DIRECTIONS:
From Goldyke, head directly east on a good road. Follow for 7½ miles to Paradise Peak (elevation 8650 feet).

Paradise Peak, a minor camp, first formed in the teens. The North Star Mine was dug 1000 feet into the side of the mountain and yielded low-grade ore that had small values in gold, silver and copper. The mine closed after only a year. The area remained quiet until 1929, when the Paradise Peak Mining Company began to rework the old mine. The company was incorporated in that year, and was organized by John Reinmiller of Reno. Ore mined by the company assayed from $2 to $18 per ton. The company continued to operate for a few years, but the low-grade ore was not sufficient to warrant continuing operations.

Mercury was discovered at the site in the mid-1930s. The North Star Mine was renamed the Scheebar Mercury Mine, and full-fledged operations soon began. The year 1936 was big for mercury mining, with over fifty flasks of mercury produced.

In 1943 the Scheebar Syndicate, headed by J. Benjamin Parker and Julius Redelius, was formed and took over operations. The syndicate mined over 100 tons of cinnabar ore, averaging about 16 pounds of crude mercury per ton. The company continued to be active in the district until the late 1940s. Since then only minor work has been done at the site. Collapsing remains of two tunnel mines are left, plus the rotting ruins of a number of small wooden buildings.

PARK CANYON

DIRECTIONS:
From Round Mountain, head west on Nevada 92 for 2.7 miles. Exit right (north) on Nevada 376 and follow for 21.4 miles. Exit left and follow for 1 mile. Take the right fork and follow for ¾ mile to Park Canyon.

Park Canyon, a small silver camp, originally formed in 1865 soon after the Buckeye Mine was discovered. The camp was in the North Twin River mining district, organized in 1863. The Buckeye Mine was run by the Buckeye Mining Company of New York. The mine's ore was primarily silver but also had values in gold, lead and copper. The silver ore occurred in pockets, and the ore value was extremely inconsistent. The ore was shipped to Austin until 1867, when a ten-stamp mill was moved from Yankee Blade (Lander County) to Park Canyon. The La Plata Mining Company of Reading, Pennsylvania, housed the stamps in a building of native brick and stone. The mill opened in July 1867 and operated regularly until it closed two years later.

The camp that formed around the Buckeye Mine contained a number of stone buildings and not much more. It has been long rumored that in 1867 a deposed Hawaiian queen, Queen Liliuokalani, lived in Park Canyon and supposedly owned a few mining properties. After the La Plata mill closed, Park Canyon emptied. The district had a number of revivals after 1869, the biggest occurring during 1885 and 1886. The Buckeye Mine was reopened and a few small surface operations were worked. A post office opened up on Jan. 25, 1886, but closed Nov. 11. Park Canyon remained a lonely ghost until 1905, when minor activity began again. This revival turned out to be the longest period of sustained activity in Park Canyon. It lasted until 1916, and a considerable amount of ore was removed. A new five-stamp mill, built by the Nevada National Company, processed ore from 1911 to 1913. After 1916, however, Park Canyon faded into the past.

The only additional activity took place from 1937 to 1941 on the Giant Claim, 1½ miles west of the old Park Canyon Mill site. The mine was far up the side of a steep mountain. An 800-foot tram, equipped with a 10-ton ore bin, was rigged up to bring the ore down from the mine. The mine produced $12,000 before closing in 1941. The road to the Giant Claim site is washed out, and a ¾-mile hike is required to get there. Remains of the tramline and the mine are still visible.

This is the only building left in Park Canyon.

Remains of an old ore bin and the tramway still stand in Park Canyon.

Ruins in Park Canyon are scant. The Nevada National Mill, near the mouth of the canyon, is in fairly good condition but the stamps have been removed. There is only one standing structure, a small stone cabin. The La Plata Mill ruins consist of stone foundations. The only other signs of past activity are a few scattered stone ruins and piles of old tin cans.

PEAVINE

DIRECTIONS:
From Manhattan, head west on Nevada 69 for 6.8 miles. Exit left (south) on Nevada 376 for 2.8 miles. Exit right and follow for 4 miles to Peavine.

View of the Peavine schoolhouse and ranch house taken around 1910. *(Pete Bertalino Collection–Central Nevada Historical Society)*

Peavine is a ranching settlement dating from the 1870s. By 1881 the small settlement had a population of twenty-five. A post office opened on Aug. 25, 1890, and remained operational until Oct. 5, 1895. The Peavine Ranch had a small supply store that served smaller ranches along Peavine Creek. The ranch has maintained a low-level existence, with its population never exceeding twenty-five. Today the ranch is still in operation. A number of old stone buildings are nearby.

PENELAS

DIRECTIONS:
From Ione, head northwest on a good road and follow for 9½ miles. Exit left and follow for 2 miles to Penelas.

The Penelas Mine was the biggest producer of the Bruner mining district. The mine was originally discovered by Severino Penelas in the teens. No real activity took place before 1930; major operations began in 1931. The Penelas Mining Company, headed by L. D. Gordon of Reno, purchased the mine in 1931 and continued to work it until 1942. The company built a 50-ton cyanide mill in 1935 that gained a reputation as one of the most efficient mills in the whole state. The mill was forced to close in 1940 after ore values from the Penelas Mine drastically declined. During peak operation of the mine and mill, a small camp of thirty-five formed. After the mill closed, most residents left. When the mine closed in 1942, the camp was quickly abandoned. At that time the Penelas Mine was over 900 feet deep, had almost 5000 feet of lateral work and had produced close to $900,000 in gold and silver. Nothing at all remains of the camp. Only the mill foundations and mine tailings mark the site.

PHONOLITE (Bruner)

DIRECTIONS:
From Gabbs, head north on Nevada 361 for 3 miles. Take a right onto Lodi Valley Road and follow for 10½ miles. Exit right and follow for 2½ miles to Phonolite.

Gold and silver ore was discovered at Phonolite in July 1906 by a group of prospectors who had been working the Northern Pacific range. Their ore assayed at over $2500 per ton, setting off a small rush to the area. Two major forces set up the Phonolite townsite. Bill Bruner, originally from Kansas City, was active in promoting the townsite and was named postmaster when the Phonolite post office opened on Jan. 26, 1907.

The Phonolite Townsite, Water & Light Company was also a heavy promoter of the site. The company had been incorporated in 1907 with capital of $1 million. Promotion of the townsite included plans for a city water system and an electric plant. The plans fell through when the promoters left the site. By 1909 the district had lived up to its name: Phonolite had turned out to be a phony, all talk and no ore. The post office closed July 23, 1909. Only two people were left in town: Bill Bruner, the former postmaster, and Larry Ryan, an old-timer who had claims in the area.

It was not until late 1910 that activity came once again to Phonolite. Bruner discovered new deposits and by 1911 over twenty people were back in the district. The post office reopened Oct. 17, 1910, and was renamed Bruner. Activity was limited, and the post office closed once again on Jan. 31, 1912. The next year two new mining companies were formed, with Bill Bruner in charge of both. The two companies, the Phonolite Paymaster Mining Company and the Phonolite Silent Friend Mining Company, carried on operations until 1914, when they merged to form the Kansas City–Nevada Consolidated Mines Company. The company was incorporated early the next year with backing capital of $6 million. President of the company was Walter Neff; Bill Bruner stayed on as secretary. This new burst of activity warranted reopening the Bruner post office on Dec. 28, 1915, and it continued to operate until June 15, 1920.

The Kansas City–Nevada Company owned twenty-five claims in the district. The biggest producer was the Paymaster Mine, 300 feet deep with over half a mile of lateral work. The ore was rich enough that the company built a 50-ton mill in June 1919 to treat it. Almost $300,000 was invested in the mine and mill. These efforts paid off; the mine paid back investments. The mill was completely remodeled in 1921 to be much more efficient. In addition to treating the Bruner district ore, the mill also had a contract with the Broken Hills Silver Corporation Mine, 12 miles away.

The company ran into financial trouble during 1924 and was forced to fold. Walter Neff maintained control over the mineral rights, and in 1925 he organized the Golden Eagle Mining and Milling Company. That company worked the old Kansas City–Nevada Company's property. A 4-inch water pipeline was constructed 8 miles across Lodi Valley to Lebeau Creek, but the water supply went dry during summer months. The Golden Eagle property was worked on a low level through 1929 before the company gave up and left the district. The 50-ton mill burned down in early 1930. With the mill gone, there was not much interest paid to Phonolite.

There are few remains at Phonolite. The huge cement foundations of the mill dominate the site. The ruins of two wooden cabins also stand. The Paymaster Mine is only 200 feet from the mill ruins. A small group of men are now carrying on a low-level operation at the mine. The site is marked "no trespassing," so be sure to ask the men at the mine for permission before exploring.

PINE CREEK

DIRECTIONS:
From Belmont, continue north on Nevada 82 for 15 miles to Pine Creek.

Pine Creek was a stage stop on the Belmont–Austin stageline from the 1860s until the early 1880s. During this time a small ranch was built at the site along with a few other buildings. The stage station was a stone structure, as were the ranch buildings. The area never had a population in excess of twenty-five. A post office was active at Pine Creek from 1873 to 1875, then again from 1879 to 1881. Although the Belmont–Austin stage stopped running in the 1890s, the site has been maintained as a ranch ever since. The original stage station buildings, used as ranch headquarters, stood until the early 1970s, when it was destroyed by fire. Another two-story building was built at Pine Creek early in the century and served as a boardinghouse and a summer home. This building stood just to the left of the present ranch house. Tasker Oddie, while Nevada's governor, owned Pine Creek and used the large wooden house as a summer home for a number of years before leaving the area. The ranch was also owned by O. K. Reed, of Kawich fame, when he controlled most of central Nevada's cattle industry.

Today only one of the original buildings remains, used for cold storage. The ranch is presently owned by the Hage family. A talk with owner Wayne Hage is rewarding, for he knows a lot about the history of the area.

PIONEER

DIRECTIONS:
From Beatty, head north on US 95 for 5½ miles. Exit left and follow for 1¼ miles. Take the right fork and follow this road for 2 miles. Exit left and follow for 1 mile to Pioneer.

Rich gold ore was discovered on the northwestern edge of the Bullfrog district in 1907. Two mines were started, the Mayflower and the Pioneer. A camp begun in 1908 between the two mines grew at an amazing rate, acquiring a population of 1000 by 1909. A post office opened March 2, 1909, and Pioneer was officially a town. Two newspapers, the *Pioneer Press* and the *Pioneer Topics,* started in early 1909 but folded in August 1909.

Pioneer in February 1909. *(Nevada Historical Society)*

Only a few buildings remain in Pioneer. A disastrous fire in 1909 destroyed most of the town, and not much was rebuilt.

The Pioneer Consolidated Mines Company purchased the Pioneer Mine and eleven other claims in 1909. The company, incorporated in May of that year in Wyoming, had William Tobin as president and mine offices in Pioneer. The Pioneer Mine was 430 feet deep and had over 15,000 feet of branch tunnels. The ore, assayed at up to $20 a ton, consisted mostly of gold plus minor values in silver. In 1913 the company built a ten-stamp mill along with a 30-ton cyanide and amalgamation mill to treat the Pioneer Mine ore. The mine partially collapsed in December 1914 and was shut down along with the mills.

The booming town was devastated in May 1909 when a fire swept through the tinder-dry wooden buildings. Although soon partially rebuilt, the fire had taken the life out of Pioneer; the town never really recovered. By 1911 the population was down to 300, and the downhill trend continued.

The Consolidated Mayflower Mine Company gained control of the Mayflower Mine and ten other claims after the fire. The mine area contained two tunnels over 1000 feet and four shafts ranging in depth from 100 feet to 350 feet. The ore was not quite as rich as the nearby Pioneer Mine, assaying at an average of $17 per ton. The mine closed down in 1928 after producing $400,000.

Reopening of the Pioneer Mine in May 1915 gave a small lift to sagging Pioneer. The Pioneer Consolidated Mines Company reorganized in May 1918 and was appropriately renamed the Reorganized Pioneer Mines Company. It continued working the Pioneer Mine until 1931. During its period of operation, the mine produced over $500,000 in gold and silver.

Photo of Pioneer taken only a few weeks before the May 7, 1909, fire that leveled the town. *(William Metscher)*

A smaller company, the Indiana Mines Exploration Company, also was active in Pioneer for a while. The company owned claims adjoining the Mayflower and Pioneer mines. It sank a 500-foot shaft and built a 75-ton amalgamation mill. In 1930 the company merged with the Reorganized Pioneer Mines Company.

After Pioneer Mine closed in 1931, the town died. The post office ceased operations Jan. 26, 1931. From then on, only an occasional leaser worked the area. After 1940 no activity was done in Pioneer. The ruins of Pioneer are scant. Only one building still remains, along with ruins of the mines and mills. The harsh desert climate has practically obliterated the site. Only a long search turns up the townsite layout, which is strewn with rubble and faint sunken foundations. Difficult access makes this ghost town not really worth the trip.

POTOMAC (Cimerron) (San Lorenzo)

DIRECTIONS:
From Liberty, continue north for 3½ miles. Exit right and follow for 4 miles to Potomac.

Potomac, one of the earliest camps in Nye County, formed in October 1863. The discoverer was J. P. Cortez, who had also discovered La

The insides of the Potomac Mill today present many good exploration possibilities.

Libertad (Liberty Mine). Cortez named the small camp San Lorenzo, after the nearby spring. Two arrastras were constructed at the spring to process the ore from the San Lorenzo mines and the nearby Liberty Mine.

Spanish activity ended in the 1870s and the small camp only saw intermittent activity afterward. The site became fairly active during the 1940s and early 1950s when the owners, E. M. and Mabel Booth, employed a small crew to work three mines here. A number of wooden cabins were built during this period, all still standing. Work on the shafts totaled over 700 feet; more than $15,000 was produced before the mines closed.

Remains are fairly extensive, although quite modern. In addition to the cabins, there are also mine ruins. The Potomac Mine still has its galvanized steel covering. Inside are the remains of a small, crude concentration system. Be careful when driving to Potomac: the road is extremely rough and sandy.

POTTS

DIRECTIONS:
From Belmont, continue north on Nevada 82 for 37 miles. Exit right and follow for 1½ miles. Exit right and follow for ¾ mile to Potts.

Potts, a small and very prominent ranching settlement, was named for William Potts, who first organized the ranch. The Potts ranch achieved a reputation as one of the best cattle operations in the state. A post office opened at the settlement on Aug. 12,

Stone dugouts remain at the old ranching settlement of Potts.

This house was headquarters for the Potts family ranching empire. Surrounding land is still used for grazing.

1898, and continued to operate until Oct. 31, 1941. Potts was also the site of a ranger station.

The ranch complex was abandoned a number of years ago, but the remains are still very interesting. The ranch house still stands in fairly good condition. A number of stone dugouts and two other buildings also remain. An old corral, complete with a rare old slaughter wheel, is just to the west of the buildings. The range around the site is still used by a number of other ranches in the area. Potts is well worth the trip—and do not miss Diana's Punch Bowl, just south of the site.

PRITCHARD'S STATION

DIRECTIONS:
From Moore's Station, continue north for 1 mile. Bear left and continue for 4¾ miles. Exit right and follow for 1½ miles to Pritchard's Station.

Pritchard's Station is a well-rewarded find after leaving the car, due to the treacherous road and hiking the last three fourths mile to the site. The old stage station is in excellent condition. It was located on the old Tybo–Eureka stage run, active from the 1870s until the turn of the century. In February 1874 a post office was organized at Pritchard's Station but was rescinded in April 1894. In addition to the station, there are a few old corrals and an old foundation, apparently the remains of a stable. The road to Pritchard's Station is extremely soft and treacherous. But the site is a definite must, well worth the required caution and the short hike to get to the remains.

PUEBLO

DIRECTIONS:
From Round Mountain, head west on Nevada 92 for 2.7 miles. Exit right (north) onto Nevada 376 and follow for 21.4 miles. Exit left and follow for .1 mile. Take the left fork and follow for 1½ miles to Pueblo.

Pueblo formed in 1863 shortly after discoveries were made in nearby Park Canyon. Nothing substantial was discovered at the camp, and soon the site was abandoned. It was not until 1905 that the town came back to life. A wandering prospector found a skeleton of a man next to one of the two

The still impressive Pritchard's Station house is in the middle of nowhere. The short hike required to reach the site is well worth it, for not too many people visited the site, then or now.

This is one of the few remains of the boom town of Pueblo.

streams near the old Pueblo townsite. An old gold pan was lying next to the dead man. The prospector panned the dirt, and it assayed at $5000 per ton. Within a matter of weeks, a camp of sixty tents had sprung up. By 1906 more than a dozen wooden frame buildings had been built; the town's population was 500. Unfortunately for Pueblo, the veins discovered in 1905 were very shallow and had been worked out by the next summer. The town emptied as fast as it had filled, and within weeks the site was completely abandoned.

Not too much remains of Pueblo. A few dilapidated wooden buildings still struggle to stand. A couple of old wrecked cars are also scattered among the ruins. Fresh water is available here.

QUARTZ MOUNTAIN

DIRECTIONS:
From Gabbs, head north on Nevada 361 for 9 miles. Exit right and follow for 3½ miles to Quartz Mountain.

Initial discoveries in the Quartz Mountain area took place in early 1920, but no activity was started until 1925. Work then began on three mines. One was found to contain a high-grade ore shoot of lead and silver, starting a small rush to the district. Within months almost 500 people were gathered around the base of Quartz Mountain, and by June 1926 a townsite had been platted. Soon the booming town had its own newspaper, the *Quartz Mountain Miner*. A number of buildings were moved here from other towns that had died. The town of Rawhide, deserted after the disastrous fire of 1908, supplied a few buildings, including a saloon and a barbershop.

Automobiles were plentiful in Quartz Mountain, making it much easier for anxious prospectors to travel to the site. Trucks were utilized to haul out the mined ore and to bring back supplies and water, of which Quartz Mountain had very little. The mail was relayed through Broken Hills (Mineral County), which had been revived by the Quartz Mountain boom. By the end of the summer of 1926, the town had a number of cafés and saloons, three grocery stores, two barbershops and five general merchandise stores. In response to pressure from the residents, a post office opened June 7, 1927.

Over fifteen mining companies were active in the district between 1926 and 1930. Some only maintained a claim or two, others were large operators. There were four mining companies working the area in 1926, but all four folded within a year. One of those, the Goldfield Quartz Mountain Mining Company, built a small mill during May 1926 to

Only this pile of rubble marks the business district of Quartz Mountain. A two-story hotel once stood here.

treat ore from the company's two 140-foot tunnels. The company gave up during the fall of 1926. George Wingfield, a prominent Nevada mining expert, owned the San Felipe Mining Company, which controlled fourteen claims in the district. The property was transferred in September 1927 to the San Rafael Consolidated Mines Company, which was incorporated on Aug. 17, 1927, as the consolidation of four mining companies that had earlier worked the district. The four companies were the San Rafael Development Company, Calico Quartz Mountain Mining Company, San Felipe Mining Company and Exchequer Quartz Mountain Mining Company. The property of the San Rafael Consolidated Mines Company encompassed twenty claims in the district. There were two shafts among the property, one of 600 feet and the other 400 feet, with 6500 feet of lateral workings.

The only building left in once prosperous Quartz Mountain is this small, warped cabin.

Another major company in the district was the Quartz Mountain Mines and Milling Company. Incorporated in January 1928, it gained control over the Quartz Mountain Metals Company and the San Rafael Consolidated Mines Company. A new vein, the Lease, was discovered by the company. This vein, along with the other claims, produced over $300,000. The company operated three major mines. The San Rafael Mine, which followed the newly discovered Lease vein, was dug to a depth of 450 feet and produced over $250,000 in gold and silver from 1920 to 1927. The Calico shaft was a little over 400 feet. The third mine, the Quartz Mountain Metals Mine, was just under 300 feet. Although the properties looked promising, the ore deposits were so small that by 1930 the company had left the district.

A few other small companies also worked Quartz Mountain during 1929, but life seemed to have left the town. The post office closed Jan. 15, 1929, and soon the town was empty. The ghosts of Quartz Mountain have rarely been disturbed since. Until recently a number of buildings still stood, but only two wooden cabins remain now. The townsite is very easy to locate, for it is marked by large piles of wooden rubble from the recently collapsed buildings. One of the ruins is a two-story hotel. At least ten fallen buildings are distinguishable on the flat below the Quartz Mountain Mine. Ruins from the mines abound in the area and are well worth investigating. Plan to spend a long time here, for the site is spread out and nothing should be missed. The site is one of the more interesting of Nye County's numerous ghosts, even though there is not an abundance of ruins. The road to Quartz Mountain is quite sandy, so exercise caution.

RALSTON

DIRECTIONS:
From Stonewall, go back the same way you came in and continue straight for 3 miles to Ralston.

Ralston, a minor station on the Las Vegas and Tonopah Railroad, was established in September 1907 when the L.V.&T. R.R. completed its rails through the site. When minor silica mining operations were begun nearby, a camp of about fifteen formed at the station. A small store and saloon were about the extent of Ralston's growth. After the L.V.&T. R.R. stopped running in 1914, the nearest railroad was the Bullfrog-Goldfield. Ore was shipped through Cuprite and Bonnie Clare. The year 1926 was the peak of Ralston's silica production; over forty-five carloads of ore were shipped. Production in early 1927 was very poor, adding to the troubles of the already faltering B.-G. R.R. When it stopped running in January 1928, all interest in Ralston faded and the lonely camp was left to the ghosts. Nothing remains at the site except scattered wood scraps.

RAY

DIRECTIONS:
From Tonopah, take US 95 west for 1½ miles. Exit right and follow for 4 miles. Exit left and follow the dirt road for 5 miles to Ray.

Ray was first discovered on Christmas Day 1901 by Judge L. O. Ray, who found rich silver ore in the mountains north of Tonopah. Judge Ray filed for six claims in the area, naming them the Hornsilver, Ladysmith, Boomerang, Jenny Belle, Christmas Gift and Teddy Roosevelt.

Judge Ray was originally from Iowa. After graduating from college, he worked in Colorado as a mining engineer. He arrived in Tonopah in 1901, where he met Jim Butler. The two men worked together for a few months before the judge struck out on his own. Before the discoveries at Ray, the judge had already made a small fortune selling rich claims that he had filed on around Tonopah.

In February 1902 ore assaying at $240 a ton was discovered. Soon almost 200 miners flocked to the area to work the new mines. Judge Ray decided to sell his claims during April 1902; the Ray and O'Brien Gold Mining Company purchased the holdings. Because of the judge's faith in his new camp, he accepted Ray mining stock as the bulk of his payment.

The Ray and O'Brien Gold Mining Company had a very strong board of directors, including Jim Butler as president and Judge Ray as general manager. The company immediately began intensive prospecting in the Ray area and soon uncovered a rich new ore body. This led to the most serious development of the Ray area. The largest mine at Ray had a 300-foot shaft with a 100-foot air shaft. At the 160-foot level of the shaft, stoping of

Judge L. O. Ray's ore discoveries led to formation of a camp named for him. This photo shows the lower section of Ray as it was in 1901. *(Nevada Historical Society)*

Although Ray lasted only a little more than a year, there was quite a bit of activity during that period. This photo of Upper Ray shows some of the mining that took place. Note the fancy carriage in the center of the photo. *(Nevada Historical Society)*

94

ore deposits was instituted. The ore was not only rich in silver but also rich with lead.

Because of Ray's location, there was a problem transporting silver ore to Tonopah. The only available transportation was by wagons, and the road from Ray to Tonopah made even this almost impossible. There were plans to build a suitable road to Ray, but before they could be put into effect, the ore at Ray faded, and the plans were scrapped. After the ore began fading, the only shipments from Ray took place in February 1903—a last gasp from a dying town.

Because of Ray's short life, no substantial buildings were erected. Absolutely nothing remains except faint depressions at the site. Small tailing piles on the hillside mark Judge Ray's claims. The road to Ray is extremely rough, with many sandy areas.

REPUBLIC

DIRECTIONS:
From Black Spring, head south on Nevada 89 for 3.1 miles. Exit left and follow for 2 miles to Republic.

Republic was one of a number of very small camps that sprang up in Nye County wherever a mine was located. The Republic group consisted of four mines. The Cipac Mine was the richest and oldest, a fair producer during the early 1900s but panned out in little more than two years. It was not until the late 1930s and early 1940s that interest was revived in the Republic Group. Tom Hyland was the first to begin working the area. He sank a 200-foot shaft and did a small amount of lateral work. The ore from the mine had from 8 to 22 ounces of silver per ton.

The second person to come to the Republic district was William Farris, who sank a shaft half a mile west of Hyland's mine. Farris mined 12 tons of ore, which averaged 40 ounces of silver per ton. These operations were short-lived. After Hyland and Farris left the district in the late 1940s, only limited activity took place. In addition to the mine ruins, three buildings still stand along the canyon road.

REVEILLE (GILA) MILL

DIRECTIONS:
From Warm Springs, head east on Nevada 375 for 1 mile. Exit right and follow this road for 12½ miles to Reveille Mill.

The Gila Mill, dating from 1869, was built 12 miles west of Old Reveille because this was the nearest source of abundant water. The main part of the complex was a ten-stamp mill, but originally there was a smaller five-stamp mill at the site. The two mills both stopped production in late 1869

The old Reveille Mill stands as a lonely sentinel over the expanses of the Reveille Valley. The mill makes for interesting exploration.

when the company owners lost their financial backing. The ten-stamp mill was reopened in 1875 when the Gila Silver Mining Company acquired a number of mining properties and needed a place to process their ore. The mill continued to run until 1879.

The mill did not reopen until 1904, soon after initial discoveries were made at New Reveille. The mill operated off and on until 1948. Today the mill is quite dilapidated. A number of small wooden buildings surround the mill, probably former housing for the mill's employees. A spring with fairly heavy flow at the site was used to spray the stamps in the mill to keep down the dust. The ruins of the smaller five-stamp mill are only 100 feet from the Gila Mill. Even though the Gila Mill was not actually a town, it is included here because it was an important part of Reveille's history.

REVEILLE, NEW (Morristown)

DIRECTIONS:
From Warm Springs, head east on Nevada 375 for 7 miles. Exit right and follow for 9 miles. Exit left and follow this road for 12 miles to New Reveille.

New Reveille formed in early 1904, a number of years after Old Reveille had faded into oblivion. The new site was platted directly across the Reveille mountain range from Old Reveille. The camp that sprang up in 1904 was originally called Morristown, after one of the discoverers. Rich lead ore had been located at the site, and soon a number of mines were being worked.

The camp had grown enough by the summer of 1904 that a post office, called Morristown, was opened on Aug. 29, 1904. Initial excitement slowly faded, and Morristown became comatose. The post office was renamed New Reveille on June 13, 1905, in hopes that the name change might help the dying camp. It was new discoveries that revived the camp. New Reveille reached its peak in 1909 when almost fifty people were working the lead mines. The ore from the mines was sent to the Gila Mill, located in Reveille Valley to the west.

The camp soon faded again, and the post office closed on Dec. 31, 1911. Limited activity took place at the site as late as 1945 but was never prolonged. Total production for the New Reveille mines was just over $30,000, with most of the values being in lead. At the present time a great deal of new activity is underway here by the Golden Arrow and Keystone Company, the same company that has been doing revival work at Old Reveille. Most buildings at the site have been torn down, but a few stone and adobe ruins remain along with a number of mine hoist frames.

REVEILLE, OLD

DIRECTIONS:
From Warm Springs, head east on Nevada 375 for 19½ miles. Exit right and follow this road for 8 miles to Old Reveille.

Old Reveille was one of the earliest settlements in Nye County. Ore was discovered here in August 1866 by three prospectors: Arnold, Fairchild and Monroe. Their ore assayed as high as $1500 per ton, and soon people began to flock to the newly formed district. The camp that sprang up was named Reveille, after the prominent newspaper, the *Reese River Reveille*. By the following summer over forty mines were being worked in the district, with the ore shipped to mills in Austin. The richest of these mines was the Gila, which produced over $500,000 in gold and silver before closing in 1891. The small town had a population of 150; business establishments included a boardinghouse, two stores and a blacksmith shop. A post office opened on Sept. 24, 1867, and remained in operation until Dec. 14, 1868. It reopened on July 19, 1870, and remained open until Aug. 21, 1880, except for a short closing in the summer of 1875.

After the Reveille (Gila) Mill was built in 1869, some 12 miles to the west in Reveille Valley, ore from the Reveille mines was shipped there. This greatly decreased shipping costs. During Reveille's prominent years, over 950 claims were made in the hills around the town. There were a number of important mines, of which the best producers were the Gila, Joliet, Good Hope, Liberty, and Fisherman. The Gila was the largest, with a main shaft of over 500 feet and a tunnel over 1000 feet.

Water was always scare in Reveille. There were a number of springs and wells, but the flow was never enough to provide the town sufficiently. Wood was also scarce; wood for the buildings had to be brought in by freight lines from Eureka, almost 130 miles away. All of Reveille's mines closed in 1880, and the town quickly faded. In that year Thompson and West reported that the town still had thirty

Lower (Old) Reveille in 1905. A few years later a few more substantial buildings were built. *(United States Geological Survey)*

Remains of a horse whim at the Gila Mine in Old Reveille, photographed in the 1930s. *(MacKay School of Mines/University of Nevada at Reno)*

One of the many stone ruins that abound around Old Reveille. Approximately thirty of Old Reveille's stone remains are scattered throughout the site.

residents and contained a hotel, a butcher shop and a livery stable in addition to saloons and boardinghouses from the earlier development.

Reveille received a new lease on life when the post office went back into business on June 12, 1882, continuing to operate until April 30, 1902. Reveille never came close to its former activity but still managed a meager existence. Even after the post office closed in 1902, a number of people remained in the town. When discoveries were made at New Reveille in 1904, a few people chose to live in Old Reveille. As late as 1911 the town still had over twenty people. But soon after the mines closed at New Reveille, Old Reveille quickly faded, awakening to no more "reveilles." Total production for the Reveille district, including the old and new towns, was over $4 million.

New cyanide leaching work is presently going on at the site. While production values are good, it is highly doubtful that anyone will be moving back to

This schoolhouse is the only remaining structure in Old Reveille. It is now being used for storage by the company that is carrying on leaching operations here.

the district. While visiting the site, I met up with the mining company watchman—the only person living there—and he very helpfully provided a grand tour of the Reveille site. The ruins here are very interesting. There is only one complete building, the wooden schoolhouse, which is in excellent shape because it had been inhabited for a long time and then converted for storage. All of the other ruins in Reveille are stone. An overall look at the site reveals the town's layout. A small church and cemetery were on the hill to the west of the ruins, but that site has vanished except for faint raised mounds. Reveille is always cool, a relief after driving through hot and dusty Railroad Valley. The site is well worth the trip, and a talk with the watchman is very rewarding.

RHYOLITE

DIRECTIONS:
From Beatty, head west on Nevada 58 for 2 miles. Exit right and follow Nevada 90 for 2.3 miles to Rhyolite.

Although Rhyolite was relatively short-lived, its history of dramatic rise and swift fall is one of the most fascinating of any ghost town in Nye County. Rhyolite formed soon after Frank "Shorty" Harris and Eddie Cross made rich discoveries in the summer of 1904 in the hills west of the eventual townsite. Soon a small camp sprang up, called Bullfrog. Another camp, called Rhyolite, formed a mile to the north. Rhyolite was staked out in November 1904 and officially platted on Jan. 15, 1905. Within a month an unknown person, rumored to be Bob Montgomery, offered free lots to merchants. A small tent city sprung up, with numerous saloons, cafés and boardinghouses.

An unofficial post office was established in early 1905 in Len McGarry's general store. In February of that year it was moved to Bill Porter's grocery store on growing Golden Street. He "delivered" the mail by yelling out the names of the addressees, a process that normally took hours and was extremely inefficient. The official U.S. post office, housed in a 10′ x 12′ tent, opened May 19, 1905, with Anna B. Moore as postmistress. With the growing clientele, the post office outgrew a number of new offices before moving into the basement of the John S. Cook Bank Building in 1908.

Water, a rare commodity in the Rhyolite area, was carted in at a cost of $2–$5 per barrel. It was not until June 26, 1905, that an efficient water system was brought to Rhyolite. The Indian Springs Water Company formed in 1905 and soon was piping in water from Indian Springs, 5 miles to the north. Six weeks after the Indian Springs Company reached Rhyolite, the Bullfrog Water Company completed a water system pipeline to Rhyolite from Goss Springs, 12 miles away. This pipeline had a daily flow of 200,000 gallons. A short time later a third water company, the Bullfrog Water, Light and Power Company, also became active in the district. The company controlled thirteen springs, which had a flow of one million gallons. Water pressure was strong enough to support a fire hydrant system with 70 pounds of pressure. Only a year after Rhyolite had been bone-dry, the town had an abundance of the precious liquid.

During March 1905 a number of small camps in addition to Bullfrog and Rhyolite were developing within a radius of a few miles. Squattersville, a small tent city, was set up between Rhyolite and Bullfrog and eventually merged with the southern part of rapidly expanding Rhyolite. A mile below Bullfrog was Orion, later called Amargosa City, which contained eighty tents and had a population of 160. Bonanza, another small camp, was at the south end of Ladd Mountain. All of these quickly faded as attention focused on booming Rhyolite.

By the spring of 1905 four stagelines were bringing supplies to Rhyolite. Best known was the Kitchen stage, which brought supplies from Goldfield, 80 miles north, at a cost of $18 a ton. The first auto-stage, run by the Tonopah and Goldfield Auto Company, became active in May 1905. Judge William Stewart, a famous lawyer, moved to the Rhyolite area that spring, bestowing a sense of prestige on the growing city. Rhyolite built its first school in early 1906; the enrollment soon reached ninety. The school was blown off its foundation in September 1906 but was soon reset. By May 1907 the number of pupils had swelled to 250. Soon a $20,000, two-story brick school was built, with three classrooms on the first floor and one classroom and an auditorium on the second.

Rhyolite reached its peak in 1907 and 1908. Its population then was estimated to be 8000 to 12,000. During this time two weekly newspapers and one daily competed for favor in Rhyolite. The

When this photograph of Rhyolite was taken on May 1, 1905, the town was already booming although no substantial buildings had yet been constructed.

weekly *Rhyolite Herald* was the first in town and was also the last to fold. It began publication on May 5, 1905, and continued until June 23, 1912. The *Bullfrog Miner*, after being published in Bullfrog for a little over a year, moved to Rhyolite on March 30, 1906. The *Rhyolite Daily Bulletin* began publication on Sept. 23, 1907, but did not last long; it folded on May 31, 1909. Two magazines were published in Rhyolite toward the end of the town's zenith. The first was the *Death Valley Prospector,* first issued in November 1907, then renamed the *Death Valley Magazine* the next month and published monthly until it folded in October 1908.

Rhyolite was served by three railroads during its peak years, an honor rarely bestowed on any Nevada city. The first to reach Rhyolite was the Las Vegas and Tonopah, which began regular service on Dec. 14, 1906. The railroad was strongly backed by then Senator William A. Clark and his relative, J. Ross Clark. The Bullfrog-Goldfield Railroad, the second to arrive in Rhyolite, was run by John Brock of Tonopah. He had already made a name for himself with the prominent Tonopah and Goldfield Railroad. The B.-G. R.R. was the weakest of the three, but it was the first to complete a depot in Rhyolite. The depot was 24′ × 72′ and was completed in April 1908, just before the L.V.&T. R.R. completed their own fancy depot. The third of the railroads, the Tonopah and Tidewater, never went as far as Rhyolite but had a station at nearby Gold Center. That station opened in October 1907, and the newly formed T.&T. R.R. soon became the best established railroad in Nye County, lasting into the 1940s.

In January 1907 a network of 400 electric street light poles were installed, and soon Rhyolite was brightly lit twenty-four hours a day. By March 1907 Rhyolite's post office had the seventh largest clientele in Nevada. A number of very impressive buildings were built in 1907 and early 1908. These included the $90,000 John S. Cook Band Building and the $50,000 Overbury building. H. D. and L. D. Porter, who operated mercantile stores in Nevada, built a new store in Rhyolite in 1907. During its peak Rhyolite had forty-five saloons, an opera house, a number of dance halls, two electric light

By November 1905 Rhyolite was well established and on its way to becoming the metropolis of southern Nevada. Many sturdy structures were built during the summer of 1905, including the large two-story hotel in the left portion of the photo. *(Nevada Historical Society)*

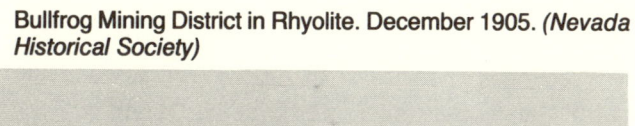

Bullfrog Mining District in Rhyolite. December 1905. *(Nevada Historical Society)*

101

Rhyolite was at its peak in January 1908. The major buildings shown here are the Overbury Block and the John S. Cook Bank (both in the center) and the solid concrete jail (lower right corner). *(Nevada Historical Society)*

plants, a two-story Miners' Union Hall with a 60-foot front, a slaughterhouse, two railroad depots, numerous stores and countless other buildings, both wooden and brick. The Rhyolite Foundry and Machine Supply was organized in June 1907 to build cars. Parts were brought in, but the company folded before production began. Rhyolite even had its own stock exchange for a while in 1907.

During Rhyolite's brief stardom over eighty-five mining companies were active in the hills around the city. There were seven major mines: the Montgomery–Shoshone, Denver, National Bank, Eclipse, Polaris, Gibraltar and Tramp. Of these, the Montgomery-Shoshone was the most productive. The mine was discovered by a Shoshone Indian Bob Montgomery had sent to stake a claim for him. When Montgomery began to work the claim, he kept running into talc deposits, which frustrated him. But one day, after a heavy rain, he happened to take a look at the dissolving talc pile and found gold. The talc ore assayed from $3000 to $6000 a ton. Soon afterward, Montgomery sold the mine to Charles Schwab for a reported $5 million. Schwab then built a large mill and also convinced the L.V.&T. R.R. to run a rail line by the mine, making it worthwhile for Schwab to mine lower value ore because he incurred no extra cost for transportation.

The financial panic of 1907 killed Rhyolite. Most of the town's investors were from the East, and when they withdrew their backing all of the mines were forced to close. The devastating effects of the panic did not reach Rhyolite until the spring of 1908. Then the trains were almost always filled to capacity with people leaving town. The city emptied as fast as it had been populated only a few years earlier. Rhyolite suffered a fire on Aug. 19, 1908, that leveled the red-light district and spread to parts of the eastern business district. By the end of 1909, the population was well below 1000. The Montgomery–Shoshone Mine, the last real hope of survival for Rhyolite, closed after producing close to $2 million. The only mine left in operation was the old

Tramp Mine, just north of Bullfrog. The Sunset Mining and Development Company worked the mine for a while but finally gave up in the early teens. The railroads continued to operate and the clientele continued to decline, until an average of only two or three people took the trains each day.

The population had shrunk to six hundred seventy-five by 1910 and continued to fall rapidly during the next two years. Street lights were shut off on April 30, 1910, although the power company operated until 1916. Earle R. Clemens, editor of the *Rhyolite Herald*, wrote a touching editorial in the April 8, 1911, issue, his last before leaving to work in California: "GOODBYE: It is with deep regret

Rhyolite began to decay very rapidly after being abandoned. This photo, taken in the 1920s, shows the already collapsing remains of the Cook Bank, the Overbury Block and the H. D. and L. D. Porter Store. The L.V.&T. R.R. station is in the background. Most of the city had been leveled, evidenced by the huge empty spaces between the buildings. *(Western History Research Center/University of Wyoming)*

All that remains of the once impressive Overbury Block are these crumbling foundations.

The pride of Rhyolite was its two-story schoolhouse, now only gaunt walls.

These crumbling ruins are all that remain of the Porter Store, built in 1906. The flat area beyond the store, once filled completely with buildings, hardly bears a trace of the hundreds of structures.

that I announce my retirement from the newspaper field in the Bullfrog district. It has been my lot to remain here while all my erstwhile contemporaries have fled, one by one, to more inviting localities, and now it is my time to say goodbye.... May prosperity follow you everywhere, and catch up with you, too, and may prosperity again reign in Rhyolite—the prettiest, cosiest mining town on the great American desert, a town blessed with ambitious, hopeful, courageous people, and with a climate second to none on earth. Goodbye, dear old Rhyolite." After Clemens left the paper was continued by the Rhyolite Printing Company, then finally folded on June 22, 1912.

The L.V.&T. R.R. and the B.-G. R.R. consolidated in July 1914 in an effort to maintain service to Rhyolite, but it was a losing cause. The railroad struggled on for a few more years and finally ended service in 1918. The last freight train left Rhyolite on August 17, the last work train on October 31. The post office continued until the population fell below twenty-five, when the postmaster, Anna Moore's husband, decided it was no longer needed; on Sept. 15, 1919, the office closed. The population of the almost dead town had shrunk to fourteen by the beginning of 1920. Two years later only ghosts roamed Rhyolite's deserted streets.

During the 1920s and 1930s, Rhyolite remained almost the same. The only semblance of a revival took place in 1928, when the Rhyolite Consolidated Mines Company was formed and began work on a number of mines on Bonanza Mountain. The company was backed by capitalists from Virginia and Georgia, but they withdrew their support in 1930 and the company folded. The empty buildings in Rhyolite were full of furniture, and the bank floors were covered with official records and worthless stock. The only building occupied during this period was the old L.V.&T. R.R. depot. Wes Westmoreland had purchased it in 1925 and had opened a casino and bar. The other buildings in town were left to the mercy of the harsh desert wind.

The railroad station is now maintained by Westmoreland's sister, Mrs. H. H. Heisler, who runs a small museum and curio shop in the station. The bottle house, constructed of 51,000 beer bottles, is one of the few other buildings still in fairly good condition. In addition to a few small wooden structures, the only other substantial remain is the jail. The more impressive ruins in Rhyolite include the John S. Cook Bank, the $20,000 school and the Porter store. The front of the Cook building ruins was altered by a movie company to a Spanish style. Grills drilled into the window frames seemed to weaken the front, and a large section of it collapsed the following year. The Rhyolite–Bullfrog cemetery is half a mile south of the Bullfrog townsite. It contains many interesting gravestone styles, including numerous wooden headboards.

It is almost unimaginable, while standing amid Rhyolite's ruins, that this desolate site was once filled with over 10,000 people and rows and rows of buildings. One feels a deep sense of emptiness and amazement at the total devastation that has almost

The statuesque remains of the John S. Cook Bank show how harsh desert conditions can destroy the most impressive of structures.

Many wooden headboards are scattered throughout the Rhyolite-Bullfrog Cemetery, some of which are still legible.

completely leveled the once bustling city. Shock also seems to overwhelm a visitor. Rhyolite is clearly one of the best ghost towns in Nye County and in the state. If there is a single town that exemplifies how fast life can change in a mining town, Rhyolite is that town. *Don't miss it.*

ROSE'S WELL (Palmer's Well)

DIRECTIONS:
From Beatty, head south on US 95 for 15½ miles. Exit right and follow this faint road for ¼ mile. Exit left and follow for ½ mile. Take a left and follow for ¾ mile to Rose's Well.

Rose's Well was dug in the early 1900s by G. W. Rose and E. E. Palmer, both of whom ran a small freight line from Las Vegas to Beatty. Their 210-foot well yielded over 100 barrels of cool water each day. The well was known as both Rose's Well and Palmer's Well until Palmer's death. At the stage station not only water but good meals and shelter for horses and tired travelers were available. Rose's Well was the only spot between Beatty and Las Vegas that offered such commodities.

When the Las Vegas and Tonopah Railroad was built, Rose's Well became an important way station. The railroad reached Rose's Well in July 1906. Before further construction could be done, a strike of tie shippers stopped all work; Rose's Well was the end of the line for almost all of July. This created a flow of travelers going to and from Rhyolite and led to further development of Rose's Well. After railroad construction resumed, the small settlement continued to be an important stop until the railroad reached Gold Center. Then the station was downgraded to a water stop. The station and small complex continued until the L.V.&T. R.R. folded and tore up its rails in 1918–19. Rose's Well was then quickly abandoned.

Today, the site is virtually nonexistent. The only marker is the old well, now dry. Scattered wooden boards show that buildings once did exist. The site is so extremely dry and desolate that it is hard to imagine a once busy railroad station here.

ROUND MOUNTAIN (Gordon)

DIRECTIONS:
Located 2¾ miles east of the junction of Nevada 92 and Nevada 376. Round Mountain is 54 miles north of Tonopah.

Gold was discovered at Round Mountain as early as 1905, but it was not until February 1906 that more substantial discoveries aroused sincere interest. In February 1906 three men—Louis Gordon plus Morgan and Scott—discovered high-grade gold ore on a hill known as Round Mountain. A small camp formed at the base of the mountain and was named after Louis Gordon. The Gordon post office opened here on June 28, 1906, and soon the camp's population was close to 400. A weekly newspaper, the *Round Mountain Nugget*, began publication on June 2, 1906, but did not last long. A number of major mining companies became active in the Round Mountain district during this period. On March 4, 1907, the name of the growing town was changed to Round Mountain. Two adjacent smaller townsites were laid out, Shoshone and Brooklyn. However, Round Mountain was growing so fast that the plans were changed and a larger, single townsite was platted.

By 1907 there were daily stages to Tonopah. Fresh freight supplies arrived daily. The town contained many wooden structures housing mercantiles, saloons, brokerage agencies, a school and a substantial library. That same year also witnessed discovery of the Dry Wash Placers, just below the rich Round Mountain mines. Discoverer Thomas Wilson, a resident of nearby Manhattan, consoli-

Round Mountain in 1906, only weeks after its founding. *(Kay Butler Collection/Central Nevada Historical Society)*

dated his placer claims into the Round Mountain Hydraulic Mining Company in 1907. Water for the operation was at first piped in from Jefferson and Shoshone creeks; in 1915 a new and more efficient pipeline was built to Jett Canyon, across Smoky Valley. These placers provided a large portion of Round Mountain's total production figure.

Two mining companies began operations in Round Mountain soon after its discovery in 1906. Round Mountain Mining Company was the principal operator of the district and also the earliest, being incorporated in March 1906. The company, with Louis Gordon as president and general manager, had offices in Round Mountain and in San Francisco. The company controlled almost 1000 acres of mining claims, which ranged from gold to silver, from lode deposits to placers. The company built a 180-ton stamp mill near the Sunnyside Mine, which was the largest mine in the district. Sunnyside had a 1000-foot incline shaft and miles of lateral work. The ore values were low, averaging about $7 per ton, but mining was economically feasible because the mill could treat over 1100 tons of low-grade ore daily. In 1914 the company bought out the Round Mountain Sphinx Mining Company, which controlled the Los Gazabo claim. This claim proved to be a valuable addition. Production for the company during the first ten years (1906–16) was a little over $3 million. The Sunnyside Mine and Mill continued to operate until 1921.

The second mining company to come to Round Mountain was the Fairview Round Mountain Mines Company, incorporated on June 25, 1906. Louis Gordon was president of this company, too. Fairview controlled twelve claims in the district, including major mines named Daisy and Fairview. A six-stamp amalgamating mill built next to the Daisy Mine had a daily capacity of about 50 tons of ore. It was not until 1919 that other large mining companies came to the district.

Fairview Extension Mining Company was incorporated in July 1919 and was controlled by Fairview Round Mountain Mines Company interests. Louis Gordon was also president of this company, which controlled three major claim groups: the Alta, Shot and Blue Jacket (purchased by the company from the defunct Round Mountain Blue Jacket Mining Company). The company carried on mainly surface operations. The Blue Jacket Mine was only about 100 feet deep but in total the Blue Jacket group produced almost $100,000 before operations were curtailed in the early 1920s.

Nevada Gold Development Company was the next major company to move to the Round Mountain district. Incorporated in July 1925, the company took control of the Tom Wilson placers. A

Round Mountain in 1914, near its peak. *(Nevada Historical Society)*

shaft dug on one of the company's other claims eventually reached a depth of 300 feet, with lateral workings of 400 feet. Ore from the mine only averaged $2 per ton. The company was absorbed into the Nevada Porphyry Gold Mines Company in 1928.

Round Mountain Mining Company was reorganized in 1926 and renamed Round Mountain Mines Company, which was incorporated in February of that year. The company enlarged the old Sunnyside Mill to 200-ton amalgamation size. The mill also contained twenty stamps, a small Huntington mill and a few smaller tube mills. The company continued to conduct hydraulicking operations, mostly in the spring when there was an abundance of water. Over $200,000 was spent on the Jett Canyon water pipeline to Round Mountain, which enabled the placers to produce for a number of more years.

In 1928 the company gave its option to the newly formed Nevada Porphyry Gold Mines Company. This new company consolidated all of the mining activity in the Round Mountain district and even today controls most of the mining properties. In 1935 underground mining was deemed too dangerous and was curtailed in favor of surface operations. A small placer mill was built in the early 1950s. Hopes were high that the placering would once again be profitable, but the ore values were extremely poor and the mill closed in 1957. Round Mountain was quite ghostly until recently, when life has come back to the little town.

Extensive new surface operations were begun on the side of Round Mountain in the early 1970s. The din of heavy machinery is ever present as the area is worked around the clock. During the summer of 1979, it was reported that almost $100,000 in gold was being removed each week. Although this activity has led to a rise in population, Round Mountain still remains a quiet little town with many interesting buildings.

On the hill just behind town are two mills, both very dilapidated but still standing. A large number of abandoned mines are scattered all around the town. At present the total production figure for the Round Mountain mines is easily in excess of $10 million,

This quaint old building in Round Mountain is still occupied and cared for.

and current activity will push this figure higher. Gas and food are available. Plan to spend a day wandering through picturesque Round Mountain.

ROYSTON (Quincy)

DIRECTIONS:
From Tonopah, take US 95 west for 2.4 miles. Then take Nevada 89 north for 23.2 miles. Exit left and follow for 5 miles. Exit right and follow for 2 miles to Royston.

Royston was a small boom town that quickly formed in 1921 when word spread that $20,000 in silver had been taken from a 24-foot shaft in only six weeks. The camp was originally called Quincy, but the name was changed to Royston soon after the discovery. The Hudson Mining and Milling Company staked seventeen claims in the district, including the Golden Eagle Mine and the Best Chance Mine. The company was incorporated in April 1921 by the Walker brothers of Salt Lake City, Utah. Actually, the company was organized in early 1919 but was not large enough for incorporation until two years later. Hudson Mining had leased a few of its Royston-area claims to the Hudson Leasing Company in 1919. That company ran at a loss and folded that same year. Hudson Mining then began serious operations. A vein assaying at $90 a ton was discovered and before the boom of 1921, over $40,000 in silver was removed.

By 1921 Royston had a population of 300 and a small business district. A planned post office did not receive government approval before the town was practically abandoned, and thus the project was dropped.

Some of the mines, including the Golden Eagle remained open and operated periodically. The Super Six Mining Company leased a number of claims from the Hudson Company but gave up after a short period of unprofitable activity. After that only the Golden Eagle Mine was worked. B. F. Betts leased the property after the Super Six Company folded. He worked the mine on a low scale until the Western Leadfield Mining Company purchased the property from the Hudson Mining and Milling Company in 1926. The new company enlarged the Golden Eagle shaft to 300 feet deep and did over 1200 feet of branch tunnel work. Betts continued prospecting the area and in 1927 located another rich claim, just south of his old claim. He leased it to Frank Tabakacci. The Western Leadfield Mining Company gained control of the property in late 1927 and sank a 350-foot shaft; the project was abandoned as the ore values sank.

The last company to work the district was the Royston Turquoise Mines Company, Incorporated. The company, organized in 1929 by Salt Lake City residents Bryce Sewel and Frank Keller, obtained a permanent lease on some holdings of the defunct Hudson Company. (Former heads of that company still maintained a one-fourth interest in the Royston Turquoise Mines Company.) The company merged in 1930 with Royston Royal Blue Turquoise Mines, Incorporated. The companies both folded in 1931 and the district was quiet until 1948, when some minor activity was done but without realizing a profit. After work was curtailed in late 1948, the district was abandoned forever.

Even though there had been mining activity in the Royston district after 1923, the townsite was never populated to any extent. The remains of Royston are almost nonexistent and are extremely hard to locate. The only site markers are tailing piles from the various mining ventures. On the flat below the remains of the Golden Eagle Mine are scant wooden scraps—the only remains of Royston. The site is not very interesting and is not really worth the long trek.

RYE PATCH

DIRECTIONS:
From Tonopah, take US 6 for 5½ miles. Then take Nevada 376 north for 11 miles to Rye Patch, located on the east side of highway.

Rye Patch, in addition to being the water supply for the Hannapah district and for the town of Tonopah, was also a ranching and mining area. The Sam Jack mining group was located on a ridge just east of the Rye Patch pumping station. This group consisted of fourteen claims owned by Earl Mayfield and Jack Clark. A number of shallow shafts were dug; the ore assayed at $5 per ton. Not much development was ever done on these claims. A number of small ranches in the Rye Patch Wash represent the only activity left in the area.

SAN ANTONIO (San Antonia) (San Antone)

DIRECTIONS:
From Tonopah, head east on US 6 for 5½ miles. Then take Nevada 376 north for 33.7 miles. Exit left and follow for 3 miles. Exit left and follow for 7 miles to San Antonio.

San Antonio was a small stage station built around a group of springs. As early as 1845 Frémont had stopped at the springs on his way to meet up with Kit Carson and a group of prospectors. San Antonio was a major stop on the Ione–Belmont stage. After gold was discovered in the nearby San Antonio mountains, the stage stop became a small town as miners began to move to the district. A two-story station-hotel was built in 1865. The district's main mine was the Liberty Mine. A stamp mill built at San Antonio to treat some of the ore from the mine operated until 1866 and then was moved to Belmont, where new strikes had been made.

San Antonio soon had a fair-size business district and a population of about 100. A freight line to Austin was set up; shipping cost $30 per ton. Even after the Liberty Mine closed in 1868, San Antonio remained active. The population dropped below fifty, but the stage station was still an important stop for travelers heading toward new strikes in southern Nevada. The San Antonio post office opened on May 14, 1873, and served the district until Jan. 25, 1888. San Antonio then sank close to ghosthood, with only an occasional traveler stopping at the station. The owner of the station and half a handful of others remained at the site.

The station was saved for a while when new strikes in 1896 in Esmeralda and Nye counties led to increased stage travel. The small town came to life once again; the post office reopened April 8, 1896, and San Antonio was put back on the map. Initial strikes at Tonopah and Goldfield in the early 1900s created a large flow through the district. Then the railroad was built, almost ending stage travel. Compounded with this was the arrival of the automobile in the West. The station and town struggled on for a few more years, but when the post office closed on July 14, 1906, the end was in sight.

Soon only the stationmaster was left in San Antonio; by 1910 even he had departed. Time and the harsh desert sun has not been kind. The site was on the San Antonio Ranch until even the ranch was abandoned in the 1960s. All that remains of the once impressive stage station are crumbling walls. The station partially burned, and without a protecting roof the remains decayed very rapidly. A number of smaller ruins from the business district are scattered around the old stage station. The site is marked by two large, very old poplar trees, the only green in the whole valley. San Antonio lends itself to interesting photos and exploration.

SAN CARLOS

DIRECTIONS:
From Bonnie Clare, go back to Nevada 72. Take a left (east) and follow for 2¼ miles. Exit left and follow for ½ mile. Take the right fork and follow for 2 miles to San Carlos.

San Carlos served as a water stop on the Bullfrog-Goldfield Railroad. It was established in October 1906 and used until the railroad folded in January 1928. The Las Vegas and Tonopah Railroad passed just west of San Carlos but had its water stop at Wagner. San Carlos never amounted to anything more than a water stop, and even this vanished as soon as the B.-G. R.R. folded. Nothing at all remains here.

SAN JUAN

DIRECTIONS:
From Ione, head north on Nevada 21 for 24.6 miles. Exit right and follow this road for 4 miles to San Juan.

Silver ore was discovered at the head of San Juan Canyon in 1862 by the same group of prospectors who, only weeks earlier, had discovered rich ore in nearby Washington Canyon. A quick camp of fifty sprang up here, but the veins were extremely shallow and lasted only a month before fading out. The camp quickly folded and most residents moved to Washington, which was having better luck.

The canyon remained quiet until the 1930s, when fairly intensive operations were begun. The first was the St. Elena claim group, originally filed on in 1872. The claim was owned by Clara Williams. She hired a small crew that worked a new mine to a depth of 110 feet and over 500 feet of lateral workings. Nothing of value was removed from the mine, and Mrs. Williams soon gave up. The second group was the Bi-Metallic group, owned by S. H. Linka. It consisted of three different claims: Bi-Metallic No. 1, McIntyre Mine and the Tiger group. Bi-Metallic No. 1 was never really worked. The McIntyre, which consisted of the St. Louis, Richmond and Henry George shafts, also was a financial flop. The only producer was the Tiger group, which had shafts of 40 feet and 30 feet. After producing about $500, the ore ran out and the Bi-Metallic group ceased to exist.

The only decent producer during this revival was the Grand View Mine. Work began in 1947, and soon the mine was over 100 feet deep and was equipped with a Gordon-Smith compressor and a track and car. A large stone cabin was built here to house the six men working the mine. The mine produced over $11,000 in silver before closing in 1950.

Only the large stone cabin is left in San Juan Canyon. Nothing at all remains of the earlier operations. Only the well-weathered mine headshafts show that mining ever took place here.

SAWMILL (Willow Creek Ranch)

DIRECTIONS:
From Moore's Station, continue north for 5 miles. Follow the left fork, keeping right, for 24 miles to Willow Creek Ranch, site of Sawmill.

The small camp of Sawmill grew around a small sawmill. The operation never expanded, and later the site was incorporated into a ranch. The Willow Creek Ranch, smaller than the original operation, has been operating off and on during the last fifteen years. A number of ranch buildings remain at the site, including the old ranch house. There is no trace of the sawmill.

SHAMROCK

DIRECTIONS:
From Ione, take the dirt road directly south from town and follow for ½ mile. Take a left at the fork and follow for 1½ miles to Shamrock.

Initial discoveries of rich gold, silver, copper and lead deposits in Shamrock Canyon were made by P. A. Havens in 1863. It was not until 1867, however, that a few fairly large mines were started. The Indianapolis Mine and the North Star Mine, also known as the Phillips Mine, were 200 feet and 300 feet respectively. Production was erratic, and by the turn of the century, all work was given up on the mines. An earthquake in 1932 collapsed the shafts, ending forever any thought of reopening the mines. Mercury deposits discovered in 1907 by J. L. Workman were a big boost for nearby Ione and led to the first major development of the canyon. The Shamrock Mines Company, based in Salt Lake City with mine offices in Ione, bought twenty-one claims in the canyon in 1923, and activity in Shamrock became more consistent. The company was incorporated in 1923; L. E. Elggren was president and John Bluth, who lived in Salt Lake City, was secretary.

The company built a small mill in 1923 and operations began. A tunnel shaft revealed that the ore carried values in both silver and gold. By 1926 the tunnel was over 1000 feet long. Work began on branching tunnels to reach veins discovered during the early 1920s. The company remodeled the 1923 mill to use the Vandercook mercuric cyanide system. The mill had a 75-ton capacity, which sometimes was not large enough and the overflow ore was sent to the Pioneer Mill in Ione.

The main operation during the next few years was the tunnel mine. By 1928 the tunnel was over 1700 feet long. The company discovered another low-grade cinnabar deposit in 1929, but the ore was not rich enough for prolonged production. In 1929 the mill was again changed, this time from a cyanide

Shamrock Canyon's rich Nevada Cinnabar Mine as it was in 1905. The small camp of Shamrock is in the foreground and also extended to the left. *(United States Geological Survey)*

plant to a flotation system. Activity in the area faded in late 1929; by 1930 only leasers were working the area. Recently the Iron Mercury Mining Company has been working the cinnabar deposits in the canyon. The company has been operating off and on during the last ten years.

Ruins are scarce in Shamrock Canyon, for the area never developed into a real camp. The mill has been used recently by the Iron Mercury Mining Company and is still in good condition. Otherwise, there is nothing of much interest in the canyon.

SILVER BOW

DIRECTIONS:
From Tonopah, head east on US 6 for 32 miles. Exit right and follow for 3 miles. Bear right and continue for 4 miles. Exit left and follow for another 4 miles. Exit right and follow for 3½ miles. Exit left and follow for 8 miles to Silver Bow.

Initial silver discoveries in the Silver Bow district were made in November 1904. Additional discoveries in 1905, and George Wingfield's presence in the district, led to a rush to the area. The camp soon became home for over 300 people. George Wingfield and George Nixon platted the Silver Bow townsite in early 1905, and soon the town became a supply center for the district. A stageline to Tonopah was set up with a fare of $7. A post office opened Sept. 27, 1905, and the town took on an air of permanence.

Silver Bow had a terminal problem with claim jumping. One of the better known incidents involved Edward Johnson and Hugh Fulton, the best of friends. Their heated argument about a claim that neither owned ended up on Silver Bow's main street, where Johnson shot and killed Fulton; the death was later ruled self-defense. Claim jumping kept Tonopah's deputy sheriffs traveling back and forth from Silver Bow to arrest the offenders. But these incidents did not slow Silver Bow's growth. By the fall of 1905 the town had stores, many saloons, and a few general merchandise emporiums.

The *Silver Bow Standard* began publication in September 1905. Editor Leslie Smaill, in an attempt to focus attention on Silver Bow, printed the headline of the Jan. 6, 1906, edition with ink that had been mixed with gold assaying at $80,000 per ton. Smaill had planned to print the whole paper with

This 1905 photo shows Silver Bow in its infancy. It is one of the few photos that exist of the camp. *(United States Geological Survey)*

the special ink, but he figured that the cost of printing an entire edition "would amount to a sum far in excess of the real value of the entire plant, editor, force and all." The purpose of the paper was to show that the ore in Silver Bow was no fluke, as was feared with the nearby Golden Arrow property. The gold used in the paper headline was mined from the Reed and Robbe claim, half a mile north of Silver Bow.

In the Silver Bow district silver was clearly dominant over gold. A ratio of $1 in gold to $3 in silver was average, but some claims had as much as twenty times more silver than gold. In 1906 Silver Bow began a quick slide. Most of the mines had panned out, and only a couple of the larger mines remained open. By the next year fewer than thirty people were in the district, and only the Silver Bow Belle Mining Company continued operations. The post office closed on Nov. 30, 1907. By the end of 1907, the district was abandoned.

A small revival in 1913 warranted building a two-stamp mill and brought twenty-five people back to the district. The revival died before the beginning of 1914, and once again the site belonged to the ghosts. The last revival took place in the 1920s. The Blue Horse Mining Company organized in late 1920, built a 20-ton Gibson mill and sank two shafts, one 30 feet and the other 150 feet. Neither turned out to be worthwhile, and the mill closed in 1921.

The Virgin Gold Mining Company, with T. L. Mahoney of Los Angeles as president, was also active in the district but never was successful. Its holdings were sold in 1928 to the newly formed Silver Hoard Mining Company, which owned four claims in the district. Silver Hoard dug a number of shallow shafts and short tunnels and contemplated building a 50-ton mill. But the ore faded before mill construction started.

The last company to work the Silver Bow area was the Silver Bow Consolidated Mining Company, organized in early 1929. The company purchased the old Blue Horse Mining Company's holdings. The richest mine was the old Blue Horse Mine, 150 feet deep with 1500 feet of lateral work. A fifty-ton flotation mill was built in 1929. It ran sixteen hours a day and employed eleven men. The ore taken from the claims and processed in the mill assayed at $15 to $20 per ton. As was typical for the Silver Bow area, the ore deposits were shallow. By 1930 activity in the district had ceased, this time for good.

The remains of Silver Bow are not very extensive. A few wooden cabins still stand, seemingly from the later revivals. There are mine hoists from some of the mines. Silver Bow is quite hard to reach, for the road is extremely sandy and treacherous. Four-wheel-drive is recommended.

SILVER GLANCE

DIRECTIONS:
From Hannapah, continue northwest for ½ mile to Silver Glance.

Silver Glance was Hannapah's sister camp. The mainstay of the camp was the Silver Glance Mine, discovered in 1905. The townsite was set up in 1906, and the real estate promoters who had worked Hannapah also promoted Silver Glance. They were even less successful here than at Hannapah. Closing of the Silver Glance mine in 1909 signaled the end of the camp, although revivals did take place in later years.

In 1919 the Silver Glance Mine was reopened and worked by the Silverzone Mines Company, run by William Gray and J. S. Clark. They used the glory-hole method, following a 150-foot ore shoot that was 125 feet deep. Gray and Clark leased out their holdings after 1920; by 1921 the leasers had given up. The Silverzone Extension Mining Company was also active in the district during 1919. The company had been organized in 1919 by George Quigley, O. G. Walther and J. W. Hanson, all of Tonopah. They owned five claims just west of the Silver Glance Mine. A 400-foot shaft sunk in 1919–20 led to ore that assayed as high as $145 per ton. By 1922 the ore had faded, and the company folded in late 1922. The district was silent until 1928.

In 1928 the Silver Glance Mining Company was incorporated and purchased the old Silver Glance Mine from Gray and Clark. Intensive exploration of the mine rewarded the new owners with a rich new ore body that yielded almost $300,000 in silver during 1928. Unfortunately the ore body was in a pocket, and by early 1929 the pocket had been emptied. When the company folded in that year, so did Silver Glance.

Only a few substantial buildings were ever built at the townsite, and no sign of these remain. The only marker of what used to be Silver Glance is the Silver Glance Mine glory hole. The townsite was platted just south of the mine, but no matter how hard you search, the townsite is completely unlocatable.

SPANISH SPRING

DIRECTIONS:
From Tonopah, head east on US 6 for 5½ miles. Then take Nevada 376 north for 13.3 miles. Exit right and take Nevada 82 north for 12 miles. Exit left and follow this road for 3¼ miles to Spanish Spring.

Spanish Spring, a little-known stage stop on the Tonopah–Manhattan stageline, was nevertheless one of the most important stops on the run. The stage got water here for the horses before the tough climb over the mountains to booming Manhattan. The stageline was abandoned in late 1907 after Manhattan began to decline. One stone cabin and some scattered wooden remains mark the site. The spring still flows here but very slowly, and it gathers in a stagnant pool. Do not plan on getting any drinking water here.

SPRINGDALE

DIRECTIONS:
From Beatty, head north on US 95 for 9½ miles to Springdale, on the east side of the highway.

Springdale was a train stop on the Bullfrog-Goldfield Railroad, but the meadowy area had been occupied long before the steel ribbons were laid. During the 19th century Indians camped at the site. After they left, a number of small ranches were built in the fertile area. The coming of the railroad in the winter of 1906 put Springdale on the map. A station house and a water tank were built here, for the site had a very good water supply needed by the steam engines of that era.

A small settlement grew around the railroad, and a post office opened on Feb. 19, 1907. Springdale received another big boost that year when a boom at nearby Pioneer brought a small rush of prospectors to the area. Springdale became a railhead for booming Pioneer and was soon enjoying a brisk, prosperous shipping business. By the summer of 1907 Springdale had four saloons, a number of restaurants, a hotel, a livery stable and a popular red-light district with fourteen girls. Springdale had

Springdale's two-story station indicated the town's importance as a shipping terminus. *(Nevada Historical Society)*

an extremely large Independence Day celebration in 1907 that included a Wild West show from Goldfield. Over 1000 people from surrounding mining camps showed up, and a good time was enjoyed by all.

Springdale remained an important stop on the B.-G. R.R. until Pioneer began to decline late in 1911. At the beginning of that year, Springdale still had a population of seventy-five; by the end of 1911, the population had shrunk to around ten. The post office closed on Jan. 15, 1912, and soon only the trains disturbed Springdale's slumber. Even the trains stopped running in 1928, and Springdale faded into history.

A ranch opened at the site and a few gas stations served travelers until 1958, when new highway US 95 bypassed the area. The buildings that are left are now on the ranch.

STARGO

DIRECTIONS:
From Antelope, continue north, bearing right and follow this road for 4 miles. Exit left and follow this poor road for 6 miles to Stargo.

Stargo was a little-known mining camp on Stargo Creek in Little Fish Lake Valley. The mining camp formed in the early 1900s. No rich ore was ever found, and the camp died as quickly as it had formed. A few small stone and wooden cabins were built during the site's short period of activity. The camp had vanished from all maps by 1910, and hardly a trace remains today. Only one completely flattened stone cabin marks the site.

STIRLING (Sterling)

DIRECTIONS:
From Lathrop Wells, head east on US 95 for 30 miles. Exit right and follow this road for 7 miles to Stirling.

Stirling was an extremely short-lived mining camp, lasting only from 1908 to 1909. There had been activity in the mountains around Stirling as early as 1869. After a short while the Timber Mountain mining district was organized, encompassing the north end of the Spring Mountain range. The Sterling Mine was opened, and a small five-stamp mill was constructed to treat the ore. This activity was extremely limited, and the district was abandoned in 1870.

The town of Stirling was formed in April 1907 when the Ore City Mining Company reopened the Sterling Mine and began intensive operations. Both gold and copper ore were found in the old mine and in other newly discovered claims in the area. A townsite was platted at the base of Mt. Sterling in April 1907. The town soon had twenty-five people. Supplies were brought in from the Las Vegas and

Tonopah Railroad, 7 miles to the north. Water was obtained from Big Timber Spring, on the backside of Mt. Sterling. The *Reno Evening Gazette* remarked, in its May 3, 1907, issue, that Stirling appeared to be a promising camp. A post office opened on June 3, 1907, just as the small boom at Stirling was dying out. The town struggled into 1908, but after the post office closed on Feb. 13, 1908, the town folded.

Only scant ruins are left. No buildings remain, but rubble is scattered over the site. There are some meager mine ruins on the side of Mt. Sterling. The road to Stirling is extremely rough and is impassable during wet weather.

STONE HOUSE (Smith's Station)

DIRECTIONS:
From Belmont, continue north on Nevada 82 for 7 miles. Exit left and follow this road for 1½ miles to Stone House.

Stone House was a stop on the Belmont–Austin stageline for a number of years. The two-story stone station was built in the early 1860s and was used by weary travelers for the next thirty years. The station was constructed by L. D. Smith and was the scene of many memorable dances. The dances took place in the ballroom on the second floor and attracted people from as far away as Hot Creek. L. D. Smith was killed on March 6, 1869, after a gun battle with E. L. Musick, whom Smith employed. The dispute occurred over a team of oxen that Smith had purchased from Musick and was planning to resell, which upset Musick. Musick followed Smith down the road from Stone House and killed him. Smith, who was from Tennessee, left a wife and two children, who stayed and operated the station for a number of years. For many years after Smith's death, the station was known as Widow Smith's place. After the stage run was stopped in the mid-1890s, the station was bought by an Indian family named Hooper. They erected new buildings around the old station house, and the small complex was used as a ranch. Albert Hooper and his father, Tim, did a lot of prospecting in the hills west of the station. They staked a number of claims, but

Once-proud Smith's Station, at Stone House, is now sadly in disrepair and could collapse at any moment.

none turned out to be really prosperous. After his father died, Albert continued to run the ranch until the mid-1960s. The ranch has been abandoned since then and is now owned by the nearby Pine Creek Ranch.

Remains at the site are fairly extensive and interesting. The old station house is in relatively poor condition—there is no floor on the second level, and a wooden cabin has been built inside the station's shell. Although strong-looking from the outside, a quick look inside reveals large cracks, showing that the building is not going to last too much longer. A number of newer wooden cabins also remain near the station house. Stone House is a definite must because the beauty of the station house should not be missed; hopefully it will remain standing. Spring water is available at the site.

STONEWALL (Fork's Station)

DIRECTIONS:
From Beatty, head north on US 95 for 53½ miles. Exit right and follow this road for 1 mile. Continue straight for 3 more miles. Exit right and follow this road for 1½ miles to Stonewall.

A small silver strike was made on the north side of Stonewall Mountain in August 1904. By the end of that year, 150 people were living in the camp. The town and the mountain had been named for General "Stonewall" Jackson, famous for his "stonewall" stand at the Civil War battle of Bull Run. The Las Vegas and Tonopah Railroad set up a station here called Fork's Station. The initial burst of activity quickly subsided. By the end of 1905, only a handful of inhabitants were left. A two-stamp mill was built here during the early 1900s.

Several small ore shipments were made after the short boom collapsed, but the district was practically abandoned until the Yellow Tiger Consolidated Mining Company moved into the area in 1917. The company was a consolidation of Desert Chief Consolidated Mining Company, New Goldfield Sierra Mining Company and Red Lion Consolidated Mines Company. The new company was originally known as the Yellow Tiger Mining Company, but the name was altered after reorganization and incorporation.

The company had sixteen claims in the Stonewall district, covering almost 280 acres. These claims were in two groups, the Stonewall and the Sterlag groups. The mainstay of the Stonewall group was the Stonewall Mine, which reached a depth of 500 feet before closing. The shaft followed a rhyolite and

The small camp of Stonewall never achieved prominence but was the scene of a fair amount of activity for a number of years. This is a 1915 photo of the camp. *(William and Phillip Metscher)*

lime-porphyry vein that varied in width from 7 feet to 22 feet. The ore assayed at an average of $20 per ton. The gold-and-silver–bearing vein was intersected by the Sterlag tunnel, which was dug to a length of 1100 feet. The ore from the tunnel contained an average of 16 ounces of silver and 2 ounces of gold per ton. The company curtailed operations in September 1920 when financial backing failed. The company was back in business a year later, and by 1925 the Sterlag tunnel had been extended to over 5000 feet. The company left the district in 1926 to concentrate efforts on its property in the Goldfield mining district. The Stonewall area has been dead ever since.

The only remains at Stonewall are the mine ruins at the site of the Sterlag tunnel. Nothing else is left. Stonewall is a disappointingly bland site, especially after an extremely rough ride to get here.

SULPHIDE

DIRECTIONS:
Located inside the Las Vegas Bombing and Gunnery Range, 3 miles northeast of Jamestown. Off-limits to the public.

Sulphide sprang up during the early 1900s, one of a group of mining camps that included Jamestown, Trappman's Camp, Wilson's Camp, Wellington, Kawich and Gold Crater. Sulphide was the smallest of these and was the first to fold. Sulphide reached peak population of twenty-five before excitement in the district crumbled. Since the camp did not last long or grow to any extent, no substantial buildings were built. In 1910 Sulphide was still on highway maps, but by 1912 it was gone for good. Because of its location, a present-day status report is impossible. I doubt anything could be left of the small, short-lived camp.

SUNNYSIDE (Whipple Ranch)

DIRECTIONS:
From Lund (White Pine County), head south on Nevada 38 for 30 miles to Sunnyside.

Sunnyside was—and is—a small settlement in the southern part of the White River Valley. It started as a ranch owned by a man named Horton. The ranch was built in the 1880s, and soon a small settlement surrounded it. A post office opened July 10, 1880, to serve the whole White River Valley. The small settlement never really grew but did have a small mercantile store providing supplies for the many ranches in the valley.

The Horton Ranch was bought by John Lytle Whipple in the fall of 1904. He moved his family to Sunnyside from Lund after Christmas of that year. Whipple had 200 beef cattle on the ranch during 1904 and 1905; he sold them in DeLamar, a mining town in Lincoln County. Whippe took over O. H. Snow's mail contract in 1904 and ran the route from Pioche to Sunnyside, a trip that took two days by buggy.

Whipple worked this route for two years before hiring a man for the job. By a quirk of fate, this turned out to be a very profitable decision for Whipple. The hired man lost a horse on one of his trips in February 1906. Whipple was forced to go out and search for the lost animal. While searching, he found an outcropping of rock that turned out to be high-grade silver ore. This was later developed into the Silver Horn Mine, 4 miles north of the mining camp of Bristol. Whipple sold his mine to an English mining company in March 1906 for $10,000, using the money to pay off the ranch. He maintained an interest in the mine, which provided him with a small cash flow. Whipple also had a group of claims, the Silver Dale group, located next to the Silver Horn Mine. He sold these claims in late 1906 to the same English company for $3500.

Whipple was officially appointed postmaster at Sunnyside on Sept. 27, 1917, a post he held until Jan. 31, 1933, when the post office closed. A school was also located at Sunnyside. When the ranch was short of hands, the teacher would cancel classes and the children and the teacher would both help out. Whipple bought back the Silver Horn Mine and the Silver Dale claims in the spring of 1920 but spent most of his time at Sunnyside.

John Whipple's son, Clair, leased the ranch from his father in 1935 and purchased it in 1940. In 1945 Sunnyside still had a population of twenty-seven, most of whom worked on the ranch. Clair Whipple and his wife, Lila, ran the ranch until 1962. They sold the property to the Johnson family, who are the present owners of the site. Not much else remains except the ranch complex and a few log ruins. The ranch is in a beautiful setting and is well worth the trip. Camping facilities are available at the Warm Springs Camp, southwest of Sunnyside.

TATE'S STATION

DIRECTIONS:
From Round Mountain, head west on Nevada 92 for 2.7 miles. Exit right (north) on Nevada 376 for 19 miles to Tate's Station.

Tate's Station was an important stop on the Austin–Belmont stage in the 1880s and the 1890s. The station was organized in 1886 by Thomas Tate and his wife. Tate also had a contract for mail delivery that he fulfilled for over thirty years. He was influential in getting the first school in Smoky Valley. Buildings at the station included the stone station house, a small lodging building and a number of stables. The Tates closed the station in 1901. Eventually the site was incorporated into a ranch, which is still in operation today. The old station house and one of the sod stables remain on the ranch.

TELLURIDE

DIRECTIONS:
From Beatty, head south on US 95 for 1 mile. Exit left and follow this road for 1 mile. Bear left and continue for 2¾ miles. Exit right and follow for ¼ mile. Exit left and follow for 2 miles. Exit right and follow for 1½ miles to Telluride.

Telluride was another of the small camps that sprang up in the hills east of Beatty during the early 20th century. Telluride was founded around the same time as nearby Fluorine, and for a while the two camps were rivals. But Telluride soon faded and slowly disappeared. The camp last appeared on maps in 1910. During its peak Telluride had a population of twenty-five. Nothing substantial was ever built, and only some small tailing piles mark the site.

TOLICHA (Monte Cristo) (Clarkdale) (Quartz Mountain) (Vignola's) (Carr's Camp)

DIRECTIONS:
Located 4 miles southeast of Monte Cristo Springs, inside the Las Vegas Bombing and Gunnery Range. Off-limits to the public.

Tolicha was another of the many camps that sprang up in the Pahute Mesa area just after the turn of the century. Tolicha was prospected during 1905, but the district remained fairly quiet until 1917 when two men, Jordan and Yaiser, found rich gold and silver ore on the northern slope of Tolicha Peak. One of the larger claim groups, the Life Preserver group, was leased by George Wingfield for a while. After Wingfield left, Eric Harvey took over the lease and installed a Gibson mill.

Harvey continued to work the lease at a profitable level until 1923, when the property was purchased by the newly formed Landmark group. In January 1923 Charles E. Knox, president of the group, purchased the Life Preserver claims. He died soon after, and the property was transferred to James W. Gerard. The group sank a 150-foot shaft, which was equipped with a hoist from a mine in Hawthorne. The vein followed by the mine, containing mainly gold with traces of silver, produced ore that assayed at $25 per ton. A short tunnel was dug but proved unprofitable. The Landmark group continued to be worked until 1926, when J. A. Logan and H. L. Gilbert of Tonopah purchased the property for $50,000. They had disappointing results and gave up in 1927, leaving the district totally abandoned.

The Landmark claims were leased during the 1930s, bringing Tolicha back to life. The Landmark Mine was reopened and worked until the 1940s. The mine turned out to be a profitable investment, producing $750,000 during the fourteen years of production. The mine was eventually dismantled for salvage. Just before the site was incorporated into the bombing range, a visitor reported that one building remained. Only a few were ever built in Tolicha, one being the ever-present saloon.

A few other small camps were active in the immediate Tolicha area. The largest was Quartz Mountain, 3 miles southeast of the Landmark group. Formed in 1905, the camp saw limited activity for almost thirty years. In 1950 a number of buildings still remained at the site. Another camp formed just north of Tolicha Wash. Clarkdale, named after one of its founders, came into existence in the early 1930s. Six mines, with a total depth of 700 feet, were active during this period. In 1933 one shipment of ore brought a return of $1000. The ore did not last long, and by the end of 1937 the camp was abandoned.

Carr's Camp, located on a ridge just west of Clarkdale, was also active during the 1930s. The camp was owned by C. J. Carr, who had located the Yellow Gold Mine in 1931. The camp consisted of a number of shacks, a storehouse and not much

Remaining buildings of the Quartz Mountain camp, located near Tolicha. The photo was taken in 1950 just before the site was incorporated into the Las Vegas Bombing and Gunnery Range. *(William Metscher)*

more. Mine operations were fairly extensive, but no lasting deposits were ever found. By 1939 the camp was deserted. The last camp in the district formed at the Wyoming–Scorpion claim group, 1½ miles north of Carr's Camp. The claim group was owned by H. B. Kleinstick of Daniel, Wyoming. The mainstay of Kleinstick's holdings was a 100-foot shaft mine with 40 feet of lateral work. The ore assayed at an average of $5 per ton. A few cabins were built at the mine, but the ore ran out and the camp was abandoned in the early 1940s. All of the sites are now off-limits inside of the Las Vegas Bombing and Gunnery Range.

TONOPAH (Butler)

DIRECTIONS:
Located at the junction of US 6 and US 95, 207 miles northwest of Las Vegas.

Tonopah Springs, later the site of one of the richest silver booms in the West, was an Indian camp ground for many years, long before Jim Butler spent a chilly night here. A number of stories exist as to how Butler discovered the silver ore. The most popular version is that Butler's mule wandered away, and when Butler found the ornery critter, he noticed an outcropping that appeared to be heavily laced with silver. Butler took a number of samples. The date was May 19, 1900. This quiet start belied the actual importance of the discovery. Butler firmly believed he had discovered an important silver deposit, but he had trouble convincing the assayer he visited in Klondike. The assayer told him the samples were worthless, consisting mainly of iron, and he threw them into the back of his tent.

Butler was still convinved that his find was genuine. On his way back to his Monitor Valley ranch, he stopped at Tonopah Springs once more to gather samples. Back at his ranch, Butler put the samples on his windowsill. Not too much later, Tasker Oddie, later to be governor of Nevada, stopped at the ranch and spied the ore samples. He offered to pay for another assay, and Butler agreed to this. Butler, in turn, offered Oddie a quarter interest of the assay. Oddie heartily agreed. He took the ore samples to William Gayhart, an Austin assayer, and offered Gayhart a quarter interest of his quarter. Gayhart found the assay to run as high as $600 per ton. When Oddie was notified of the value of the samples, he immediately sent an Indian runner to

Butler's hay ranch to alert him of the rich find. Butler did not react rapidly—he stayed at his ranch to complete the hay harvest and did not even bother to file claims on the lode site!

News of the discovery traveled to Klondike, and soon scores of eager prospectors were searching around Tonopah Springs, to no avail, for Butler's lode. Butler finally went to Belmont, and on Aug. 27, 1900, he and his wife filed on eight claims near Tonopah Springs. Six of these —the Desert Queen, Burro, Valley View, Silver Top, Buckboard and Mizpah—turned into some of the biggest producers the state has ever had.

Work was begun on the Mizpah Mine in October 1900, and a camp called Butler formed nearby. Butler decided to lease out all of his claims for one year, from December 1900 to December 1901. Soon the cry of, "Jim, how about a lease?" was heard throughout the bustling camp. Oddie and Butler were partners, receiving a 25 percent royalty on all gold and silver mined from the Butler claims.

The town of Butler began to grow by leaps and bounds. The first stagecoach, coming from Sodaville, arrived in Butler on March 24, 1901, with seven passengers. It was a two-day trip, with an overnight stay at Crow Springs. The camp consisted of seven shacks, a number of tents and a population of sixty. A post office, named Butler, opened at the booming camp on April 10, 1901; it was not until March 3, 1905, that the post office changed its name to Tonopah.

By the summer of 1901, Butler was beginning to make its mark on Nevada's silver-production figures. The mines around the town produced almost $750,000 in gold and silver in 1901, and for the next forty years were consistent producers. The town now had six saloons, restaurants, assay offices, lodging houses, a number of doctors, lawyers and a rapidly swelling population that stood at 650. A news organ came to the town on June 15, 1901, when W. W. Booth, who had published a paper in Belmont, set up the *Tonopah Bonanza*. It listed Butler as place of publication until March 11, 1905, when the name was officially acknowledged as Tonopah. Booth also acted as the postmaster until March 1905.

The year 1902 was also very prosperous for the booming town. Jim Butler had sold out the claims, which were all consolidated and gave birth to a new company, the Tonopah Mining Company. It was incorporated in Delaware, with stock listed on both the Philadelphia and San Francisco exchanges. The company, J. H. Whiteman president, controlled 160 acres of mineral-bearing ground around the Tonopah district. The company also had holdings in the Tonopah-Goldfield Railroad and controlled mining companies in Colorado, Canada, California and Nicaragua. The mine workings at Tonopah consisted of three deep shafts with over 46 miles of lateral workings. The deepest of the three shafts was 1500 feet. The ore mined at the site was shipped to Millers, where it was treated in a 100-stamp mill. This facility was used by the company's mines until suitable treatment facilities were built at Tonopah.

The Tonopah–Belmont Mining Company was also formed in 1902. The company was based in New Jersey and had C. A. Heller as president. The company's property, eleven claims covering over 160 acres, was on the east side of the property owned by the Tonopah Mining Company. There were two deep vertical shafts, 1200 feet and 1700 feet, with lateral workings covering almost 39 miles. The company also had to ship its ore to Millers until 1912, when its own 60-stamp mill was built at Tonopah. The mill had a capacity of 500 tons; during its years of activity (1912–23) it was regarded as one of the country's best equipped and most efficient silver cyanide mills.

These two mining companies were the mainstays that provided the financial boost to push Tonopah to prominence during 1902. There were some dark days for Tonopah that year. A month-long epidemic plagued the town; before it had passed, fifty of Tonopah's residents had died. By the end of 1902, the town had recovered and the population stood at over 3000. The booming town supported more than thirty saloons, a few churches, a school, two newspapers and numerous other business establishments. Stages from all over the state began to arrive in Tonopah. One was held up on the outskirts of town— Tonopah's only stage robbery. Wyatt Earp was a resident of Tonopah during 1903 and 1904, running the Northern Saloon and helping out the law every once in a while.

Any fear of Tonopah being just another quick boom, destined to collapse, vanished in late 1902 and early 1903. Substantial new ore deposits were located deep in a number of the already active mines, including the Montana–Tonopah, Desert Queen, North Star and Tonopah Extension. The

This very early photo of Tonopah was taken only a short time after Jim Butler had staked his claims. *(William Metscher)*

Tonopah in May 1901 already had a number of fair-size buildings. *(Central Nevada Historical Society)*

huge volume of ore being mined in Tonopah's rich mines led to shipping problems, for the only mills at that time were in Millers. It was decided to build a narrow-gauge railroad; construction started in late 1903. The 60-mile-long railroad connected Tonopah with the Carson and Colorado branch of the Southern Pacific Railroad at the Sodaville junction. The railroad was officially opened on July 25, 1904, followed by three days of jubilant celebration. In 1905 the railroad was enlarged to standard gauge. When the rails were extended to Goldfield in the fall of 1905, the railroad was organized and named the Tonopah and Goldfield Railroad.

In May 1905 Tonopah became the county seat in place of almost empty Belmont. The town continued to grow. John Brock dominated most of the mine ownership in Tonopah. In addition to controlling a number of prosperous mining companies, he also was acting president of the Bullfrog-Goldfield Railroad and the Tonopah and Goldfield Railroad.

Two major mining companies achieved prominence in Tonopah during the next few years. The

View of Tonopah soon after its formation in 1901. *(William Metscher)*

This is one of the first loads of ore shipped from the newly discovered Tonopah mines. The ore was shipped to the railroad siding at Sodaville, from which it was sent to smelters. *(William Metscher)*

Tonopah Extension Mining Company was formed in Arizona and had its main offices in New York City. The company controlled almost 700 acres of mineral-bearing ground in the Tonopah district, most on the west side of the Tonopah Mining Company's property. The company had three major shafts with about 33 miles of lateral work. The three mines—the No. 2, Victor and McKane—were all over 1500 feet deep. The deepest, the Victor, was almost 2200 feet. The company built a thirty-stamp cyanide mill in 1910, which was later enlarged to fifty stamps.

The second major new company was the West End Consolidated Mining Company, incorporated in Arizona. West End controlled 185 acres on the southwest side of the Tonopah Mining Company's property. The company also controlled the Halifax–Tonopah Mining Company and leased land from Jim Butler. There were three main shafts on the company's property, the deepest more than 1400 feet. The company built a cyanide mill in 1911 that had a daily capacity of over 200 tons. In addition to these four big companies, there were close to twenty other well-established mining companies active in the district during the 1910s and the 1920s.

By 1907 Tonopah had become a regular city, with modern hotels, electric and water companies, five banks, schools and hundreds of other buildings. Newspapers began to play a larger role in the town, and a number of rivalries arose. The best-known of these rivalries was between the *Tonopah Sun* and the *Tonopah Daily Bonanza*. The Sun had begun in 1904 as a weekly but was changed to a daily on Jan. 10, 1905. The *Daily Bonanza* was run by W. W. Booth, who also controlled the weekly *Tonopah Bonanza,* which had folded on Christmas Day, 1909. Booth's daily began publication Oct. 24, 1906, and soon the two papers were fighting tooth and nail. During this same period three other weeklies were being published.

The Mizpah Hotel, the landmark of present Tonopah, was completed in 1908 and opened with great fanfare on November 17. Over $200,000 was spent on the hotel, which boasted baths, steam heat and crude elevators. Not all was glitter in Tonopah, however. Feb. 28, 1911 lives as the darkest day in the town's bright history. A mysterious fire, small but smoky, broke out at the bottom of the 1200-foot shaft of the Belmont Mine at seven in the morning. A number of men had already gone below before the seriousness of the situation was realized. The fumes were extremely toxic. Calls to the hoist operator came in slowly at first but soon became frantic. Although many men were brought to safety, seventeen perished in the mine. All died not from the fire but from the choking fumes. A number of the dead had actually made it to the hoist lift but were so weakened that they fell out of the cage to their deaths at the bottom of the shaft. Actual damage to the shaft was only $5000. The cause of the deadly fire was a candle left on a pile of dry timber by a careless night watchman. This was the only major mining incident in the Tonopah mines. The Belmont Mine was soon reopened. It produced $38 million in silver and gold before another fire in 1939 closed the mine for good.

W. W. Booth remained a controversial figure as Tonopah continued to progress. In 1916 he was brought to court on a libel suit after accusing a district attorney of being dishonest, among other things. He lost the case and was sentenced to six months in the county jail. The other newspaper

1902 photo of the Tonopah *Miner*'s main office, soon after it started publication. The paper's first issue was on June 19, 1902. A weekly was printed until the paper folded on Nov. 5, 1921. *(William Metscher)*

Later photo of Tonopah, about 1904, when the town was well established as the new mining force in Nevada. *(William Metscher)*

editors were outraged, and their voices were heard. Booth was released after serving only a month and was eventually pardoned. Booth's *Daily Bonanza* came upon hard times during the 1920s. On Nov. 16, 1929, the paper was sold to Frank Garside, who had been in charge of the *Tonopah Daily Times* since its origin on Dec. 1, 1915. Garside consolidated the two papers into the *Tonopah Times-Bonanza*. Booth soon left Tonopah and moved to Hawthorne, becoming editor of the *Hawthorne News*. The *Tonopah Times-Bonanza* was a daily until April 2, 1943, when it was changed to a weekly, as it is today.

Tonopah's mines maintained very high yearly production until the Depression brought a slowdown. Mine production from 1900 to 1921 (the peak years) was almost $121 million. The biggest single year was 1913, when almost $10 million in gold, silver, copper and lead was mined. By World War II only four major mining companies were operating. At the end of the war, even these companies had left. The final blow came in 1947 when the Tonopah and Goldfield Railroad folded and its rails were torn up.

Not much mining activity has taken place in Tonopah since then. In 1968 Howard Hughes and his Summa Corporation bought 100 claims in Tonopah, including the Mizpah Mine, Silver Top Mine and Desert Queen Mine. Hopes for a mining revival soon faded after core samples and nothing more were taken. New molybdenum discoveries north of Tonopah could bring active mining back to Tonopah. Also, a number of the old mines have recently been retimbered. With the recent rise in gold and silver prices, reopening the mines seems inevitable. As of now, total production from the Tonopah district is just over $150 million, a figure few other places could boast.

Tonopah is the largest town in Nye County; 2500 people live here. This figure could begin to grow dramatically since the Anaconda project is bringing new life to Tonopah. The deposits are believed to

This 1906 photo of Tonopah shows the extensive settlement. The wide road in the foreground is the main street. *(William Metscher)*

Tonopah during the winter of 1906. The gathering of carriages seems to indicate a Sunday service. *(William Metscher)*

1913 view of Tonopah taken from the Desert Queen Mine, owned by the Tonopah Belmont Development Company. *(William Metscher)*

Later shot of Tonopah after the town had begun to decline.

This is the Tonopah-Goldfield Railroad station as it was during the 1920s. The station was the victim of arson in August 1980; only the cement walls of the railroad safe remain. The Central Nevada Historical Society had discussed using the building as a museum and still plans to use the huge metal safe doors from the building for their archive vault.

The old Tonopah Cemetery as it was in the late 1940s. The Central Nevada Historical Society has recently restored it and done research to mark most of the previously unknown graves. *(Central Nevada Historical Society)*

be large enough to last for at least twenty years. Many buildings still remain from the boom era, including the newly renovated Mizpah Hotel. West of town is the old town dump, which is available for digging; old bottles, a few coins and a lot of broken pottery still remain here. Other points of interest include the Nye County Court House, built in 1905 at a cost of $55,000 on land donated by Jim Butler; the old Tonopah Public Library, built in 1912 and now the oldest active library in Nevada; St. Mark's Episcopal Church, built in 1906 and one of the better known landmarks in Tonopah; and the ruins of the old 500-ton Belmont Mill, on the east side of Mt. Oddie. Supplies of all sorts are available in Tonopah as well as reasonably priced lodging.

TOYAH

DIRECTIONS:
From Ione, head east on Nevada 21 for 8¼ miles. Exit right and follow for 4¼ miles. Exit right again and follow for 3½ miles to Toyah.

Toya, a stop on the Belmont–Ione stage run during the 1860s, was located at the highest point of Ophir Canyon. The station served as a rest stop for the horses after the tough climb up the mountain. Only a large wooden cabin and a small stable were ever built here. Later, very limited mining took place near the site.

Hardly a trace remains of Toyah. Some scattered test tailing piles mark the general area along the road where the station was; nearby, but hard to see, are some very faint wooden remains. This is all that is left of Toyah.

TRANSVAAL (Nyopolis)

DIRECTIONS:
From Beatty, head north on US 95 for 4½ miles. Exit right and follow this poor road for 11 miles to Transvaal.

Transvaal was an extremely short-lived mining town that had one of the most incredible booms—and one of the fastest declines—of any town in Nye County history. Initial discoveries were made in the northern section of the Beatty Wash in March 1906. A small tent camp, called Nyopolis, soon formed. By the beginning of April the tent camp had been renamed Transvaal, which meant "across the river," a clear reference to Transvaal's location across the Amargosa River from Beatty and Rhyolite.

By the second week of April, Transvaal had over

seventy-five tents. Business establishments at the camp included four saloons, an assay office, a lumberyard, lodging houses and a number of broker and real estate offices. Two newspapers, the *Transvaal Miner* and the *Transvaal Tribune*, began publication during early April. Transvaal reached its peak during the third week of April, when 700 to 800 people were living in the tent city. Stages for Beatty left from Transvaal every morning, charging $5 per person.

The swift and dramatic collapse of Transvaal occurred in the first two weeks of May 1906. When it was discovered that there was no ore at Transvaal, the people left in droves. Both papers folded in early May, and by the third week of that month the site was totally abandoned. Absolutely nothing remains; the town did not last long enough for any permanent buildings to be erected. The site is difficult to reach and is very unrewarding.

TRAPPMAN'S CAMP

DIRECTIONS:
Located 4 miles east of Mt. Helen, inside the Las Vegas Bombing and Gunnery Range. Off-limits to the public.

Trappman's Camp was a mining camp that formed on Pahute Mesa after silver and gold ore was discovered there in June 1904 by Hermann Trappman and John Gabbard. A small camp of about fifteen men soon formed around the discovery site. Wood and water was obtained from Antelope Springs, 9 miles away. The Trappman Mining Company, newly formed and based in Goldfield, moved into the district in July 1905. During the course of the next month, the company's five employees sank a 50-foot shaft. Ore from the shaft continued an ounce of gold and 4 ounces of silver per ton. The company continued to work the shaft in hopes of finding richer deposits. When none were found, the company folded in late 1905.

Only a few persistent prospectors remained in the district, and even they had left by the summer of 1906. Because of the limited activity here, nothing even close to substantial was ever built. The miners' small stone dugouts were about the extent of the development. When the mining company moved in, a small wooden cabin was built to house the five men working the mine. Since there never was much at the camp, it took only a few years for the site to completely vanish. Without anything to haunt, even the ghosts have left Trappman's. The site is now inside the Las Vegas Bombing and Gunnery Range, off-limits to the public.

TROY

DIRECTIONS:
From Nyala, continue north on the Currant–Nyala road for 9 miles. Exit right and follow this road for 3 miles to Troy.

The first ore in the Troy area was discovered in May 1867 by Alexander Beatty. He sold his claims to a Yorkshire, England, mining company in 1869 and moved to Butterfield Springs, where he started a prosperous ranch. The Old English Gold Corporation built a twenty-stamp mill in 1870 and began operations. The stamp mill, at a site 5½ miles west of the Troy Mine, cost over $500,000 to construct. It was equipped with Stetefeldt furnaces and was finally completed in 1871.

The camp that grew up around the huge stamp mill soon had a few stores, an express office, a boardinghouse and some cabins. An unofficial post office was formed in 1870, but it was not until Feb. 18, 1873, that a U.S. post office opened. By 1871 the population of Troy was well over 100.

The English mill handled ore from both the Troy Mine and the Lock Mine. The Troy Mine comprised two separate mineral lodes, the Troy and the Gray Eagle. The mine shaft was over 500 feet deep with many branch tunnels. Although the Troy Mine is more than 1000 feet higher than the camp, a constant problem with water seepage in the mine eventually led to abandoning it in 1913. The Lock Mine, three quarters of a mile south of Troy, also had a 500-foot shaft, only horizontal. The Lock Mine was never a big producer. The two other main mines in the district were the Clifton and the Blue Eagle. The Blue Eagle had a 500-foot vertical shaft and a branch tunnel over 700 feet long. Overall, the only big producer was the Troy Mine. The ore mined in the area contained silver, gold, copper and small amounts of lead.

The stamp mill operated for six months, closing in 1872 because of extremely low-grade ore. The equipment was sent to Ward in White Pine County. The English company pulled out of Troy soon after. Around seventy miners stayed on to prospect the different sites along the canyon. The post office was

This is all that remains of the once impressive Troy Mill.

Only this crumbling brick wall marks the old Troy Bank.

operational until Aug. 7, 1876. Even after the post office closed, some people still remained, although no ore was shipped out. Freight was brought once a week from Eureka, indicating that there was still some faint interest in Troy. A small revival attempt took place in 1908 when new ore deposits were found in the Lock Mine and the Blue Eagle Mine. The post office reopened on April 24, 1908, and managed to stay open until Feb. 28, 1913. The amount of ore taken out was small but was enough to keep the town going a little longer. Slowly the revival died out, and by 1915 Troy belonged to the ghosts. The town woke from its sleep for a short spell when the call went out for metal prior to World War II. The mines were reopened by Joseph Hafen of Provo, Utah, in 1936 to help boost prewar production. He built a small flotation mill in 1936, which was enlarged to 50-ton capacity ten years later. The mines maintained fairly steady production until 1949, when they were shut down and the town was once again abandoned.

Troy still has a few inhabitants. Three of the remaining buildings are occupied by sportsmen. The stream flowing through the ruins and down the canyon is full of fish. There are five standing buildings, four of stone from the original settlement and the other a remnant of wartime operations. The ruins of the mill, directly opposite the buildings, comprise huge concrete foundations along with the unique remains of the Stetefeldt furnaces. Many faint foundations remain at Troy plus a number of interesting dumps in which to dig. All of the mining apparatus remains at the Lock Mine. Most of the mine workings are left from recent operations. The road to Troy is fairly rough but is passable with a four-wheel-drive. The first sign of Troy is the Lock Mine, located high up on Troy Mountain.

TWIN SPRINGS

DIRECTIONS:
From Warm Springs, head east on Nevada 375 for 10½ miles to Twin Springs.

Twin Springs is a small ranching settlement that dates from the late 1870s. The ranch does not have any real history except that it has been active for over 100 years. A number of old buildings still remain at the ranch along with newer ones. The present population of the ranch is about ten. The site is interesting to explore because it is still set up as it was long ago.

TYBO

DIRECTIONS:
From Warm Springs, head north on US 6 for 8 miles. Exit left and follow this road for 3½ miles. Take the left fork and follow for 3 miles to Tybo.

Original discoveries were made in the Hot Creek range in 1866. One of the discovery sites was

In 1875 Tybo had not really developed, but the Bunker Hill Mine, in the foreground and right, was a consistent producer. *(Nevada Historical Society)*

The most developed area of Tybo in 1875 was Upper Tybo, which included a number of falsefront buildings on the main street. *(Nevada Historical Society)*

named Tybo, derived from the Shoshone *tai-vu* meaning "white man's district." The first major ore discovery was made in 1870 by Dr. Gally and M. V. B. Gillett. The discovery was later developed into the Two-G Mine.

It was not until 1874 that a small camp began to form in Tybo Canyon. The first settler in the canyon had been John Centers, who moved to the canyon in August 1866. A small lead smelter was built in the canyon in 1874, and in the next year the Tybo Consolidated Mining Company was formed. The company built another smelter and a twenty-stamp mill before the end of 1875. Tybo Consolidated controlled three major mines near the camp: the Casket, the Lafayette and the original Two-G. The Two-G was the deepest of the three, having been dug to a depth of 450 feet before closing in 1883.

By the summer of 1876, the small town had boomed to a population of almost 1000. The town had been divided, because of constant racial problems, into three separate sections: Irish, Central European and Cornish. Buildings in the town in 1876 included five stores, a number of saloons, two blacksmith shops and a post office, which opened on Sept. 3, 1874. The *Tybo Sun,* under the management of a Mr. Ragsdale, began publication on May 19, 1877. Ragsdale sold the paper in early 1878 to William Taylor, who operated it for a short time and then sold out to William Love and D. M. Brannan. They continued to publish the weekly until declining interest forced the paper to fold on March 14, 1880.

A big blow, but a financial boost, came to Tybo in 1879 when the Tybo Consolidated Mining Company decided to close its two smelters, which employed 400, and build a crushing and roasting mill. The mill had a daily capacity of 80 tons but did not employ nearly as many men. This caused a drop in population, but nevertheless in 1880 three hotels, two restaurants, an express office and an assay office were built. A brick schoolhouse, which had twenty-five students, was also built. And a jail, seldom used, was constructed. From 1877 to 1880 Tybo was the top producer of Nye County and was second only to Eureka in total lead production for the entire state.

The Tybo Consolidated Mining Company ran into problems in early 1881 when the quality of the ore dropped drastically. The mill closed down and the company worked just the mines. But soon the company was forced to fold. By the end of 1881, only 100 people were left in Tybo Canyon, and the outlook for the future looked bleak. During the next twenty-five years, Tybo barely managed to cling to life. A number of different mining enterprises attempted to profitably work the Tybo district, but all quickly failed. In the 1880s and the 1890s, most of the activity in Tybo was limited to small groups of residents working some of the 100 claims made during the town's boom. The post office remained open through all of this and continued to serve the dwindling populace until July 14, 1906.

The town's perseverance was rewarded for a while in 1906 when the Nevada Smelting and Mines

The house pictured here in the 1910s still stands today in Tybo. *(Western History Research Center/University of Wyoming)*

Many mines were located in the Tybo district. Upper Tybo is just past the mine and mill, with Railroad Valley in the distance. *(Western History Research Center/University of Wyoming)*

Ruins of a large stamp mill, at one time instrumental in Tybo leading in ore production.

Corporation began work in Tybo Canyon. The company had been incorporated in May 1906 with capital of $5 million. Max Berrheimer was president. The company took over the old Tybo Consolidated Mining Company's holdings and began new operations. Profits were extremely low, and the company left the district in 1908. The town was almost completely abandoned; there were only four residents by 1911.

Tybo was given another lease on life when the Louisiana Consolidated Mining Company began to work a few of the mines. The company, incorporated in May 1912 with Julius Sieghart as president, owned property in Tybo and also in Reveille and in the Oreota district (Mineral County). The company obtained a twenty-year operating agreement on the Tybo Mine and the nearby Diminick Mine. A 75-ton concentration mill built in 1917 operated until late 1918. At the end of 1919, a flotation plant and a lead smelter were installed; these operated until 1921. The company faltered in 1921, and by 1922 flow of ore from the mines had stopped. The company left the district in 1922 to work its other properties. Soon Tybo was emptied again, with only rows of deserted, decaying buildings acknowledging that people had ever been here.

The last revival at Tybo started in 1926 when the Keystone–Hot Creek Mining Company purchased property in Tybo Canyon. The company leased this property to the Treadwell–Yukon Company, Ltd., which built a 350-ton concentration mill and a new smelter during 1929. The mill was soon processing over 300 tons of lead ore daily. Another company,

The old Trowbridge Store, on what used to be main street, became a dance hall during the 1930s.

Many buildings are still at the Tybo townsite. This one is in poor condition and may collapse very soon.

the Tybo Dominion Mines, Inc., also became active in the district, purchasing the Old Dominion and the Jumping Jacks claim groups. The company was incorporated in 1928 with Irving Farrington as president. Operations never really got off the ground, and the company quietly folded in 1929.

The Treadwell–Yukon Company became the core of the Tybo revival. Over seventy-five people came back to Tybo during 1929, and the post office was reopened on February 11 of that year. Treadwell–Yukon built a number of two-story boardinghouses for the miners and brought in some prefabricated houses for the executives. During the next eight years, the mill processed over 500,000 tons of lead ore. The company sank a 1500-foot shaft during those eight years. While it was being dug, some small silver deposits were discovered. The revival ended in 1937 when the company closed the mill, which was dismantled shortly afterward. Total production for the Tybo district was an amazing $9.8 million—amazing because Tybo's best years of production were when lead and silver prices were extremely low. If the ore had been mined today, the value would have come close to tripling.

Even today, Tybo is not a complete ghost. A handful of people still make their home in the peaceful, beautiful canyon. Tybo is one of the better ghost towns in Nye County. There are extensive mine and mill ruins scattered throughout the canyon. Many buildings remain, most still in very good condition. Among the better remains is the old Trowbridge store, changed from a store to a miners' recreation hall during the last revival. The cemetery is on a small hill at the mouth of the canyon and should not be missed. The Tybo charcoal kilns, further up Tybo Canyon and difficult to reach, are well worth the tough drive. Tybo, on the whole, is one of the top ten ghosts in Nye County.

UNION (Union Canyon)

DIRECTIONS:
Located 1 mile east of Berlin and well marked.

Union, a minor camp, sprang up in Union Canyon during 1863. The camp faded quickly and was virtually nonexistent during the 1870s and 1880s. Union was revived when rich gold deposits were discovered in the hills around Berlin. Some of the

Union Canyon in June 1907 was at its peak. Almost all of the residents were employed at the Berlin Mine and Mill. *(Nevada Historical Society)*

Barbed wire protects the melting remains of an adobe house that was occupied by the Kennedy family. This is one of the more substantial remains in the canyon!

miners working in the Berlin Mine settled in Union Canyon because it was far enough from the mine and mill to be quiet but close enough to walk to work.

The little settlement reached its peak during 1904 and 1905. During this period there were over twenty buildings, including a town hall, schoolhouse, mercantile store and even a small mill. The town hall was a large one room log structure. The building was later moved to Berlin in 1910 by Bob Dixon, who used it for a combination bar and boardinghouse. The schoolhouse was just a small log cabin; in 1902 the enrollment was twelve, with Celia Peter as teacher. Miss Peter lived in what is now the only remaining building in Union. The mercantile store was run by a Mr. Lennox and was actually a combination store and saloon. It closed during 1910 when the miners' strike in Berlin emptied the town. The mill, known as the Cirac Mill, was owned by the Cirac family, all of whom resided in the canyon. One of the family, Louie Cirac, owned the most imposing structure in Union: a two-story brick building with a large room on the second floor that frequently served as a dance hall. Louie and three of his brothers later became the first to patent the stop-and-hold lock for automobiles, making them the most notable people to have lived in Union. The small town also had another small saloon located next to the Cirac Mill and run by a Chinese man named Sam "China" Wing. A post office was formed but was rescinded before operations began.

The ruins of another mill are at the mouth of Union Canyon. This was the Mayette Mill, run by the Mayette family. The Mayettes had a house in the canyon surrounded by fruit trees and a large garden, with running water supplied from a nearby spring.

The camp was active until late 1910, when the miners went on strike at the Berlin Mine. The company refused to grant them a pay hike and closed down the mine. Both Berlin and Union Canyon were soon emptied. The years have not been kind to Union. The site is almost completely obliterated. Other than the still-standing adobe house, the only ruins marking the site are one partial adobe wall, which used to be part of the Kennedy house; the cement foundations of the Cirac Mill; and some scattered lumber north of the adobe house. Broken glass and rusted tin cans mark the

The schoolteacher's home in Union Canyon is the only standing building in town. It was last occupied about twenty years ago.

site of the Lennox mercantile store, and broken beer bottles and a dugout shelter are all that remains of Sam Wing's saloon. Union is now part of the Berlin–Ichthyosaur State Park. The site is patrolled by State Park rangers who try to protect what is left of the site from further vandalism.

UPPER TOWN (Carrolton)

DIRECTIONS:
Located in Upper Six-Mile Canyon, six miles north of Hot Creek. No passable roads reach the site.

Upper Town was a small settlement that sprang up in 1867 soon after the twenty-stamp Old Dominion Mill was put into operation to process ore from Hot Creek and Tybo. The mill burned down in late 1867, with damage of over $90,000. It was decided not to rebuild the mill, and Upper Town was quickly abandoned. There were never more than ten people at the mill site, and nothing substantial was built there. Only very faint stone foundations now mark the site of the mill.

VAN NESS

DIRECTIONS:
From Barcelona, backtrack for 1 mile and then exit right. Follow this extremely rough road for 2 miles to Van Ness.

Van Ness was a small mining camp 2 miles from Barcelona. The camp was owned and run by the Raymond Van Ness Mining Company. C. E. Van Ness, both president and manager, had his offices in Tonopah. The other two officers of the company, secretary-treasurer Dr. William Reece and construction engineer P. Shelby, were both from Los Angeles.

The company had six claims in the district and began working them in the early 1920s. The claims consisted of cinnabar ore mixed with granite and shale. The ore contained a high concentration— almost 5 percent—of mercury. The workings of the company included two shafts, both approximately 100 feet deep. The shafts followed a vein of ore varying in width from 4 feet to 6 feet. In 1929 Van Ness Mining built a 40-ton Gould rotary furnace to help smelt the mercury out of the ore. That same year the company became active in the Ellendale district. The cinnabar ore slowly ran out, and by 1935 the camp was abandoned.

There are a number of interesting ruins at Van Ness. The two mines retain most of their workings. Ruins of a number of miners' cabins are scattered around the mines. I was told the ruins of an old Spanish fort were half a mile north of Van Ness, but after trudging through the area for a number of hours, I was not able to locate it; perhaps someone else will be luckier and find this rare relic of early Nevada history. The road to Van Ness is very rough and had a number of washouts. It is passable only with four-wheel-drive.

WAHMONIE

DIRECTIONS:
Located inside the Las Vegas Bombing and Gunnery Range, 35 miles southeast of Beatty. Off-limits to the public.

Early activity in the Wahmonie district was extremely limited. Some small discoveries were made in 1904. A small mine, the Hornsilver, was opened but closed after only two months. It was not until W. R. McRae (McCrea) and Mark Lefler, who were traveling by automobile, discovered a lode of high-grade silver and gold ore just south of the old Hornsilver Mine that sustained activity came to the district.

McRae and Lefler made their discovery in February 1928. By mid-March there were over 200 people on the flat below the Hornsilver Mine. The district grew rapidly because of Wahmonie's accessibility by automobile. During the first months of Wahmonie's existence, the town was made up of only tents. There were a number of stores and saloons, all operating out of tents. The Gilbert brothers, who also ran a grocery store in Wahmonie, built an electric light plant to serve the small town. A post office opened on April 2, 1928, and Wahmonie reached its peak soon after. During the summer of 1928 Wahmonie's population was as high as 1500, but this figure dropped very quickly during the fall. Almost 1500 claims were made in the Wahmonie area, but only a few were good producers.

Five mining companies were active in Wahmonie during its short period of prominence. The major one was the Wahmonie Mines Company, incorporated on March 5, 1928, with George Wingfield, prominent in Nye County's mining history, as president. The company purchased the claims of Wahmonie's founders, McRae and Lefler, plus four other claims: Buckhorn No. 1, No. 2 and No. 3 and the Jumbo. The Hornsilver Mine was reopened and dug to a depth of 500 feet, with over 1300 feet of lateral tunnels. The ore from the mine had as much as 20 ounces of gold and 650 ounces of silver per ton. The company installed a 25-h.p. hoist and a compressor at the mine. But the excitement was short-lived, for the ore quickly ran out. The Wahmonie Mines Company struggled into 1929 but soon folded.

Another prominent company in Wahmonie was the Original Wahmonie Gold Mines Company, which purchased eight claims in the district in March 1928. These claims included two at Kane Springs, the Black Metal claims, the Big Boy, the Duke, the Little Girl, the King and the Prince Ajax. The richest of the eight was the Kane Springs group, which had two shafts (180 feet and 60 feet) and produced ore with half an ounce of gold and 36 ounces of silver per ton.

The remaining three companies were only minor contributors to Wahmonie's production total. The Wahmonie Development Company, incorporated in March 1928, purchased the Victory Six claim,

This 1928 photo shows the boom town of Wahmonie, a "flash in the pan" that faded almost as soon as it had formed. *(Nevada Historical Society)*

Wahmonie was expected to boom, at least by this office that sold lots in the town. *(Nevada Historical Society)*

half a mile south of Wahmonie. The company also leased the Buckhorn No. 3 claim from the Wahmonie Mines Company but had to give up the lease after only two months. The company was run by W. Fording, Frank Richardson and W. H. Thomas, all from Tonopah. Nothing of value came from the claims, and the company quickly faded into oblivion.

The next company that tried to scratch a profit was the Wahmonie Monterey Mines Company, formed in March 1928 with Joseph Snelson as president. The company purchased the Monterey claims and the Early Bird group. After losing its Early Bird option in July 1928, the company continued to work the Monterey claims until mid-1929. Financial troubles then forced the company to fold.

The last company to work the district was the Reorganized Booth Mining Company of Goldfield, Nevada. It was a latecomer to the district, not arriving until May 1928, a few months after the initial excitement. The company had originally been incorporated in 1912 and had a number of claims in the Goldfield district. In 1928 the company decided to expand by buying a two-year lease from Wahmonie Mines Company on the Buckhorn No. 3 claim, recently abandoned by the Wahmonie Development Company. The lease stipulated that the Booth company would receive 100,000 shares of Wahmonie Mines Company stock only after the Booth company had sunk a 300-foot shaft and completed 600 feet of branching tunnels. The Booth company fulfilled the requirements, but no worthwhile amounts of ore were uncovered and the company left the district in May 1929.

Departure of the Booth company signaled the end of Wahmonie. The post office closed on April 30, 1929; the district was practically empty by the end of 1929. Only a handful of people remained behind, patiently searching for ore that was not there. By 1931 everyone had given up and the district was abandoned.

The only substantial building ever at the townsite was a wooden boardinghouse. The site is only a few miles from Yucca Flats, the atomic testing site. Wahmonie has not had any visitors since the Las Vegas Bombing and Gunnery Range was incorporated in 1950. Now probably not even the ghosts dare to haunt the site.

This is one of the better remains at Warm Springs. Not too much of real historical interest is left in the small town.

WARM SPRINGS

DIRECTIONS:
Located on US 6, 49 miles east of Tonopah.

Warm Springs was originally a stopping place for freighters and stages traveling to Eureka and Elko. The first settler came to the site in 1866 and built a small stone house next to the warm, soothing springs. The small settlement never grew to any size, but after the turn of the century, a store and a lodging house were built here. Warm Springs continued to serve a small number of weary desert travelers. During the 1920s the town reached its peak. On Jan. 19, 1924, a post office opened at Warm Springs. Although it closed on June 29, 1929, there always was—and still is—a fairly consistent amount of travelers stopping at Warm Springs.

Today only a handful of people still live here. A combination saloon/gas station serves the residents, travelers and workers from the Keystone cyanide leaching operation. There are a number of remains from the beginnings of Warm Springs.

WASHINGTON

DIRECTIONS:
From Ione, head north on Nevada 21 for 32 miles. Exit right and follow this road, keeping to the right, for 10 miles to Washington.

Original discoveries made in 1860 in Washington Canyon were later developed as the Warner Mine. Further discoveries in 1862 and 1863 led to a fairly active rush to the area. A townsite was platted in 1863, and soon Washington had three saloons, a bakery, a livery stable, two stores and the first billiard hall in Nye County.

The Washington, or Columbus, mining district was organized in 1863. A $40,000 ten-stamp mill was built in the same year. The rush was over by late 1863; the stamp mill was closed when the flow of ore stopped. Many of the mines were not developed until the early 1870s after capitalists began to invest in the Washington mines. A number of Spanish miners continued to work a few mines, but by 1865 the mines had all closed down.

The remaining inhabitants of Washington Canyon turned to agriculture for a living. The rich soil in the canyon was excellent for root vegetables and cabbage, marketed in Austin and Ione. The abundance of trees in the canyon led to altering the stamp mill into a sawmill. It enjoyed a long production period during which time the sides of Washington Canyon were denuded of trees.

There was a small revival of silver mining during 1870. A post office was opened on July 29, 1870, but only lasted until Aug. 27, 1872. After the mines closed in late 1872, only a handful of people remained in the canyon. By the beginning of the 1880s, the entire canyon belonged to the ghosts.

The canyon remained empty until 1918, when the Warner Mining and Milling Company reopened the Warner Mine and began new operations. The company was run by A. O. Jacobson and A. P. Swoboda, both from Salt Lake City, Utah, and both were also officers in the Columbus–Rexall Mining Company and the West Toledo Mining Company. In addition, Jacobson ran his own mining company, the Jacobson Mining and Milling Company, active elsewhere in Nevada. The Warner Mining and Milling Company purchased twenty-one claims covering over 400 acres. These included three tunnel mines plus the Warner Mine shaft. The ore from the district was mainly quartz and carried high values in silver, with smaller amounts of lead and copper. The company worked the Warner Mine from the old depth of 100 feet to over 600 feet. A diesel engine was installed at the mine. A new cyanide and concentration plant was built, which utilized a crusher, rolls, tables and cyanide tanks. A 1500-foot aerial tram was strung from the Warner Mine to the mill. The company continued to operate the mine until 1922, when financial backing was withdrawn and the company folded. The canyon was then only visited by cool breezes.

The district was reopened in the early 1930s when a small revival took place. Another small mill was constructed, along with a tram that ferried the ore from the mine high up on the canyon to the mill on Washington Creek. This activity was short-lived, and by 1937 the district was once again abandoned. A small tungsten mine was worked from 1956 to 1957. Then Washington became ghostly again.

The ruins of the three mills remain in the canyon, plus a number of stone ruins left from the 1860s development. Although the remains are scant, the site is extremely interesting and is well worth the long trip. This is a great area for the ghost town enthusiast to do some uninhibited exploration; possibilities are almost unlimited.

WELLINGTON (O'Brien's)

DIRECTIONS:
Located 6 miles northeast of Gold Crater, inside the Las Vegas Bombing and Gunnery Range. Off-limits to the public.

Wellington was a short-lived mining camp established in August 1904, shortly after gold was discovered in the nearby hills. The camp of twenty-five only existed for a few months before the ore ran out. A number of buildings and a mill were built at the site. For a while the camp was known as O'Brien's, for one of the first settlers. After the camp was abandoned in early 1905, no other activity ever took place. As late as the 1920s, a number of buildings and the mill still stood. No present-day report is available because of the site's location.

WHITE CAPS

DIRECTIONS:
From Manhattan, head east for ¼ mile. Exit right onto a poor dirt road and follow for 2½ miles to White Caps.

White Caps was a small mining center a few miles from Manhattan. The White Caps area was first worked in 1915 by the White Caps Mining Company, incorporated in June 1915 with backing capital of $200,000. The company purchased two claims originally owned by the Dexter White Caps Mining Company and then built a ten-stamp mill and a 75-ton cyanide plant. During the first full year of production, the company produced a surplus of $120,000. Ore from the mine assayed from $40 to $120 a ton.

The company was reorganized in early 1918, with John G. Kirchen replacing A. G. Raycroft as president. Long litigation initiated by the Morning Glory Mining Company concerning a few rich claims were finally resolved in May 1918 in favor of the White Caps Mining Company. By 1918 the company had $100,000 ore sales but expenditures of over $250,000. The main shaft was dug to a depth of 650 feet, but the ore values sank to $10 to $13 a ton. Total production for 1918 fell to $87,000, and this trend continued as the yearly production continued to diminish.

As the shaft was dug deeper, the ore became increasingly more difficult to process. High amounts of arsenic began to appear in the ore, requiring an oxidizing roast before the ore could be put into the cyanide tanks. Plans were in motion to change the mill to accommodate the arsenic ore, but the mill closed in January 1920 and the ore was sent to other mills in Manhattan. The mine was worked periodically during the next ten years, and the shaft was eventually dug to a depth of 1300 feet. But the ore values just were not good enough to offset the milling and shipping costs, and the company closed down operations.

Another company worked the White Caps area before selling out to the White Caps Mining Company. This was the White Caps Extension Mines Company, which owned thirteen claims adjacent to the White Caps Mining Company's property. The company's most important property was a 500-foot vertical shaft run by a 50-h.p. Dendrie–Boltoff hoist and a large compressor. The property seemed very promising, but the gold ore veins were short and the company sold out at a loss. White Caps Mining continued operations on the property for a while, then ceased activity when no new major ore bodies were discovered. A flotation mill was built at the White Caps Mine in 1935 during a short revival. The mill was destroyed by fire in 1936 but the mine was still worked until 1940. Total production from

The White Caps Mine as it was in the 1920s, before the mine and mill burned down. Nothing remains of the mill, and only a gaping hole marks the mine. (William Metscher)

This was the elegant home of the White Caps Mine superintendent. The roof has recently collapsed and the house is now deteriorating.

The building to the left served as the White Caps assay office; core samples still litter the floor. At the right is the sawmill that cut lumber for mine supports.

the White Caps Mine from 1918 to 1940 was just over $2.7 million.

The White Caps property was recently purchased by Argus Resources, which reactivated the White Caps Mine in the spring of 1980. Tests show that around 20,000 tons of ore remain between 1100 feet and 1300 feet in the mine. The company also plans to dig a new shaft to follow the White Caps limestone formation. The operation looks very promising.

Remains at White Caps are very extensive and extremely interesting. Two buildings are in fairly good condition. One is the old assay office, still filled with core samples taken from the mine. The other building served as housing for the mine motors. A huge iron wedge roasting furnace marks the site, looking like a lonely sentinel. At the top of the hill behind the White Caps Mine are the remains of a house that belonged to one of the company's officers. It was fairly elegant at one time, but recently the roof has fallen in and the wood frame is quickly deteriorating. When visiting White Caps, be extremely cautious. The 1300-foot shaft of the White Caps Mine is in the open ground in front of the two remaining buildings and cannot be seen until you are right on top of it. I almost drove right into the shaft; only a hard slam of the brakes saved a long, long trip down. White Caps is a must for the ghost town hunter, with many different areas to delight the explorer.

WHITE ROCK SPRING

DIRECTIONS:
Located inside the Las Vegas Bombing and Gunnery Range, 5 miles southwest of Oak Springs.

White Rock Spring was another of the many small mining camps that sprang up during the early 1900s in southern Nye County. The small camp of ten was located at a source of fresh water. Most of the residents worked in mines in nearby Oak Springs. There was one small mine just south of the White Rock Spring camp, at Captain Jack Spring. It was never a producer, and when Oak Springs folded, so did White Rock Spring. By 1910 the site was abandoned. A present-day report on White Rock Spring is impossible because of its location.

WILLOW CREEK

DIRECTIONS:
From Nyala, head south on the Currant–Nyala Road for ½ mile. Exit left and follow for 2¾ miles to Willow Creek.

The Willow Creek mining district is in the Quinn Canyon Mountains. Willow Creek, although barely remembered, was the scene of quite a bit of activity. The first mining claim was located by Charles Sampson and David Jenkins in June 1911. They named their claim the Rustler and worked it until the middle of 1912. The Rustler claim was dormant until April 1913, when the workings were bought by George Wingfield. He began extensive mining operations and shipped over 40 tons of ore from the claim. The ore assayed at $8 in gold and $65 in silver per ton. A discovery of free gold in April 1913 created a great deal of excitement. The free gold was discovered in the Melbourn vein by Steve Pappas and W. Blackwell.

The Willow Creek mining district comprised seven separate claim groups. The first was the Gold Spring claims, located in Gold Canyon, 2 miles north of Osterlund Camp in Willow Creek Canyon. The Gold Spring group was made up of five claims that had vertical veins containing free gold laced with heavy amounts of green talc. A 25-ton mill was built in Gold Canyon in 1914 and produced $10,000 before it was closed in 1915.

The Last Chance claim was about one eighth mile west of the Gold Spring group. This claim was the property of William Wittenburg and Dr. Weller, both residents of Goldfield. A crosscut tunnel was dug to hit a 6-inch vein of gold-bearing white quartz. The claim was abandoned after the tunnel reached 175 feet without too much success.

The main development of the Willow Creek mining district was done by the Willow Creek Mining Company. It was formed by George Wingfield after he purchased the Rustler claim and five other nearby claims. The Rustler became the company's main property, with a 50-foot shaft and 120 feet of branch tunnels. The biggest shipment by the mining company took place in October 1913 when a 500-pound shipment of free gold ore returned almost $20,000. Total production for the Rustler claim was just over $50,000.

The remaining four claims—the Queen of the West, Mayflower, Melbourn and Battle Axe—were smaller workings and, except for the Melbourn

Mine, not very productive. Ore at the Battle Axe claims ran only $6.40 per ton. Activity in the Willow Creek mining district continued until late 1914, when the Willow Creek Mining Company stopped production.

The area remained dormant until 1917, when new discoveries of rich gold ore warranted reopening the district. The Gold Spring claims were purchased by the Gold Spring Mining Company, run by people living in Salt Lake City and managed by W. L. McMullen of Nyala. In addition to the claims, the company also owned a five-stamp amalgamation and concentration mill that produced concentrate worth as much as $100 per ton. The company worked the Gold Spring area until 1922, then folded.

The district was silent until 1926, when the Nyala Gold Mines Company was organized. The company purchased a gold mine adjacent to the Nevada–California Metals Corporation's properties. The gold ore removed from the mine assayed from $200 to $2000 a ton. The company also purchased the five-stamp mill previously owned by the Gold Spring Company. Nyala Gold Mines planned to build a 60-ton mill, but the ore faded before construction even started and the idea was dropped. The company folded in 1927, leaving the Nevada–California Metals Corporation as the only company working the Willow Creek district.

Nevada–California Metals was organized in 1927 and purchased eight claims at Willow Springs, including four from Steve Pappas. The gold ore, mined from a 600-foot tunnel, assayed as high as $75 a ton. After an initial investment of a few thousand dollars, the company cleared $11,000 before folding in late 1927. The last activity in the district took place in 1928 when the Gaston Gold Company began limited operations on a group of claims south of the Nevada–California claims. The company curtailed activity in late 1928 and the district was totally abandoned.

Scattered ruins remain at Willow Creek. Only one structure still stands, but piles of rubble are at the site. The Gold Spring site in Gold Canyon is marked only by small piles of tailings. The road tends to be very rough; use extreme caution.

WILSON

DIRECTIONS:
From Pine Creek, continue north on Nevada 82 for 26 miles to Wilson, located on the Monitor Ranch.

Wilson's was a small stage station on the Belmont–Eureka stageline. The station was located near the beginning of Stonebarger Creek, named after the family that ran a ranger station on the creek in Lander County. The Wilson stage station was named for Isaac J. Wilson, who later became the first postmaster. A post office opened at the site on July 18, 1898. A number of buildings were erected here, including a small ranch. The post office closed on Aug. 31, 1899. The stage run stopped after the turn of the century, but Wilson's continued on as a ranching settlement.

Today the Wilson site is known as the Monitor Ranch and is run by the Zimmerman family. In addition to newer dwellings, a few unique wood-and-mud barns still exist at the ranch.

WILSON'S CAMP

DIRECTIONS:
Located 10 miles east of Wellington, inside the Las Vegas Bombing and Gunnery Range. Off-limits to the public.

The small mining settlement of Wilson's Camp started after fairly rich gold and silver ore was discovered on the north slope of O'Donnell Mountain. The discoveries were made in May 1904, and soon a small camp of about twenty-five formed. A number of short tunnels and shallow shafts were dug, and the ore removed from these mines assayed from $110 to $180 per ton. These mines were on the Pittsburg claim group, owned by men named Reed and Slavin. The largest mine was over 300 feet deep. The ore averaged six times more silver than gold. Although the ore was rich, the problem was shipping it out. The roads to and from Wilson's Camp were extremely primitive; the ore had to be sacked and brought out by horse or sometimes a daring buckboard driver.

This difficulty put a damper on the camp's development. By July 1905 only five miners remained to work the mines. The camp did not become a complete ghost until late 1906, when all hope was given up. Because of the camp's location and the hard trek to bring in supplies, only one wooden building was ever constructed here: a fairly small, one-story boardinghouse. A number of miners lived in the boardinghouse; others did make some small stone shelters in which to live. Ten years after activity stopped in the Wilson district, not a sign was left of the small camp. The ghosts must have left the vanished camp long before the site was incorporated into the Las Vegas Bombing and Gunnery Range.

Glossary of Mining Terms

Adit A level mine opening that is driven into the side of a mountain or hill. The word is normally used interchangeably with tunnel.

Amalgamation The process of extracting gold and silver from crushed ores by merging with mercury. The mercury is later recovered through heat and used over and over again.

Arrastra A circular rock-lined pit in which broken ore is crushed by stones attached to horizontal poles that are in turn fastened to a pole in the middle. The system is turned, normally, by mules or horses.

Assay A test of ore or metal to determine the exact amount of valuable minerals contained in it.

Ball Mill An ore-crushing system that utilizes a cylindrical tube in which there are steel balls or bearings. The ore is crushed as it passes through these bearings.

Calcining Furnace A furnace for roasting ore to drive off excess sulphur before final smelting.

Chilean Mill A grinding mill with three heavy wheels in a circular pan.

Claim An area 600' × 1500' (20 acres) on public land that has been staked off and claimed by a prospector or miner.

Concentration The process by which the metallic part of ore is separated from the waste rock. The separation is done by various methods, including dry, water, oil flotation and magnetic separation.

Concentrator A type of plant that utilizes concentration to separate ores. A rocking motion, along with strong jets of water, carries off the refuse while the heavier minerals remain behind.

Counterbalance A hoisting system used in very deep shafts. The weight of the lowering car helps pull up the other car. This system may also be used in tramways that go from a mine to a mill.

Crosscut A tunnel driven at right angles to an ore body.

Cyanide Process A process used to extract gold from very finely crushed ore. A cyanide of potassium solution is used, which dissolves the gold. The gold is recovered by introducing metallic zinc into the cyanide solution.

Drift An underground passage that follows a vein or orebody.

Dry Washing A process involving separation of heavier minerals from waste by means of a vertical rocking motion.

Finisher Jigs Used to save the smaller particles of ore in a stamp mill or concentrator.

Flake Copper Very thin pieces of native copper.

Float Gold Loose ore that has broken away from the main lode.

Flotation A process by which the valuable metallic sulphide minerals are separated from the ore. The crushed ore is mixed with acid and oil, then agitated. The minerals float off, leaving the worthless refuse behind.

Free Milling Ore Ore that yields minerals by such simple means as Cyanidation or amalgamation.

Gallows Frame The timber or steel framework located over the opening of a shaft. The frame (also known as a head frame) is wrapped with a hoisting rope to bring both ore and miners up and down.

Glory Hole A large open pit from which ore is removed.

Gravity Stamp A stamp in which the piston of the stamp is raised by a cam and then is dropped by gravity.

Hardinge Mill A cone-shaped cylinder that rests horizontally and is half filled with small rocks. The ore is crushed as the mill is revolved.

Horse Whim A windlass operated by horses. Used in very small operations.

Huntington Mill Almost identical to the *Chilean Mill*.

Jig A machine used in concentrating ore by means of a vibratory motion, which is aided by strong streams of water to carry off the refuse. Heavier minerals sink to the bottom.

Nissen Mill This mill utilized an individual stamp worked in its own circular mortar box to crush rock to sand size.

Placer Mining This type of mining extracts a heavy mineral that is trapped in gravel or dirt by exposing the mineral to a hard stream of water.

Reverberatory Furnace A smelting furnace in which an extremely hot flame is put on the ore from below and is reflected back from the roof onto the top of the ore.

Roasting A process of cooking ore to release sulphur and other volatile elements. Also known as calcining.

Stoping A process by which an orebody is broken down above a drift. This process allows miners to break the ore much quicker.

Stetefeldt Furnace A furnace used for chloridizing and roasting silver ores and also for roasting fine copper ores low in sulphur.

Tailings The gravelly or rocky refuse left from a mill's operations. Some small operations also left tailing piles, heaps of ore of lower quality, not necessarily worthless.

Tube Mill A steel cylinder half-lined with steel balls is the basic concept of the Tube Mill. Rotating the tube crushed the ore.

Windlass A device for hoisting from a shaft, by means of wrapping a large rope or cable around a drum with crank handles on it.

Bibliography

The books listed below represent only the major sources used in compiling this book. Countless manuscripts, files and personal interviews also served as excellent references, but to list all of these other sources would be much too lengthy.

UNITED STATES GEOLOGICAL SURVEY BULLETINS

Ball, S. H., *A Geological Reconnaissance in Southwestern Nevada and Eastern California*, Bulletin 308.

Emmons, William, *Reconnaissance of Mining Camps in Nevada*, Bulletin 408.

Ferguson, Henry, *Geology and Ore Deposits of the Manhattan District, Nevada*, Bulletin 723.

Hill, James, *Mining Districts of Western United States*, Bulletin 507

———, *Mining Districts—California and Nevada*, Bulletin 594.

Ransome, Frederick, *Preliminary Account of Goldfield, Bullfrog and Other Mining Districts in Southern Nevada*, Bulletin 303.

———, *Bullfrog District, Nevada*, Bulletin 407.

Spurr, Josiah, *Geology of Nevada South of the Fortieth Parallel*, Bulletin 208.

UNIVERSITY OF NEVADA PUBLICATIONS

Armstrong, Robert D., *A Preliminary Union Catalogue of Nevada Manuscripts*, 1967.

Carlson, Helen S., *Nevada Place Names*, University of Nevada Press, 1974.

Couch, B. F., and J. A. Carpenter, *Nevada's Metal and Mineral Production, No. 38.* 1943.

Kral, Victor, *Mineral Resources of Nye County, Nevada.* Geology and Mining Series, No. 50, 1951.

Vanderburg, W. O., *Placer Mining in Nevada.* Geology and Mining Series, No. 27, 1936.

OTHER SOURCES

Ashbaugh, Don, *Nevada's Turbulent Yesterday, A Study in Ghost Towns*, Westernlore Press, 1963.

Averett, Walter R., *Directory of Southern Nevada Place Names*, privately printed, 1962.

Beebe, Lucius M., and Charles Clegg, *U.S. West, the Saga of Wells Fargo*, E. P. Dutton & Company, 1949.

Bruner, Firmin, *Some Remembered . . . Some Forgot. Life in Central Nevada Mining Camps*, Nevada State Park Natural History Association, 1974.

Cook, Fred S., *Legends of Nye County*, privately published.

Davis, Sam P., *The History of Nevada*, 2 volumes. Elms Publishing Company, 1965.

Florin, Lambert, *Ghost Towns of the West*, Superior Publishing, 1971.

Fox, Theron, *Nevada Treasure Hunters Ghost Town Guide*, Harlan-Young Press, 1961.

Harris, Robert P., *Nevada Postal History*, privately published, 1973.

Kelly, J. Wells, *First Directory of Nevada Territory (1862)*, Talisman Press, 1962.

Labbe, Charles, *Rocky Trails of the Past*, privately published, 1960.

Lincoln, Francis Church, *Mining Districts and Mineral Resources of Nevada,* Nevada Newsletter Publishing Company, 1923.

Lingenfelter, Richard E., *The Newspapers of Nevada,* John Howell Books, 1964.

Mack, Effie, *Nevada,* Arthur Clark, 1936.

Murbarger, Nell, *Ghosts of the Glory Trail,* Desert Magazine Press, 1956.

Myrick, David, *Railroads of Nevada and Eastern California,* Volume Two, Howell-North Books, 1963.

Paher, Stanley, *Nevada Ghost Towns and Mining Camps,* Howell-North Books, 1970.

Stevens, Horace, *The Copper Handbook—A Manual of the Copper Industry of the United States and Foreign Countries,* Volumes 2, 3, 4, 5, 6, 7, 8, 9, 10, the Government Printing Office.

Weed, Walter, *The Copper Handbook—A Manual of the Copper Mining Industry of the World,* Volume II, 1912–13, the Government Printing Office.

———, *The Mines Handbook and Copper Handbook,* Volumes 12, 13, 14, 15, 16, 17, 1916–26, the Government Printing Office.

Weight, Harold and Lucile, *Rhyolite, the Ghost City of Golden Dreams.* Calico Press, 1953.

Writers' Program, *Nevada, A Guide to the Silver State,* Binfords & Mort Publishers, 1940.

Index

Asterisk (*) indicates towns highly recommended by the author

Adams, John, 36–37
Adaven, 5
Advertiser (Ione), 53
Airshaft Mine, 76
Aladdin Divide Mining Co., 9
Ala-Mar Magnesium Co., 33
Alexander Co., 47
Alexander Mine, 47, 48
Allen, F. P., 35
Allen, Henry, 52
Allred, 5
Amargosa, 5–6. *See also* Original
Amargosa City, 25, 99
American Carrara Marble Co., 29
American Eagle Mine, 76
Anaconda Mining Co., 63
Ancram, 6
*Antelope, 6
Antelope Mines Co., 7
Antelope Springs, 6–7
Antelope View Mine, 7
Antimony mining, 74
Appache Hannapah Mines Co., 49–50
Arctic Mine, 55
Argentore, *see* Jett
Argonaut Mine, 33
Argus Resources, 71, 143
Arizona Mine, 14
Arrowhead, 7–8
Arrowhead Annex Mining Co., 8
Arrowhead Bonanza Mining Co., 8
Arrowhead Consolidated Mining Co., 8
Arrowhead Esperanza Mines Co., 8
Arrowhead Extension Mining Co., 7–8
Arrowhead Inspiration Mines Co., 8
Arrowhead Mining Co., 7, 8
Arrowhead Syndicate Mines Co., 8
Arrowhead Wonder Mines Co., 8
Ashmeadow, 8–9

Ashton, 9
Athens, 9
Atwood, 9, 46
Auriferous Mine, 7
Auto-stages, 5, 32, 46, 99

Bailey, Edith, 28
Bailey brothers (miners), 6–7
Baird, Jules, 40
Ballinger, W. S., 82
Bannock, *see* Hannapah
*Barcelona, 10
Barcelona Mine, 10
Bare Mountain, 40
Barieu, Walter C., 68
Barium mining, 38
Barnes, Thomas, 55
Barnes, T. J., 76
Barnes Park, *see* Jackson Mining District
Barrett, 11
Barrett, J. T., 11
Bart, J. I., 64
Bartlett, *see* Northumberland
Battle Axe Mine, 143–44
Baumann's, *see* Minnimum's
Baxter's, *see* Baxter Spring
Baxter Spring, 11
Bay State Mine, 76
*Beatty, 11–12
Beatty, Alexander, 27, 129
Beatty, Montillus Murray (Jim), 11–12, 13
Beatty Bullfrog Miner, 12
Bell (state senator), 20
Bell, Billie, 20
Bellehelen, 13–14
Bellehelen Consolidated Mines Co., 14
Bellehelen Development Corp. 14
Bellehelen Extension Mining Co., 14
Bellehelen Merger Mines Co., 14

*Belmont, xiii, 14–20, 54
Belmont Courier, 15–16
Belmont Mine, 14, 17, 124
Belmont Silver Mining Co., 15
Benton, Donald, 39
*Berlin, 20–21
Berlin-Ichthyosaur State Park, 20, 137
Berlin Mine, 20, 136
Berrheimer, Max, 134
Berryman, E., 74
Best Chance Mine, 109
Betts, B. F., 109
Big Henry Gold Mining Co., 35, 36
Black Diamond Mine, 76
Black Dog Mine, 44
Black Hawk Mine (Manhattan), 66
Black Hawk Mine (Morey), 76
Black Spring, 21
Blackwell, W., 143
Blake's Camp, 22
Blanchard, Benjamin, 75
Blue Bell Mine, 78
Blue Eagle Mine, 46, 129, 130
Blue Eagle Spring, 22
Blue Horse Mining Co., 113
Blue Jacket Mine, 107
Bluth, John, 111
Boardmen, Russell, 50
Bob, *see* Lodi
Bodrow, Louis, 16
Bonanza, 99
Bonita, 22
*Bonnie Clare, 22–24
Bonnie Clare Bullfrog Mining Co., 22
Booth, E. M. and Mabel, 88–89
Booth, John, 15–16
Booth, W. W., 121, 124–25
Boston Mine, 33
Bowler, Fred, 24
Bowler Mine, 24
Bowlerville, 24
Bradford Siding, Calif., 8
Bradley, Frank, 55
Bradshaw, Mark G., 37
Brady, S. H., 56
Branigan, T. F., 37
Brannan, D. M., 132
Brock, John, 100, 122
Brohilco Silver Corp., 39
Broken Hills, 91
Broken Hills Silver Corp., 86
Brong, "Alkali Bill," 5
Brooklyn, 106
Brooklyn Mine, 47, 48
Browne, Frederick, 49
Browne's Camp, 24
Bruner, *see* Phonolite
Bruner, Bill, 85–86
Bryan, W. C., 42
Buckboard Mine, 121

Buckeye Mining Co., 84
Bullfrog, 6, 24–27, 42, 99
Bullfrog-Goldfield Railroad, 6, 12, 13, 22, 23, 42, 51, 55, 93, 100, 104, 110, 114, 115
Bullfrog Mine, 82
Bullfrog Miner, 12–13, 25–26, 100
Bull Moose Mining and Milling Co., 40
Bunker Hill Mine, 44
Burmball Mine, 82
Burmeister, J., 82
Burn, Thomas, 47
Burns, Tom, 46
Burro Mine, 121
Butler, *see* Tonopah
Butler, Jim, xiii, 17, 93, 120–21, 124, 128
Butler, J. W. S., 37
Butler Mine, 9
Butterfield Marsh, 27
Butterfield Spring, 27

Cactus Consolidated Silver Mines Co., 27
Cactus Leona Silver Corp., 27–28
Cactus Nevada Silver Mines Co., 27
Cactus Range Gold Mining Co., 28
Cactus Silver Mine, 28
Cactus Springs, 6, 27–28
Calico Quartz Mountain Mining Co., 92
Cameron Mill, 17, 18, 19
Cambridge Silver Mining Co., 80
Canfield, R. B., 16
Canyon, 28–29
Carr, C. J., 120
Carrara, 29, 31
Carrara Marble Co., 31
Carrara Mining, Milling and Leasing Syndicate, 40
Carrara Obelisk, 29
Carrolton, *see* Upper Town
Carr's Camp, 119
Carson, Kit, 110
Casamayou, Andrew, 15
Casket Mine, 132
Cedar Mine, 76
Cedar Spring, 30. *See also* Baxter Spring
Cemeteries
    at Berlin, 20–21
    at Bullfrog, 27
    at Currant, 33
    at Ophir Canyon, 82
    at Rhyolite, 105
Centennial Mine, 57, 58
Centers, John, 132
Central, 30
Central City, 30
Charlestown, 30
Chief Kawich Mine, 60
Chispa Mine, 58
Chloride, 30–31
Chloride Mine, 7
Chloride Mining District, *see* Danville
Cimerron, *see* Potomac

Cinnabar, *see* Mercury mining
Cipac Mine, 95
Cirac, Louie, 136
Cirac Mill, 136
Clair, *see* Bonnie Clare
Clare, *see* Bonnie Clare
Clark, H. H., 26
Clark, Jack, 110
Clark, J. J., 49
Clark, J. Ross, 100
Clark, J. S., 114
Clark, Nehemiah, 72
Clark, William A., 100
Clarkdale, 119
Clay mining, 6, 8, 9
Clear Creek, *see* Antelope
Clemens, Earle R., 103-4
Clifford, 31-32, 51
Clifford, Edward, 31
Clifford, James, 31
Clifford, Joe, 41, 45
Clifford Gold Mines Co., 31
Clifford Mine, 31, 32
Clifford Silver Mines Co., 31
Cliff Spring, 60
Clifton Mine, 129
Clipper Mine, 41
Cloverdale, 32
Coen Companies, Inc., 6
Combination Mill, 15, 17, 18, 19
Congress Mine, 58, 59
Consolidated Mayflower Mine Co., 87
Continental Mines Co., 33
Cook, Fred S., 59
Copper mining
　at Currant, 32
　at Greenwater, Calif., 5
　at Jamestown, 55
　at Oak Springs, 79-80
　at Orizaba, 83
　at Paradise Peak, 83
　at Shamrock, 111
　at Stirling, 115
　at Tonopah, 125
　at Troy, 129
　at Washington, 140
Corehay, Frank, 7
Corlett, J. L., 39
Cortez, J. P., 88
Cotter Mines Co., 44
Courbat Mine, 22
Crabtree, Lotta, 20
Craig Station, 32
Crescent Mine, 44
Crockers Ranch, *see* Antelope
Cross, Eddie, 99
Cross, Ernest L., 25, 82
Crown Point Globe Mine, 59, 60
Crow Springs, 121
Crucible Gold Mining and Milling Co., 37

Currant, 32-33
Curtis, S. A., 76

Daggett, 59
Daisy Mine, 107
Danville, 6, 33-34
Darrough, James T., 34
Darrough Hot Springs, 34
Davenport, John, 57
Davis, Jack, 31
Davis, Okey, 9
Dayton Consolidated Mill, 9
Death Valley and Tonopah and Tidewater Railroad, 8, 9
Death Valley Clay Co., 8
Death Valley Magazine
Death Valley Prospector, 100
DeGrout, Henry, 53
DeLamar Lode, 68
Denver Mine, 102
Desert Chief Consolidated Mining Co., 117
Desert Queen Mine, 121, 125
Dexter White Caps Mining Co., 141
Diamondfield Black Butte Reorganized Mining Co., 82
Diamond No. 2 Mine, 60
Dignon, John, 16
Diminick Mine, 134
Divide Mining Co., 45
Dixon, Bob, 20, 136
Doctor Mine, 83
Donald, Sam, 16
Downey, P., 34
Downeyville, *see* Downieville
Downeyville Nevada Mines, Inc., 35
*Downieville, 34
Downieville Mine, 34, 35
Duckwater, 35
Duluth, 35-36
Duluth Gold Mining Co., 35, 36
Duluth Tribune, 36

Earp, Wyatt, 121
Earthquakes, 68, 111
East Belmont, 17, 18-19
East Golden Mine, 44
East Manhattan, 36
Eckley, Joseph, 53
Eclipse Mine, 102
Eden, 36-37, 51
Eden Creek Mining and Milling Co., 37
Eden Mine, 37
Ekstrom, Jack, 33
Elggren, L. E., 111
Elgin-Bellehelen Divide Mining Co., 14
Elizalde Co., 29
Ellendale, 37-39
Ellendale Mine, 38
Ellendale Star, 38
Ellsworth, 34, 39
Elsa Mining Co., 57

Emerson, John, 76
Esta Buena Mine, 39
Eucalyptus Mine, 33
Eureka Johnnie Gold Mining Co., 59
Eva, Sam, 83
Exchequer Quartz Mountain Mining Co., 92

Fairbanks, R. J. "Dad," 8, 39
Fairbanks Ranch, 39–40
Fairchild, Oscar and M. D., 15
Fairplay Prospector, 9
Fairview Extension Mining Co., 107
Fairview Round Mountain Mines Co., 107
Farcher, Charles Ira, 41
Farnsworth, Dr. A., 43
Farrington, Irving, 135
Farris, William H., 45, 95
Feenaman (miner), 20
Fenwick, J. M., 21
Ferguson, E. B. K., 79
Ferguson, Robert, 56
Feutsh, Carl, 55
Fisherman Mine, 96
Fitch, Thomas, 15
Flagstaff Mine, 39
Fluorine, 40, 119
Fording, W., 139
Fork's Station, *see* Stonewall
Fox, Pete, 8
Francisco, Barney, 44
Franz Hammel Mine, 55
Frazier Springs, *see* Frazier Wells
Frazier Wells, 40–41
Freight lines, *see* Stagelines
Frémont, John C., 34, 110
French, W. H., 8
Fresno, *see* Georges Canyon
Fulton, Hugh, 112

Gabbard, John, 129
Gabbs, 20
Gally, Dr. (miner), 132
Garside, Frank F., 67, 125
Gaston Gold Co., 144
Gates, Humboldt, 67
Gayhart, William, 120
General Lee Mine, 39
Geneva Mine, 44
Georges Canyon, 41
Gerard, James W., 119
Giant Claim, 84
Gibraltar Mine, 102
Gibraltar Silver Hill Mining Co., 58
Gila Mill, *see* Reveille Mill
Gila Mine, 96
Gila Silver Mining Co., 96
Gilbert, H. L., 119
Gilbert brothers, 137
Gilbert Clifford Gold Mines Co., 31
Gillett, M. V. B., 132

Glen Hamilton, 41
Godwaldt, William M., 67
Gold Bar, 41–42
Gold Bar Mine, 44
Gold Belt, *see* Eden
Gold Center, 6, 42–43
Gold Center Ice and Brewing Co., 42
Gold Center News, 42
Gold Center Water and Mills Co., 43
Gold Crater, 43
Golden, 43–44
Golden Arrow, 13, 22, 44–45
Golden Arrow and Keystone Co., 96
Golden Arrow Mining Co., 44
Golden Arrow Mohawk Mining Co., 44
Golden Chariot Mining Co., 55
Golden Eagle Mine, 37, 109
Golden Eagle Mining and Milling Co., 86
Golden Lion Mining Co., 66
Goldfield, 7
Goldfield Blue Bell Mining Co., 20
Goldfield Consolidated Mines Co., 7, 80
Goldfield Quartz Mountain Mining Co., 91–92
Gold Flat, 45
Gold Hill, 45
Gold Hill Consolidated Mines Co., 45
Gold Hill Development Co., 45
Gold Hill Mine, 45
Gold Hill Mining Co., 45
Gold mining
    at Antelope Springs, 6–7
    at Athens, 9
    at Atwood, 9
    at Baxter Spring, 11
    at Bellehelen, 13–14
    at Berlin, 20
    at Blake's Camp, 22
    at Bonnie Clare, 22–23
    at Cactus Springs, 27–28
    at Central, 30
    at Central City, 30
    at Clifford, 31–32
    at Currant, 32
    at Danville, 33
    at Duluth, 35, 36
    at Eden, 37
    at Ellendale, 37–38
    at Ellsworth, 39
    at Georges Canyon, 41
    at Gold Crater, 43
    at Golden, 43
    at Golden Arrow, 44, 45
    at Gold Hill, 45
    at Goldyke, 46
    at Grant City, 46
    at Grantsville, 46–47, 48
    at Hannapah, 50
    at Harriman, 51
    at Jackson Mining District, 55
    at Jamestown, 55

154

Gold mining *(cont.)*
    at Johnnie, 58–59
    at Johnnie Mine, 60
    at Kawich, 60–61
    at Liberty, 63
    at Lodi, 65
    at Longstreet, 66
    at Manhattan, 70
    at Mellan, 73
    at Mexican Camp, 73
    at Millett, 74
    at Morey, 76
    at North Manhattan, 77
    at Oak Springs, 79
    at Orizaba, 82–83
    at Pactolus, 83
    at Paradise Peak, 83
    at Penelas, 85
    at Phonolite, 85–86
    at Pioneer, 86–88
    at Pueblo, 91
    at Ray, 93
    at Rhyolite, 102–3
    at Round Mountain, xiii, 106, 108
    at Shamrock, 111
    at Silver Bow, 112–13
    at Stirling, 115
    at Stonewall, 118
    at Tolicha, 119–20
    at Tonopah, 121–28
    at Trappman's Camp, 129
    at Troy, 129
    at Union, 135
    at Wahmonie, 137–39
    at Wellington, 141
    at White Caps, 141
    at Willow Creek, 143–44
    at Wilson's Camp, 144
Gold Mountain, 15, 22, 23
Gold Park, *see* Jackson Mining District
*Gold Point, 45–46
Gold Prince Mining and Leasing Co., 43
Gold Reed, *see* Kawich
Gold Reed Mining Co., 60–61
Gold Spring Mining Co., 144
Goldyke, 46
Goldyke Daily Sun, 46
Gold Zone Divide Mining Co., 45
Good Hope Mine, 96
Good Luck Mine, 7
Gordon, L. D., 85
Gordon, Louis, 106, 107
Gordon, *see* Round Mountain
Grand View Mine, 111
*Grant City, 46
*Grantsville, xiii, 46–49
Grantsville Bonanza, 47
Grantsville Sun, 47
Grapevine Springs, 60
Graveyards, *see* Cemeteries

Gray, William, 49, 114
Green and Oder Mine, 15
Greenwater, Calif., 5
Gresham Gold Mining Co., 28

Hafen, Joseph, 130–31
Hage, Wayne, 86
Hale (investor), 31
Halifax-Tonopah Mining Co., 124
Hannapah, 49–50, 114
Hannapah Divide Extension Mines Co., 49
Hannapah Mine, 49, 50
Hannapah Silver Star Mining Co., 50
Hanson, J. W., 114
Happy Kelly Mine, 23
Hard Luck Mine, 22
Harriman, 50–51
Harris, Frank "Shorty," 24–25, 82, 99
Harvey, Eric, 119
Hatch, A. T., 39
Havens, P. A., 46, 53, 111
Hawes Canyon, 13
Hawthorne News, 125
Heisler, Mrs. H. H., 105
Helena, *see* Clifford
Hick's Hot Springs, 51
Hick's Station, 51
Highbridge Mill, 18
Highbridge Mine, 17
Homestake Mine, 42
Hooper, Albert, 116–17
Hooper, Tim, 116–17
Hooten, William, 48
Hornsilver Mine, 137, 138
Horseshoe, 51
Horseshutem Springs, 59
Horton, Martin "Pop," 22, 118
*Hot Creek, 51–52
Hot Creek Ranch Co., 52
Hot Creek Syndicate Trust, 52
Hot Springs, *see* Darrough Hot Springs
Howard, Frank, 7
Hudson Mining and Milling Co., 109
Hughes, Howard, 125
Humphrey, John C., 66
Hyland, Tom, 95

Idlewild, 52
Idlewild Mine, 57
Illinois Mine, 64, 65
Illinois Nevada Mines Corp., 64, 65
Indiana Mines Exploration Co., 88
Indianapolis Mine, 111
Indians, *see* Shoshone Indians
Indian Spring, 52
Indian Springs, 53, 82
*Ione (Ione City), xiii, 14, 53–54
Iron Mercury Mining Co., 112
Irwin, *see* Central City
Irwin, F. L., 30

155

Jackson, "Stonewall," 117
Jackson Mining District, 54–55
Jacksonville, 55
Jacobson, A. O., 140
Jamestown, 55
*Jefferson, 56–57
Jefferson Gold and Silver Mining Co., 56
Jenkins, David, 143
Jett, 57–58
Jim Graham's Camp, see Paradise Peak
Johnnie, 5, 58–59
Johnnie Consolidated Mining Co., 59
*Johnnie Mine, 58, 59–60
Johnnie Station, see Amargosa
Johns, R. L., 8
Johnson, A. P., 60
Johnson, Bob, 20
Johnson, D. S., 20
Johnson, Edward, 112
Johnson, John, 56
Johnson family (ranchers), 118
Joliet Mine, 96
Jordan (miner), 119
Jordan brothers (miners), 7
Junction, 60

Kanrobat, C. J., 56
Kansas City-Nevada Consolidated Mines Co., 86
Kawich, 60–61
Kawich Consolidated Co., 44
Keller, Frank, 109
Kendall, John, 7, 27
Kennedy Tellurium Mines Co., 28
Keyser Mine, 76
*Keystone, 45, 61–62
Keystone-Hot Creek Mining Co., 134
Keystone Mine, 61
Kiernon, J. B., 40
Kirchen, John G., 141
Kirpatrick, John, 64
Kismet Mining Co., 40
Kleinstick, H. B., 120
*Knickerbocker, 62
Knickerbocker Mill, 62
Knox, Charles E., 119
Kusic, Matt, 59

LaBarthe, Engrace, 55
Labbe, Charles, 60
Labbe Camp, see Johnnie Mine
Lafayette Mine, 132
Landers (rancher), 11
Landmark Mine, 119
La Plata Mining Co., 84, 85
Las Vegas and Tonopah Railroad, 5, 12, 13, 22, 23, 24, 29, 30–31, 42, 43, 59, 73, 77, 82, 93, 100, 102, 104, 106, 110, 115–16, 117
Las Vegas Bombing and Gunnery Range sites
    Antelope Springs, 6–7
    Cactus Springs, 28
    Cedar Spring, 30
    Gold Crater, 43
    Indian Spring, 52
    Jamestown, 55
    Kawich, 60–61
    Mellan, 73
    Oak Springs, 79–80
    Sulphide, 118
    Tolicha, 119–20
    Trappman's Camp, 129
    Wahmonie, 137–39
    Wellington, 141
    White Rock Spring, 143
    Wilson's Camp, 144–45
Lauville, 6, 62–63
Lawrence Mine, 51
Lead mining
    at Currant, 32
    at Downieville, 34
    at Jett, 58
    at Liberty, 63
    at Orizaba, 83
    at Quartz Mountain, 91
    at Ray, 95
    at Reveille, 96
    at Shamrock, 111
    at Tonopah, 125
    at Troy, 129
    at Tybo, 132, 133, 135
    at Washington, 140
Learnville, see Learville
Learville, 63
Lease Mine, 93
Lee, Calif., 63
Leeland, 63
Lefler, Mark, 137, 138
Liberty, 63
Liberty mines
    in Old Reveille, 96
    in Potomac, 88
    in San Antonio, 110
Life Preserver claims, 119
Liliuokalani, Queen, 84
Lindsay, James, 63
Linka, S. H., 111
Lippincott Mine, 23
Lisbon Mine, 39
Little Fish Lake Valley, 6
Little Giant Mine, 76
Locke, Eugene and Sarah, 64
*Lockes, 64
Lock Mine, 129, 130, 131
Lode (Ellendale), 38
*Lodi, 64–66
Lodi Tanks, see Lodi
Logan, J. A., 119
Logan, Thomas W., 67–68
Lognoz Ranch, 60
Longstreet, 66
Longstreet, Jack, 20, 66

156

Louisiana Consolidated Mining Co., 134
Love, William, 132
Lowe, Deke, 59
Lower Town, 66
Lucky Boy Divide Mining Co., 9
Lynch, Walter, 49

McCarthy (investor), 31
McCrea, W. R., 137
McGarry, Len, 99
McIntyre, Charles, 16
McIntyre Mine, 111
Mack, Thomas, 47
McKane Mine, 124
McKenna, Dan, 12
McKeon, Sam, 39
McMullen, W. L., 144
McNamara, H., 9
McRae, W. R., 137, 138
McVeigh, M. J., 7
Magazines, 100
Magnesite mining, 32–33
Magnolia Mine, 76
Mahoney, T. L., 113
Mammoth, *see* Ellsworth
Mammoth Gold Mining Co., 70
*Manhattan, xiii, 30, 36, 66–72
Manhattan Big Four Mining Co., 69
Manhattan Consolidated Mine Development Co., 69
Manhattan Copper Mining and Milling Co., 70
Manhattan Dexter Mining Co., 70
Manhattan Gold Dredging Co., 70
Manhattan Magnet, 67
Manhattan Mail, 67
Manhattan Mustang Mining Co., 70
Manhattan Post, 67
Manhattan Red Top Mining Co., 70
Manhattan Sunrise Mining Co., 70
Manhattan Times, 67
Manhattan Union Amalgamated Mines Syndicate, 69–70
Mannix, Frank, 25
Manse Ranch, 72–73
Mansfield, P. W., 33
Marble, *see* Lodi
Marble mining, 29
Martel, Albert, 61
Martel, Robert, 61
Mascot Mine, 44
Maute, Andrew, 16
Mayette family, 136
Mayfield, Earl, 110
Mayflower mines
    in Pioneer, 86, 87
    in Willow Creek, 143–44
Meikeljohn, 73
Meikeljohn, George D., 73
Melbourn Mine, 143–44
Mellan, 73
Mellan, Jess and Hazel, 73

Mellan Gold Mines Group, 73
Menzel, Joseph, 27
Mercury (cinnabar) mining
    at Fluorine, 40
    at Ione, 54
    at Paradise Peak, 83–84
    at Shamrock, 111–12
    at Van Ness, 137
Mercury Mining Co., 54
Meridian Mine, 46
Merrill, S., 47
Mexican Camp, 73
Midas, 52, 73
Midway, 73
Mighels, Roy, 67
Miller, J. H., 69
Millett, 73–74
Millett, Albion Bradbury, 74
Milone, Kathie, 59
Milton, 74
Mine Selections Co., 83
Mining, xiii, 21, 27, 29, 32–33, 38, 58, 74, 79, 80, 93, 125. *See also* Clay; Copper; Gold; Lead; Mercury; Silver; Turquoise
*Minnimum's, 74
Mizpah Hotel, 124, 128
Mizpah Mine, 121, 125
Mohawk Mine, 66
Molybdenum mining, xiii, 125
Monarch, 75
Monarch Tribune, 75
Monitor, *see* Northumberland
Monitor-Belmont Mill, 15, 18
Monitor-Belmont Mine, 14, 17
Monitor Belmont Mining Co., 17
Monitor Mine, 78
Monitor Park racetrack, 19
Monitor Ranch, 144
Montana Station, *see* Bonnie Clare
Montana-Tonopah Mine, 121
Monte Cristo, *see* Tolicha
Monterey Mine, 76
Montgomery, *see* Johnnie
Montgomery, Bob, 12, 99, 102
Montgomery-Shoshone Mine, 102
Moore, Anna B., 99, 105
*Moore's Station, 75–76
Morey, 76
Morey Mill, 33
Morey Mining Co., 76
Mormon Well, *see* Nyala
Morning Call Mine, 39
Morning Glory Mining Co., 141
Morristown, *see* Reveille, New
Mountain Champion, 15
Mount Airy Mine, 76
Mount Vernon Mine, 39
Mud Spring Station, 77
Muncey, William, 76
Murphy, John, 80

157

Murphy Mine, 80, 81, 82
Murray, P. H., 45
Musick, E. L., 116

National Bank Mine, 102
National Merger Gold Mines Co., 7
Nature Products Co., 21
Nay, Ellen Clifford, 37
Needles, see Arrowhead
Neff, Walter, 86
Nevada Bellehelen Mining Co., 13
Nevada-California Metals Corp., 144
Nevada Co., 20, 62
Nevada Gold Development Co., 107–8
Nevada Goldfield Mining Co., 22
Nevada Gold Sight Mining Co., 51
Nevada Historical Society, 19, 71
Nevada Mining Co., 55
Nevada National Co., 84, 85
Nevada Operating Co., 82
Nevada Ophir Mining Co., 81
Nevada Porphyry Gold Mines Co., 108
Nevada Smelting and Mines Corp., 133–34
Nevada Wonder Mining Co., 17
Never-Sweat Mine, 13
New Bonnie Clare Mining and Milling Co., 23
New Goldfield Sierra Mining Co., 117
New Original Bullfrog Mines Co., 82
Newspapers
  in Atwood, 9
  in Beatty, 12–13
  in Belmont, 15–16
  in Bullfrog, 25–26
  in Carrara, 29
  in Duluth, 36
  in Ellendale, 38
  in Gold Center, 42
  in Goldyke, 46
  in Grantsville, 47
  in Ione, 53
  in Manhattan, 67
  in Monarch, 75
  in Pioneer, 86
  in Quartz Mountain, 91
  in Reveille, 96
  in Rhyolite, 99–100, 103–4
  in Round Mountain, 106
  in Silver Bow, 112–13
  in Stirling, 116
  in Tonopah, 121, 124–25
  in Transvaal, 129
  in Tybo, 132
Nicholl, George, 66
Nicklin, C. W., 12, 13
Nixon, see Gold Flat
Nixon, George, 112
North Manhattan, 77
North Star mines
  in Jackson Mining District, 55
  in Paradise Peak, 83

  in Shamrock, 111
  in Tonopah, 121
*Northumberland, 63, 77–78
Northumberland Cave, xiv, 78
Northumberland Mining Co., 78
Nyala, 79–80
Nyala Gold Mines Co., 144
Nye, J. W., xiii
Nye County News, 53
Nyopolis, see Transvaal

Oak Springs, 79–80
Oak Springs Copper Co., 79
Oatman United Gold Mining Co., 9
O'Brien's, see Wellington
Oddie, Tasker, 86, 120, 121
Okey Davis, see Atwood
Old Diamond Queen Mine, 40
Old English Gold Corp., 129
Oldfield, Ed, 59
Oldham, J. W., 14
Ophir Canyon, xiii, 80–82
Ophir Canyon Mining Co., 82
Ophir City, see Ophir Canyon
Ore City Mining Co., 115
Original, 82
Original Bullfrog Mine, 82
Original Horseshoe Mine, 51
Original Mining Co., 70
Original Wahmonie Gold Mines Co., 138
Orion, see Original
Orizaba, 82–83
Orizaba Mining and Development Co., 82, 83
Oro Cache Mining and Milling Co., 37
Osterlund, C. L., 8
Ostorside, see Lockes
Overfield Mining Co., 60

Pacific States Mining Co., 14
Pactolus, 83
Padgett, Al, 59
Page, M. N., 69
Page brothers (miners), 44
Palmer, E. E., 106
Palmer's Well, see Rose's Well
Panama Mine, 40
Pappas, Steve, 143, 144
Paradise Peak, 83–84
Paradise Peak Mining Co., 83
Park Canyon, 84–85
Parman (miner), 20
Patty, Joseph, 80
Paymaster Mine, 86
Peavine, 85
Peavine, Johnny, 31
Penelas, 85
Penelas, Severino, 85
Penelas Mining Co., 85
Peoria Mine, 39
Perkins, P. V., 29

Peter, Celia, 136
Petry, William, 27
Phillips Mine, 111
Phonolite, 85–86
Phonolite Paymaster Mining Co., 86
Phonolite Silent Friend Mining Co., 86
Pine Creek, 86
Pine Creek Ranch, 117
Pioneer, 86–88
Pioneer Consolidated Mines Co., 87
Pioneer Mine, 86, 87
Pioneer Press, 86
Pioneer Topics, 86
Polaris Mine, 102
Polygamy Well, *see* Nyala
Porter, Bill, 99
Porter, George, 39
Porter, H. D., 100
Porter, L. D., 100
Porter, W. R., 49
Potomac, 88–89
*Potts, 89–90
Potts, William, 89
*Pritchard's Station, 90
Prussian Mine, 56
Publications, *see* Magazines; Newspapers
Pueblo, 90–91

*Quartz Mountain, 91–93, 119
Quartz Mountain Miner, 91
Quartz Mountain Mines and Milling Co., 93
Queen of the West Mine, 143–44
Quigley, George, 114
Quincy, *see* Royston
Quintero Co., 63, 77
Quintero Mine, 17

Ragsdale (publisher), 132
Railroads
  in Beatty, 12
  in Carrara, 29
  Danville–Eureka, 33
  terminus in Gold Center, 42
  from Tonopah, 38, 44, 122
  wreck at Bonnie Clare, 23
  See also Bullfrog-Goldfield; Death Valley and Tonopah and Tidewater; Las Vegas and Tonopah; San Pedro, Los Angeles and Salt Lake; Santa Fe; Southern Pacific; Tonopah and Goldfield; Tonopah and Tidewater; Western Pacific
Railroad Valley Co., 27
Ralston, 93
Rattlesnake Mine, 22
Ray, 40, 93–95
Ray, L. O., 40, 93
Ray and O'Brien Gold Mining Co., 93
Raycroft, A. G., 141
Raymond Van Ness Mining Co., 38, 137
Red Lion Consolidated Mines Co., 117
Red Top Mining Co., 70

Reece, William, 137
Reed (miner), 144
Reed, O. K., 60, 86
Reese River Reveille, 96
Reinmiller, John, 83
Reischke, Herman and Alvena, 79
Reno Evening Gazette, 116
Reorganized Booth Mining Co., 139
Reorganized Pioneer Mines Co., 87, 88
Republic, 95
Return Mining Co., 39
Reveille, 8, 45
  New, 96
  *Old, 96–99
Reveille Mill, 95–96
*Rhyolite, 5, 23, 42, 43, 99–106
  competition with Bullfrog, 24, 25, 26, 27
Rhyolite Consolidated Mines Co., 105
Rhyolite Daily Bulletin, 100
Rhyolite Herald, 12, 26–27, 100, 103–4
Richardson, Ben, 49
Richardson, Frank, 139
Richmond Mine, 33
Rose, G. W., 106
Rose's Well, 106
*Round Mountain, xiii, 106–9
Round Mountain Hydraulic Mining Co., 107
Round Mountain Mining Co., 107, 108
Round Mountain Nugget, 106
Round Mountain Sphinx Mining Co., 107
Royston, 109–10
Royston Royal Blue Turquoise Mines, 109
Royston Turquoise Mines Co., 109
Rustler Mine, 143
Ryan, Larry, 85
Rye Patch, 110

Sage Hen Mine, 33
St. Mark's Episcopal Church, 128
Salmon, Mattias, 47–48
Salt mining, 27
Sampson, Charles, 143
San Antone, *see* San Antonio
San Antonia, *see* San Antonio
*San Antonio, 110
San Carlos, 110
San Felipe Mining Co., 92
San Francisco Mine, 55
San Juan, 111
San Lorenzo, *see* Potomac
San Pedro, Manuel, 10, 39, 47
San Pedro, Los Angeles and Salt Lake Railroad, 40
San Rafael Consolidated Mines Co., 92, 93
Santa Fe Railroad, 59
Saulsbury Wash, 37
Sawmill, 111
Sayre, D. L., 47
Scheebar Mercury Mine, 83
Scheel, Charles, 74
Schwab, Charles, 102

Scotia Mine, 13
Scotty's Castle, 23, 24
Searville, see Learville
Seventy-Six Mine, 57
Sewel, Bryce, 109
Seymour, see Central City
Shamrock, 111–112
Shamrock Mines Co., 111
Sharp, see Adaven
Sharp, George and Mary, 79
Sharp, Thomas, 5
Sharp Ranch, see Nyala
Shelby, P., 137
Shoshone (town), 106
Shoshone Indians, 75, 102, 132
   Chief Kawich, 60
   reservation, 35
Sieghart, Julius, 134
Sierra Nevada Mine, 56
Silica mining, 93
Silver Bend Mining Co., 16
Silver Bend Reporter, 15
Silver Bow, 22, 112–14
Silver Bow Belle Mining Co., 113
Silver Bow Consolidated Mining Co., 113
Silver Bow Standard, 112–13
Silverfields Ajax Mines Co., 14
Silver Glance, 49, 114
Silver Glance Mining Co., 114
Silver Hoard Mining Co., 113
Silver Horn Mine, 118
Silver mining
   at Arrowhead, 7–8
   at Barcelona, 10
   at Bellehelen, 13–14
   at Belmont, 14
   at Cactus Springs, 27–28
   at Cedar Spring, 30
   at Clifford, 31–32
   at Currant, 32
   at Danville, 33
   at Downieville, 34–35
   at Eden, 37
   at Ellendale, 38
   at Ellsworth, 39
   at Georges Canyon, 41
   at Gold Crater, 43
   at Golden Arrow, 44, 45
   at Grantsville, 47, 48
   at Hannapah, 49
   at Jackson Mining District, 55
   at Jefferson, 56–57
   at Jett, 58
   at Liberty, 63
   at Lodi, 64
   at Longstreet, 66
   at Manhattan, 66, 69–70
   at Morey, 76
   at Northumberland, 77, 78
   at Oak Springs, 79

   at Ophir Canyon, 80
   at Orizaba, 82–83
   at Paradise Peak, 83
   at Park Canyon, 84
   at Penelas, 85
   at Phonolite, 85–86
   at Pioneer, 87
   at Quartz Mountain, 91
   at Ray, 93, 95
   at Republic, 95
   at San Juan, 111
   at Shamrock, 111
   at Silver Bow, 112
   at Silver Glance, 114
   at Stonewall, 117–18
   at Sunnyside, 118
   at Tolicha, 119–20
   at Tonopah, 120–28
   at Trappman's Camp, 129
   at Troy, 129
   at Tybo, 135
   at Wahmonie, 137–39
   at Washington, 140
   at Willow Creek, 143–44
   at Wilson's Camp, 144
Silver Palace Mines, 48
Silver Point, see Jett
Silver Top Mine, 121, 125
Silver Wave Mine, 39
Silverzone, see Hannapah
Silverzone Extension Mining Co., 114
Silverzone Mines Co., 114
Silverzone Mohawk Co., 49
Slavin (miner), 144
Smith, Alfred, 20
Smith, "Borax," 12
Smith, L. D., 116
Smith's Station, see Stone House
Smuggler Mine, 76
Snelson, Joseph, 139
Snow, O. H., 118
Southern Pacific Railroad, 122
Southgold Mine, 37
Southgold Nevada Mines Co., 37
South Prussian Mine, 56
Spanish Spring, 114
Spilman, Charles, 49
Springdale, 114–15
Squattersville, 99
Stagelines, xiii-xiv, 5, 7, 8, 11, 20, 22, 31, 32, 34, 39, 40, 47, 51, 59, 60, 64, 66, 72, 73, 76, 78, 80, 99, 106, 110, 112, 114, 121, 128, 129, 144
   Austin–Belmont, 60, 74, 86, 116, 119
   Ione–Austin, 22, 41
   Tybo–Eureka, 75, 90
   See also Auto-stages
Stargo, 6, 115
Starlight claim, 14
Star of Hope Mine, 7
Star of the West Mining Co., 55

Sterlag Tunnel, 118
Sterling, *see* Stirling
Sterling Mine, 115
Stewart, William, 26, 27, 99
Stingley, Harriet, 37
Stirling, 115–16
Stokes, John, 20
Stoneham, Charles H., 56
*Stone House, 116–17
Stonewall, 117–18
Stonewall Mine, 118
Sulphide, 118
Summa Corp., 125
Summit City, *see* Ellsworth
Sunnyside, 118–19
Sunnyside Mine, 107
Sunrise Mine, 32
Sunset Mining and Development Co., 103
Super Six Mining Co., 109
Swoboda, A. P., 140

Tabakacci, Frank, 109
Tamney, V. A., 80
Tate, Thomas, 119
Tate's Station, 119
Taylor, William, 132
Telluride, 119
Terrell, Clyde, 12–13
Thomas, W. H., 139
Thompson, Leonard, 28
Thorp, *see* Bonnie Clare
Thorp's Wells, *see* Bonnie Clare
Tobin, William, 87
Todd, Robert B., 55
Toiyabe City, *see* Ophir Canyon
Tolicha, 119–20
Tom Burns Camp, *see* Goldyke
*Tonopah, 120–28
Tonopah and Goldfield Auto Co., 99
Tonopah and Goldfield Railroad, 122, 125
Tonopah and Tidewater Railroad, 5, 8, 9, 12, 13, 40, 42, 63, 100, 121
Tonopah-Belmont Development Co., 45
Tonopah-Belmont Mining Co., 121
Tonopah-Brohilco Mines Corp., 39
Tonopah Daily Bonanza, 121, 124, 125
Tonopah Daily Times, 125
Tonopah Extension Mine, 121
Tonopah Extension Mining Co., 124
Tonopah Gold Zone Mining Co., 45
Tonopah-Kawich Mining Co., 14
Tonopah Liberty Mining Co., 63
Tonopah Mining Co., 45, 121
Tonopah Springs, xiii, 17
Tonopah Sun, 124
Tonopah Times-Bonanza, 125
Toyah, 128
Tramp Mine, 102, 103
Transvaal, 128–29
Transvaal Miner, 129

Transvaal Tribune, 129
Trappman, Hermann, 129
Trappman Mining Co., 129
Trappman's Camp, 129
Treadwell-Yukon Co., 134, 135
Trent, Walter, 81
*Troy, 27, 129–31
Troy Mine, 129
Tungsten mining, 80
Turner, A. A., 40
Turquoise mining, 27, 28, 80, 109
Twin River, *see* Ophir Canyon
Twin River Mining Co., 80
*Twin Springs, 131
Two-G Mine, 132
*Tybo, 27, 131–35
Tybo Consolidated Mining Co., 52, 132, 133, 134
Tybo Dominion Mines, Inc., 135
Tybo Mine, 134
Tybo Sun, 132

Union, 135–37
Union Amalgamated Mining Co., 69
Union Canyon, *see* Union
Upper Town, 137
Upper Weston, *see* Ellsworth

Valley View Mine, 121
*Van Ness, 137
Van Ness, C. E., 137
Victor Mine, 124
Vignola's, *see* Tolicha
Virgin Gold Mining Co., 113
Volcano, *see* Hannapah

Wagner, 110
Wahmonie, 137–39
Wahmonie Development Co., 138–39
Wahmonie Mines Co., 137–38
Wahmonie Monterey Mines Co., 139
Walker, Jack, 16
Walther, O. G., 114
Warm Springs, 140
Warner, George and Judy, 60
Warner Mine, 140
Warner Mining and Milling Co., 140
Warrior Gold Mining Co., 9
Warrior Mine (town), *see* Athens
*Washington, xiii, 140
Webster Mine, 48
Webster Mines Corp., 48
Welch, Henry, 64
Welch, Hubert, 83
Weller, Dr. (mine owner), 143
Wellington, 141
West End Consolidated Mining Co., 124
Western Leadfield Mining Co., 109
Western Pacific Railroad, 75
Western Union group, 7
Westmoreland, Wes, 105

161

Westvaca Chlorine Products Corp., 33
Whipple, Clair and Lila, 118
Whipple, John Lytle, 118
Whipple Ranch, 118–19
White, Harsha, 72
*White Caps, 141–43
White Caps Extension Mines Co., 141
White Caps mine, 71–72, 141–43
White Caps Mining Co., 69, 141
Whiteman, J. H., 121
White Rock Spring, 143
White's Ranch, see Manse Ranch
Willard, G. H., 80
Williams, Clara, 111
Willow Creek, 143–44
Willow Creek Mining Co., 143
Willow Creek Ranch, see Sawmill
Wilson, 144
Wilson, Isaac J., 144
Wilson, Thomas, 106–7

Wilson's Camp, 144–45
Windous, Tom, 33
Windous Group, 32–33
Wing, Sam "China," 136
Wingfield, George, 7, 13, 92, 112, 119, 138, 143
Wittenburg, C. F., 69
Wittenburg, William, 143
Wolftone Extension Mining Co., 70
Wonder Mine, 8
Workman, J. L., 111World Exploration Co., 49

Yaiser (miner), 119
Yellow Gold Mine, 120
Yellow Tiger Consolidated Mining Co., 117
Yount, Joseph, 72
Yount's Ranch, see Manse Ranch

Zanzibar Mining Co., 70
Zinc mining, 58